*access to history*

# Elizabeth I: Meeting the Challenge, England 1541–1603

*access to history*

# Elizabeth I: Meeting the Challenge, England 1541–1603

*John Warren*

**HODDER**
EDUCATION
AN HACHETTE UK COMPANY

Study guide authors: Sally Waller (AQA), Geoff Woodward (OCR A) and Elizabeth Sparey (OCR B).

**The Publishers would like to thank the following for permission to reproduce copyright material:** City of London, London Metropolitan Archives, page 19; Corsham Court, Wiltshire/The Bridgeman Art Library, page 189; Mary Evans Picture Library, pages 8, 14, 15, 29, 40, 74, 101, 195; Musee d'Archeologie et d'Histoire, Lausanne, Switzerland/Giraudon/The Bridgeman Art Library, page 121; © Museo Nacional del Prado, Madrid, Spain, page 21; The National Archives, ref: MPF 1/366, page 153; National Portrait Gallery, London, pages 38, 94, 117, 173, 191; Private Collection/The Bridgeman Art Library, pages 96, 163; Private Collection/The Stapleton Collection/The Bridgeman Art Library, page 70; Woburn Abbey, Bedfordshire, UK/ The Bridgeman Art Library, page 131.

Every effort has been made to trace all copyright holders, but if any have been inadvertently overlooked the Publishers will be pleased to make the necessary arrangements at the first opportunity.

Hachette Livre UK's policy is to use papers that are natural, renewable and recyclable products and made from wood grown in sustainable forests. The logging and manufacturing processes are expected to conform to the environmental regulations of the country of origin.

Orders: please contact Bookpoint Ltd, 130 Milton Park, Abingdon, Oxon OX14 4SB. Telephone: (44) 01235 827720. Fax: (44) 01235 400454. Lines are open 9.00–5.00, Monday to Saturday, with a 24-hour message answering service. Visit our website at www.hoddereducation.co.uk

© John Warren 2008
First published in 2008 by
Hodder Education,
an Hachette UK Company
338 Euston Road
London NW1 3BH

Impression number    5  4  3
Year                            2012  2011  2010

Cover photo shows a detail from the work *An Allegory of the Tudor Succession: The Family of Henry VIII*, c.1589–95 (oil on panel) by English School (16th century), courtesy of the Yale Center for British Art, Paul Mellon Collection, USA/The Bridgeman Art Library. Typeset in 10/12pt Baskerville and produced by Gray Publishing, Tunbridge Wells, Kent Printed in Malta

A catalogue record for this title is available from the British Library.

ISBN: 978 0340 965931

# Contents

# Dedication

## Keith Randell (1943–2002)

The *Access to History* series was conceived and developed by Keith, who created a series to 'cater for students as they are, not as we might wish them to be'. He leaves a living legacy of a series that for over 20 years has provided a trusted, stimulating and well-loved accompaniment to post-16 study. Our aim with these new editions is to continue to offer students the best possible support for their studies.

# 1 Meeting the Challenge: The Legacy of a Mid-Tudor Crisis?

**POINTS TO CONSIDER**

Although an assessment of Elizabeth I is at the heart of this book, her relative successes or failures cannot be discussed without an awareness of the legacy of her predecessors. For example, was the monarchy itself strong? Could it rely on the support of the political nation? Was England stable in political, social and economic terms? In particular, historians have argued over whether Elizabeth inherited a throne that was in a state of crisis. The so-called 'Mid-Tudor crisis' of 1546–58 is an historical label attached to the period from the latter years of Henry VIII to the death of Mary I and the accession of Elizabeth. This chapter discusses whether it is correct to argue that Elizabeth I faced a legacy of crisis.

## Key dates
1543   Scots forced to accept the Treaty of Greenwich
1544   Henry VIII captured Boulogne
1547   Henry VIII died
       Accession of Edward VI
       Somerset became Lord Protector
1549   Act of Uniformity
       Western Rebellion
       Kett Rebellion
       Somerset overthrown
       Warwick (later Northumberland) Lord President
         of the Council
1552   Act of Uniformity
1553   Edward VI died
       Lady Jane Grey proclaimed Queen
       Mary I took the throne
1554   Wyatt Rebellion
1558   Mary I died
       Accession of Elizabeth I

# 1 | The Mid-Tudor Crisis: Definitions

On 7 November 1558 a dying Queen Mary I named her half-sister Elizabeth as her heir. We cannot know the ailing Queen's thoughts, but she must have been close to despair. With no child of her own, she had only the memories of phantom pregnancies; there was the likelihood that Elizabeth would attempt to overturn Mary's restoration of her beloved Catholicism in the name of Protestantism; and perhaps she was aware that the young Elizabeth would rejoice at Mary's death. Ten days later, Mary was dead, and Elizabeth proclaimed queen.

What, however, was the legacy of Elizabeth's predecessors? It used to be an historical commonplace that the period from the final years of Henry VIII's reign to the death of Mary constituted a 'Mid-Tudor crisis' which was overcome in Elizabeth's reign. The main features of this supposed crisis were as follows:

- A crisis of authority, in which the monarchs were compromised by out-of-control factional fighting (often in the name of religion); similarly, the ruling class of nobles was itself shaken by rebellion.
- A social and economic crisis, marked by poor harvests, government debasement of the coinage and resulting galloping inflation.
- A foreign policy crisis, in which England's second-rate status among the European powers was all too evident.

The interaction of political, social and economic factors was allegedly sufficient to create a fundamentally structural crisis, in which the authority of monarchy and nobility was itself under threat.

> **Key question**
> How should 'crisis' be defined?

> **Key dates**
> Mary I died: 1558
> Accession of Elizabeth I: 1558

# 2 | Making the Traditional Case for a Mid-Tudor Crisis

## The reign of Henry VIII: the traditional interpretation

As Henry VIII aged dramatically, the possibility of a **minority** became stark. Minorities were fraught at the best of times, and this was not the best of times. By the mid-1540s, a potent combination of religious, political and economic problems faced the kingdom and provided an uncertain legacy for Henry's nine-year-old son Edward VI when he succeeded his father in January 1547.

### Religious problems

- Henry reigned against the background of the dramatic upheaval known as the Reformation, in which the authority of the Roman Catholic Church led by the Pope was rejected by those known as Protestants. To Catholics, the authority of the Pope guaranteed that true religious practice and doctrine had been transmitted from the days of the earliest Christian church. To Protestants, Holy Scripture – the Word of God as revealed in the Bible – was the only judge of true practice and doctrine. The Catholic Mass in Latin, and the many customs and rituals of parish life, such as the priest's blessing of the plough, or the

> **Key question**
> What are the main elements of the traditional case in favour of a Mid-Tudor crisis?

> **Key term**
> **Minority**
> The period before a monarch comes of age and is able to rule alone.

reverence displayed towards saints in the form of stone or stained glass, were condemned as unscriptural. Catholic and Protestant fought out their claims to the custodianship of religious truth in wars which engulfed continental Europe. Religious disunity, it seemed, meant political conflict, and English contemporaries understandably worried that England itself would fall victim.

- Henry had imposed his own version of the Reformation. Despite the so-called **Break with Rome** and the **dissolution of the monasteries**, the King had never espoused Protestantism, and his religious legislation, particularly the Six Articles of 1539, had maintained traditional Catholic doctrine. But opposition to Catholicism was present at the highest levels of political life, albeit hidden under a mask of compliance with the King's authority as Supreme Head of the Church of England.

## Political/religious problems

- Key members of Henry's council, including the Archbishop of Canterbury, Thomas Cranmer, and Edward Seymour, Earl of Hertford, were Protestant in all but name. Prince Edward's tutors were also of Protestant sympathy. Henry's sixth wife, Catherine Parr, was of similar mind.
- Against this grouping was the powerful Catholic faction, led by Thomas Howard, Duke of Norfolk, and Stephen Gardiner, Bishop for Winchester. The potential for turmoil at the highest levels of political life was therefore enormous.
- Sure enough, by 1546, the last full year of Henry's reign, the King had lost control of his council. The Catholic **faction** nearly succeeded in destroying Catherine Parr by trying to implicate her in the **heresy** trial of the Protestant Anne Askew, but they were outmanoeuvred by the Protestants who had secured the execution of Norfolk's son, Surrey; even Norfolk himself was imprisoned awaiting execution, and was saved only by the death of the King before the warrant could be signed.
- Henry's loss of effective control is revealed in the way his will was altered without his permission. As a result of this fraud, Hertford made sure that he was appointed Lord Protector of Edward. Also, he and his supporters were to be rewarded with significant but unspecified patronage which they claimed that the dying King had promised (the 'unfulfilled gifts' clause, which was fraudulently added to the will).

## Economic problems

The final few years of Henry's reign were also accompanied by desperate economic circumstances:

- Henry's rather pathetic and belated search for personal glory led to appallingly expensive wars with Scotland and France: the huge English army might have captured Boulogne, but, to defend it, new fortifications had to be built. To pay for these escapades, Henry sold off crown assets and **debased the coinage**.

**Key terms**

**Break with Rome**
The rejection of the authority of the Pope over the English church.

**Dissolution of the monasteries**
In 1536 all monastic property was seized by the crown; a significant portion was sold on to the nobility.

**Factions**
Rival groups of nobles.

**Heresy**
Holding beliefs in opposition to those taught by the church.

**Debasement of the coinage**
Reducing the amount of precious metal in the coinage supplied through the royal mints.

**Key dates**

Scots forced to accept Treaty of Greenwich: 1543

Henry VIII captured Boulogne: 1544

- Debasing the coinage, allied to population pressure, led to inflation and price rises which were not accompanied by a rise in wages. Peasant farmers found themselves dispossessed as wealthy landowners enclosed land and turned it over to sheep. The dispossessed poor then migrated to forest areas or suburbs where they were potentially a ready source of support for popular insurrection. And so, the King had laid the foundation for major crisis, which he then proceeded to overlay with political turmoil as he withdrew into his dotage.

## The reign of Edward VI 1547–53: the traditional interpretation

### Religious problems

Following Henry's death, Hertford, as the new and self-created Duke of Somerset, set about a thoroughgoing Protestant reformation:

- Traditional religion was attacked as a more Bible-based culture replaced the visual culture of Catholicism. Images such as statues of saints were removed from churches and long-established ceremonies banned.
- The **Roman Catholic Mass** (in Latin), which lay at the heart of Catholic doctrine and practice, was replaced under the 1549 Act of Uniformity by a service in English.

The onslaught on traditional parish life led to the Western Rebellion of 1549, in which the rebels demanded a return to the religious teachings and practices of Henry VIII's reign.

### Political problems

According to the so-called **'Whig' school of historical interpretation**, originating in the work of A.F. Pollard in the early twentieth century and refined by W.K. Jordan in the 1960s, Somerset was a liberal-minded man who genuinely wished to see increased freedom of the individual and a better life for the poor. However, economic distress led to a rebellion in eastern England – the Kett Rebellion – which may have been stimulated by the rebels' belief that Somerset was on their side. Some of Somerset's fellow nobles clearly felt the same, and this so-called 'Good Duke' was overthrown in 1549 (and later executed) by a faction led by the 'Bad Duke' John Dudley, Duke of Northumberland.

Northumberland was considered a 'Bad Duke' because 'Whig' historians doubted his religious sincerity and were convinced that his motives were those of the power-hungry, over-mighty noble. He pushed the country further in a Protestant direction only because it cemented his appeal with the young King and Archbishop Cranmer. The extent of his self-centredness and ambition was revealed in the traumatic days as the young King fell mortally ill in 1553. Northumberland persuaded Edward to disinherit his heir and older half-sister, the determinedly Catholic Mary, and, for good measure, his other half-sister, Elizabeth. Edward specified as his heir Lady Jane Grey, the granddaughter of Henry VIII's sister, Mary. Lady Jane was conveniently married

**Key terms**

**Roman Catholic Mass**
A service in which the officiating priest consecrates bread and wine. In Roman Catholic teaching it is through the agency of the priest that bread and wine become, in essence, Christ's body and blood.

**'Whig' school of historical interpretation**
A term used to criticise historians who allegedly distort their accounts of the past by imposing their liberal values on it. They are accused of implicitly judging historical figures on whether or not they contributed towards progress in the direction of liberal parliamentary democracy.

**Key dates**

Henry VIII died: 1547

Accession of Edward VI: 1547

Somerset became Lord Protector: 1547

Act of Uniformity: 1549

Western Rebellion: 1549

Kett Rebellion: 1549

Somerset overthrown: 1549

Warwick (later Northumberland) Lord President of the Council: 1549 off to Guildford Dudley, Northumberland's son. This breathtaking audacity nearly came off. On Edward's death, the council initially supported the Grey accession. Unfortunately for Northumberland, Mary Tudor escaped his clutches and was able to build up support from her power-base in Suffolk. Her appeal to the principle of inheritance as Henry VIII's eldest child was a potent one, and support for Northumberland collapsed. Attempting to capture Mary in a military action, he found his forces deserting him. The council profited from his absence by proclaiming Mary as queen and Northumberland as a 'conscienceless tyrant'. He was duly arrested. A conversion to Catholicism – further evidence of his insincerity – could not save him, and he was executed in August 1553.

## Economic and social problems

In his 1973 work *The Mid-Tudor Crisis*, Whitney Jones argued that the weakness of the monarchy, accompanied by a decline into factionalism, was itself the main cause of mounting economic and social distress in the period. This fundamental lack of political authority transformed problems such as population growth, price rises, unemployment and vagrancy into crises. Other historians have seen these problems as the symptoms of a structural instability in the economy of the country. By this token, the 1549 rebellions were economic in origin.

## The reign of Mary I 1553–8: the traditional interpretation
### Religious problems

Mary was portrayed as a politically naïve **zealot** whose reintroduction of Catholicism was widely unpopular. In particular, her burning of Protestants as heretics backfired, as she inadvertently turned them into **martyrs** and was subsequently labelled by Protestant propagandists as 'Bloody Mary'. Her Catholicism led her into domestic and foreign policy disaster as she stacked her Privy Council with Catholic nonentities whose political **acumen** was in inverse proportion to their **piety**.

### Political problems

Mary and her council faced aggressive opposition from Parliament. In part, this opposition was based on objections to her religious policy, particularly her insistence on the return of the monastic lands bought up by so many nobles. She was forced to back down over this issue before Parliament would accept the reinstituting of papal authority over the English church. Worse still was her obsession with marrying into the Habsburg family. Her suitor, King Philip II of Spain, was regarded with abject horror by most parliamentarians. The behaviour of his troops in the Netherlands had earned him a reputation for cruelty, and the prospect of an England dominated by Spanish interests was too much for many. Indeed, Mary was lucky to survive the Wyatt Rebellion, which this so-called '**Spanish Match**' provoked. Marriage to Philip then led to English involvement with the

**Key terms**

**Zealot**
One whose commitment to a cause is extreme.

**Martyr**
A person willing to suffer for faith's sake.

**Acumen**
Knowledge and experience.

**Piety**
Holding and displaying strong religious beliefs.

**Spanish Match**
The marriage between Mary I of England and Philip II of Spain.

Spanish–French war, which disastrously culminated in the loss of the last English possession in France: Calais.

Mary's reign, then, was characterised by a complete lack of positive achievement as the country was rocked by parliamentary opposition to virtually everything she stood for. It was also rocked by a social and economic crisis engendered by a catastrophic influenza epidemic and poor harvests. Pollard memorably described her reign as 'sterile': the unfeeling might add 'as sterile as her womb', since a longed-for child never arrived to secure a Catholic succession. Instead, the dying queen was faced with the prospect of the succession of her heretic half-sister and the likely extinguishing of everything she held most dear.

This picture of the mid-Tudor period apparently reveals a country lurching from crisis to crisis. Given the link between religious and political opposition, and the way in which economic discontent fuelled rebellion, the case for a full-scale structural crisis appears to be a strong one.

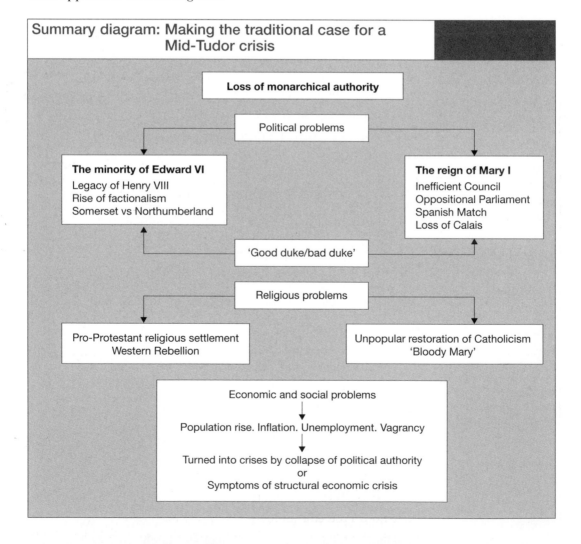

**Summary diagram: Making the traditional case for a Mid-Tudor crisis**

**Loss of monarchical authority**

Political problems

**The minority of Edward VI**
Legacy of Henry VIII
Rise of factionalism
Somerset vs Northumberland

**The reign of Mary I**
Inefficient Council
Oppositional Parliament
Spanish Match
Loss of Calais

'Good duke/bad duke'

Religious problems

Pro-Protestant religious settlement
Western Rebellion

Unpopular restoration of Catholicism
'Bloody Mary'

Economic and social problems

Population rise. Inflation. Unemployment. Vagrancy

Turned into crises by collapse of political authority
or
Symptoms of structural economic crisis

# 3 | Making the Case Against a Mid-Tudor Crisis

A major revision to the traditional **historiography** took place in the 1980s, when the work of Jennifer Loach and Robert Tittler in particular offered an interpretation which sidestepped the earlier pitfalls. In particular, they did not attempt to read into the motives of the Duke of Somerset values that suited twentieth-century liberals and made no assumptions about the respective contributions of Catholicism and Protestantism towards those very values. The resulting picture is far more nuanced, and, while it does not downplay the severity of the various crises, the case for the underpinning structural crisis and therefore for a crisis in monarchical authority is largely exploded.

## The end of Henry VIII's reign: the revisionist view

The extent of distress at the end of Henry VIII's reign should not be understated. David Loades has rightly pointed to the 'simmering discontent' in the countryside, where people could not understand why, in a time of good harvests, bread should be so expensive. Protest was held in check by the awesome personality and reputation of the King, but the question remained: what would happen when the King was gone?

It would be unwise, however, to follow traditional interpretations and accept that the ailing King was the prisoner of faction and that his will did not reflect his wishes. Eric Ives has suggested that it would have been physically impossible to have inserted clauses (including the 'unfulfilled gifts' clause) into the will, and Loach argues that the choice of members of the **Regency Council** was Henry's and that it did not represent the dominance over the King of the Seymour reformist faction. The council contained known religious **conservatives**, such as Tunstall, the Bishop of Durham, and the exclusion of the arch-conservative Stephen Gardiner was a deliberate decision which Henry made because he thought Gardiner would prove troublesome. And, although there is no evidence that Henry specified Hertford as Lord Protector, it is by no means unlikely that he did so verbally. After all, Hertford was the young Edward's uncle and so would have had every incentive to maintain the crown's authority.

## The reign of Edward VI 1547–53: the revisionist view. Duke of Somerset as Lord Protector 1547–9
### Political issues

Crises undoubtedly peppered Edward's reign, but these should be seen as the results of poor judgement by Somerset in particular and by unlucky circumstance, such as the death of Edward, rather than a crisis of authority stemming from fundamental weaknesses in the monarchy. Any Regency Council was, by its very nature, prone to factionalism; but one should not argue that it was unworkable. The authority of the head of the Regency Council, be it Lord Protector (Somerset) or Lord President (Northumberland), need not have been compromised by listening to the advice of fellow councillors. Granted, Somerset was faced

**Key question**
What criticisms might be made of the traditional, pro-crisis case for the final years of Henry VIII's reign?

**Key terms**

**Historiography**
Interpretations of the past embodied in the writings of historians.

**Regency Council**
Group of councillors ruling in the name of a monarch.

**Conservative**
One who upholds traditional values and ways.

**Key question**
What criticisms might be made of the traditional view of the Somerset Protectorate?

## Profile: Edward Seymour, Duke of Somerset c.1506–52

1536 – Seymour's sister Jane married Henry VIII
– Created Earl of Hertford by Henry VIII
1542 – Lord High Admiral
1543 – Lord Great Chamberlain
1547 – After Henry VIII died in January he was appointed
Lord Protector, created Duke of Somerset
Defeated Scots at battle of Pinkie
1549 – Protectorate dissolved; imprisoned in Tower of London
1550 – Released, rejoined Privy Council
1552 – Executed

Somerset owed his rise to the marriage of his sister to Henry VIII. As uncle to Henry's only legitimate son, Edward, he retained his pre-eminence in the Henrician Privy Council. There is considerable historical debate over the nature of his Protectorate: some see him as a well-meaning man with the sixteenth-century version of a social conscience who was overthrown by dastardly enemies; others see him as a typically greedy autocrat whose mistakes brought about his own downfall.

by a coup in October 1549 that led to his imprisonment and replacement by the Earl of Warwick (subsequently Northumberland from October 1551). But this was largely Somerset's fault. He brought about his own downfall through a combination of arrogant disregard for his fellow councillors and a series of flawed policy decisions to which he stubbornly adhered.

In September 1547 Somerset led an invasion of Scotland to force the Scots to abide by the terms of the Henrician treaty of Greenwich and so to proceed with the marriage of Edward to the even younger Mary, Queen of Scots (an English occupation of Scotland by matrimony, as the Scots readily appreciated). In fact, the Scots sent Mary to their old ally France, where a marriage with the **Dauphin** subsequently scuppered the English plans and, as we shall see, confronted Elizabeth with the prospect of a rival to her throne who was also Queen of France. However, it was Somerset's typically stubborn decision to garrison hideously expensive forts in Scotland that led to the desperate search for money and the subsequent debasement of the coinage. This contributed to a rise in prices and rents, and can be seen as one of the key causes of the Kett Rebellion of May to August 1549.

**Dauphin**
Eldest son and heir of the French King.

| Key term |

### The Kett Rebellion
Beginning with a riot at Wymondham, Norfolk, a series of rebellions affected Norfolk, Suffolk and neighbouring counties. At first sight, they appear to represent a significant attack on traditional authority, since:

Kett Rebellion: 1549

| Key date |

• They were led by those below the status of gentry (Robert Kett was a tanner and a yeoman freeholder).

- Rebels set up camps (such as Mousehold Heath) which deliberately provided an alternative system of local government.
- Rebels sought to curb the economic activities of the gentry by demanding an end to practices such as foldcourse, which permitted the gentry to pasture their flocks on tenants' land.

However, it would be an exaggeration to present the Kett Rebellion as fundamentally revolutionary, since:

- The rebels made great play of their respect for the King's laws. They claimed to oppose only those who sought to sabotage those laws (by trampling on the traditional rights of others).
- They proclaimed their support of the government's reformist religious policy by demanding a ministry which preached the Word of God.
- Their grievances against the nobility owed a great deal to the harsh ways of the Howard family, whose fall from grace in the late Henrician period left a power vacuum in eastern England.

It was Somerset's response to the Kett Rebellion which led directly to the Lord Protector's downfall. Obsessed by the Scottish campaign, he prevaricated. His apparent willingness to listen to rebel complaints about enclosure perhaps reflected a smug enjoyment of being seen by them as a socially concerned **paternalist** with the good of the ordinary people at heart. His patronage of a commission enquiring into enclosure encouraged the rebels to feel that he was on the side of the commoners. Unfortunately for Somerset, his fellow nobles thought so too. In short, he was a class traitor. Rebels were to be quashed, preferably with maximum ferocity. One hanged them; one did not talk to them. When Somerset finally did move against the rebels, the military task was given to Warwick: 3500 rebels were killed in the suppression, and Warwick received the applause of his peers.

Even worse from the perspective of fellow nobles was Somerset's ill-advised arrogance in council. He was ruling from his own household in the manner of a **regent**, rather than making decisions after consulting the council as first among equals. His Treason Act of November 1547, anachronistically seen as a 'liberal' measure because it repealed Henrician heresy and censorship laws, gave him the opportunity to govern by proclamation (in effect, by commands issued in London and the provinces) rather than through consultation.

## Religious issues

Somerset's religious legislation created confusion at best and bitter resentment at worst. By 1549 the government had imposed a religious settlement which seemed to be in part a compromise between Protestant and Catholic teachings and in part an aggressive attack on Catholicism at the level of the parish church:

- The foremost example of compromise – or mixed message – was the 1549 Act of Uniformity. It set aside the Catholic Mass in Latin and replaced it by a **Communion** service in English, but the underpinning religious doctrine was anything but

**Key terms**

**Paternalist**
Literally, a father figure and one who rules as a traditional father, making decisions with the best interests of the family in mind but without consultation.

**Regent**
A person ruling in place of a monarch (usually because the monarch was too young to rule independently or was absent).

**Communion**
The offering of the bread and wine to the congregation.

clear-cut. When the priest celebrated a Catholic Mass, his words echoed those of Christ to his disciples: offering bread and wine, Christ had said 'This is my body' and 'This is my blood', inviting the disciples to eat and drink. In Catholic teaching, the bread and wine offered to the congregation were, through the agency of the ordained priest, changed in essence to be truly Christ. Christ was, therefore, really present. But this doctrine of Real Presence was rejected by many Protestants on the grounds that Christ intended his words to be taken symbolically: the bread represented, but was not, his body: the wine represented, but was not, his blood. The Act of Uniformity imposed a Book of Common Prayer that specified the words to be said by the priest at Communion, but they were so phrased as to make it possible to take them as accepting or rejecting Real Presence. On the other hand, the Catholic practice of the priest 'elevating' the bread and wine as a sign of its transformation to body and blood was explicitly forbidden.

- Equally ambiguous was the 1549 Act permitting clergy to marry. At first sight, this was a Protestant attack on the Roman Catholic view of the priesthood as a separate caste with God-given powers acquired through ordination; Roman Catholic priests were expected to remain unmarried. And yet, the Act stated that traditional **celibacy** was to be preferred.

The 1547 Chantries Act represents more clearly a direct Protestant attack on Catholic practice. Chantries were charitable endowments that funded prayers for souls in purgatory. Somerset's abolition of chantries could therefore be amply justified by Protestant teaching, since **purgatory** was dismissed as an unscriptural fiction. On the other hand, the dissolution of the chantries meant a transfer of much-needed monies and property to the crown, and one can infer from the Privy Council minutes that Somerset's motives were more **fiscal** than theological. However, the Chantries Act also hit hard at traditional parish life. It also abolished endowments for obits (a yearly service of remembrance), 'lights' (candles lit at altars or in front of images) and altar furnishings. Similarly, in 1548 Protestant **iconoclasm** was reflected in the order for the removal of all images from churches, and some traditional ceremonies and processions were banned (such as the Good Friday 'creeping to the cross').

Overall, Somerset's religious reforms represented a profound shock to the traditionally minded. Villagers would be unlikely to appreciate the doctrinal subtleties of the new Book of Common Prayer, but they were well aware that the longstanding aural and visual culture of their parish church was largely dismantled. Services in English, with a new demand for participation from the congregation; priests wearing simpler vestments; images and rood screens removed; a simplified baptismal ritual; no more exchanging of rings in marriage; prayers for souls in purgatory banned; many feast days and processions banned; rituals banned as superstitious (including those which incorporated seasonal occupations into church life, such as the blessing of the plough,

**Key terms**

**Celibacy**
Abstaining from marriage/sexual relations.

**Purgatory**
In Catholic doctrine, a place where the souls of the dead are cleansed by suffering as preparation for heaven.

**Fiscal**
Relating to finance.

**Iconoclasm**
The destruction of those religious images which were seen by Protestants as detracting from the worship of God alone.

or the scattering of holy water on fields at seeding time). Such change was bound to be startling, but for many it was an insult to themselves, their families, their ancestors and their communities because it condemned as meaningless a style of worship which tradition had honoured.

## The Western Rebellion

The Western Rebellion of 1549 is generally seen as an angry response to Somerset's religious policy, and evidence for this interpretation seems compelling.

- The rebellion started in the West Country (south-west England) following the refusal of the villagers of Sampford Courtenay to allow their priest to use the new Book of Common Prayer for a second time.
- There had been earlier trouble in Cornwall when a royal official, William Body, had been murdered following his forcible removal of images.
- The articles of the rebels concentrated almost exclusively on religious issues. Their demands included the restoration of the Henrician Six Articles, Mass in Latin and the return of half of the ex-monastic and chantry lands to the church.

On the other hand, it would be unwise to disregard other factors. One article demanded the remitting of a sheep tax, and another wished to place a limit on the number of servants a gentleman might employ. This latter might be taken as an attack on the power of the aristocracy, and few gentlemen, if any, would have accepted the demand for the return of the monastic lands. Allied to this is the reputed slogan of the Cornish rebels, 'Kill the gentlemen and we will have the Six Articles again and ceremonies as they were in Henry VIII's time!' It may be tempting to argue from this that religion was the veneer placed on a series of political, social and economic grievances which came together in an assault on established systems of authority. This would, however, be unwise, and for the following reasons:

- The council saw the rebellion as religious in origin.
- The 'kill the gentlemen' slogan may well reflect an antagonism towards specific West Country gentry such as Carew who were both Protestant and associated with Somerset's regime.
- The importance of religious issues is reflected in the fact that the region was characterised by strong religious conservatism. The West Country was generally too remote to have developed a popular Protestantism, which usually spread where there were contacts with the court or with continental Protestantism via the ports. The rebels also complained that the new services in the new Book of Common Prayer were simply incomprehensible because they were not in Cornish.
- Established systems of authority worked well enough when Somerset finally got round to suppressing the rebellion. Neither the Kett nor the Western rebels were any match for the military forces of the ruling class.

In short, it is probably best to see the Western Rebellion as one in which a number of grievances coalesced, but whose foundation lay in resentment at the attack on traditional religion.

What part did the Western Rebellion play in Somerset's downfall? The rebellion (and similar uprisings in Oxfordshire and Buckinghamshire) revealed how widespread opposition to religious change was and no doubt encouraged pro-Catholic elements on the council to plot against Somerset. But the key element is the way in which Somerset reacted to the rebellion. Ignoring the shrewd advice of William Paget, one of the key members of the Henrician and Edwardian Privy Councils, he did not move swiftly to crush the rebels, but left it to others to do so while concentrating on his Scottish policy (or obsession).

Ignoring the advice of politically motivated counsellors such as Warwick and Paget meant that they made common cause with the Catholic faction against him. The Kett Rebellion and the Western Rebellion gave them the opportunity they needed. Paget wrote to Somerset in terms which ably reveal why Somerset had lost the support of the council:

> Society in a realm doth consist and is maintained by means of religion and law. And these two or one be wanting, farewell all just society, farewell king, justice, government … Look well whether you have either law or religion at home and I fear you shall find neither. The use of the old religion is forbidden by a law and the use of the new is not yet printed in the stomachs of the 11 of the 12 parts of the realm.

## Economic and social issues

Our discussion of the Kett and Western rebellions concluded that, although economic issues were not absent, the rebellions were not to be taken as the consequence of a collapsed or collapsing economic system, bringing down with it the systems of authority based on ownership of land. The pressures of accelerated population growth and inflation were real in the 1540s, but there is no evidence that, given decent harvests, there was anything resembling widespread starvation. On the other hand, it may be significant that 1549, the year of rebellions, did witness a poor harvest. But the difficulty with this argument is that the country as a whole was supporting a population which was no more than half of the six million supported in the fourteenth century before the arrival of the Black Death. There may have been localised pressure on grain supplies, but there is no compelling evidence that this was a factor in either the Kett or Western Rebellion.

This is not to deny that life was hard and becoming harder for all those whose wages did not match rises in prices and rents. Loades, we recall, used the phrase 'simmering discontent' to describe the countryside in the final years of Henry VIII's reign. The same applies to Somerset's Protectorship. However, this discontent was the result not of a fundamentally unstable economy, but of the way in which political and religious decisions had impacted on everyday lives. Somerset's hideously expensive military adventures made the lot of those without capital in land or trade harsher, but, without the attack on traditional religious culture, it is unlikely that the Western Rebellion would ever have taken place.

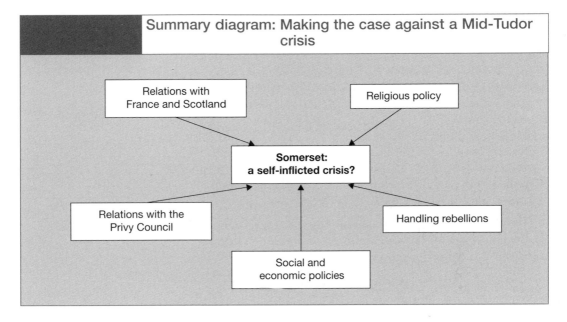

Summary diagram: Making the case against a Mid-Tudor crisis

## 4 | The Reign of Edward VI 1547–53: The Revisionist View

Key question
What criticisms might be made of the traditional view of the Northumberland regime?

### Duke of Northumberland as Lord President 1549–53
Political issues

The fundamental stability of the political system is revealed in the ability of Northumberland's government to survive and push through a reformist religious agenda despite adverse circumstances. In the first place, Northumberland was not a relative of the King and so lacked the claim of Somerset to authority over the government and country. He faced powerful adversaries, not only in the form of Catholic members of the council such as Arundel and Wriothesley, but also Somerset himself when the latter was briefly rehabilitated and restored to the council. He was therefore bound to look for allies in the council and to seek and respond to his fellow councillors' advice; part of the price he paid for his position as Lord President.

- As for his relations with fellow councillors, Northumberland accepted Paget's advice and re-established conciliar decision-making and working. All letters and state papers, including those signed by the young King, were to be countersigned by six councillors rather than simply by the Lord President (as had been Somerset's practice as Lord Protector).
- However, it would not do to overstate the contrast with Somerset. Northumberland was a more wily political operator, but his **autocratic** tendencies were no less real for being

**Key term**

**Autocratic**
Ruling without consultation or sharing power.

initially less overt. He recognised that, to safeguard his position, he had to build influence with Edward himself, and therefore through Thomas Cranmer, Archbishop of Canterbury. Edward clearly liked and trusted Cranmer, and the price for their support was Northumberland's commitment to further religious reform.

- As Northumberland's confidence in his own position increased, so did his autocratic and self-seeking ways. In February 1551, he instituted an élite force of 850 mounted cavalry who might be seen as a palace guard protecting Northumberland against a coup, since he appointed virtually every captain of these 'gendarmes'.
- In January 1552, he had Somerset executed, Catholic Bishop Tunstall sent to the Tower and Paget dispatched to the Fleet prison: a clear move against actual and potential opposition.
- Significantly, he also ended the practice of fellow-councillors countersigning documents.

It is easy to present Northumberland as venal and grasping in the unenviable Somerset mode. However, he was much more politically astute and **pragmatic**, and this meant that he was capable of taking decisions which were in the interests of stability rather than his own political need or pocket. The 'gendarmes', for instance, were abolished in October 1552 as part of a set of financial reforms.

**Pragmatic**
Making decisions on the basis of what was practical in a particular set of circumstances, rather than through theory or principle.

Key term

---

## Profile: John Dudley, Duke of Northumberland 1502–53

| 1523 | – Knighted in France |
|---|---|
| 1542 | – Created Viscount Lisle; Great Admiral |
| 1544–6 | – Led Henry VIII's forces in seizing Boulogne: became governor of the town |
| 1547 | – Created Earl of Warwick |
| 1549 | – Suppressed the Kett Rebellion and took a major role in the ousting of Somerset as Lord Protector |
| 1550 | – Treaty of Boulogne |
| 1551 | – Duke of Northumberland |
| 1552 | – Executed Somerset |
| 1553 | – Persuaded Edward VI to alter the succession in favour of Lady Jane Grey, whom he married to his son, Guildford Dudley. Abandoned by the Privy Council, he was executed by Mary I |

A skilled soldier and pragmatic politician, Northumberland was able to achieve a pre-eminent position as Lord President of the Council after the overthrow of Somerset by cultivating a strong relationship with Edward VI. Traditionally seen as lacking in principle, he recanted his Protestantism in the mistaken hope of escaping the axe.

## Profile: Thomas Cranmer, Archbishop of Canterbury 1489–1556

1529 – Wrote a treatise supporting the royal divorce
1532 – Despite being an ordained priest, secretly married the daughter of a Protestant theologian
1533 – Archbishop of Canterbury. Pronounced annulment of Henry VIII's marriage to Catherine of Aragon
1547 – Member of the Regency Council
1549 – Played a key role in drawing up the Book of Common Prayer
1552 – Played a key role in the revised version of the Book of Common Prayer
1553 – Signed Edward's will barring Mary Tudor from succession. Imprisoned on Mary's accession. Proclaimed heretic. Deprived of title
1556 – Partially recanted his Protestant ideas
1556 – Burnt at stake after repudiating his recantation

Thomas Cranmer was at the heart of the English Reformation, but he remains an enigmatic and surprisingly private figure given the importance of his role. His religious ideas reflected changes in continental Protestantism: as his ideas developed, so the Book of Common Prayer changed. He believed in the necessity and rightfulness of the Royal Supremacy over the church, but then was forced into the role of rebel against the crown with the accession of the Catholic Mary I. Although he retracted some of his Protestant beliefs in the crisis of his arrest and interrogation, he reaffirmed his Protestantism and is supposed to have thrust the hand which signed his recantation into the flames when he was burnt as a heretic: 'for as much as my hand offended, writing contrary to my heart, my hand shall first be punished therefor.'

Similarly, although Northumberland enjoyed military prestige as much as Somerset, he recognised the absolute financial need to end the French wars. The March 1550 Treaty of Boulogne handed back a thoughtfully refortified Boulogne to France and the July 1551 Treaty of Angers relinquished Edward's claim to the hand of Mary, Queen of Scots. These were bitter pills to swallow, but show that Northumberland was a *politique*: he did recognise that necessity was his master.

### Economic and social issues
Northumberland's economic policies were partly a series of responses to immediate difficulties and partly a series of sensible, statesmanlike would-be solutions to long-standing issues.

- He was initially tempted into a Somerset-style debasement of the coinage to raise much-needed funds.

- However, he subsequently (in April 1551) listened to the urgent promptings of William Cecil and attempted to curb inflation by withdrawing debased coins and issuing new ones. This depleted the crown's store of bullion; in 1552, the crown technically went bankrupt. Northumberland was obliged to sell off crown land, seize church lands (targeting clerical opponents, such as the Catholic Bishop of Durham) and melt down church plate for the re-minting of coins.
- He appointed Cecil and Mildmay to report on ways to increase crown finances and successfully cut down on embezzlement as monetary reserves were transferred out of the sticky hands of various revenue-collecting departments and into the care of Peter Osborne, who held auditing posts in both the Exchequer and the Privy Chamber.

These measures were inevitably of long-term benefit, and it is to Northumberland's credit that he was prepared to eschew short-term for long-term gain. His most effective short-term measure was of course the ending of the French and Scottish wars. However, his attempted retrenchment of crown finances was somewhat compromised by his need to keep his supporters in the council happy by selling crown land to them cheaply.

Northumberland used a judicious mixture of coercion and intervention in combating disorder. He introduced the office of Lord Lieutenant into counties to direct the suppression of unrest, and backed up this measure with anti-riot legislation: the assembly of 40 or more people for the purposes of pulling down **enclosures** was made high treason.

On the other hand, he tried to keep grain prices down by requiring JPs (Justices of the Peace) to survey grain stocks to prevent illegal exporting. He also repealed Somerset's harsh Vagrancy Act of 1547, which had condemned a persistent vagrant to the status of a slave: a punishment previously unknown to English law.

## Religious issues

Northumberland's religious legislation was risky but, from his perspective, politically necessary. As we have seen, both Cranmer and Edward were intent on further pro-Protestant reform and Northumberland recognised that, to maintain his relationship with an increasingly assertive young King, he needed to advance the Protestant cause. Under the influence of Cranmer, Northumberland's various reforms built on the attack on the traditional visual and aural culture of Catholicism that Somerset had initiated.

- Under the 1552 Act of Uniformity, the altar at the east end of a church, on which the sacrifice of the Catholic Mass was celebrated, was replaced by a wooden Communion table, sited where it was more accessible to the **laity**. The word 'altar' no longer appeared in the revised Book of Common Prayer.
- Although the words used at Communion did not explicitly deny Real Presence in the bread and wine, they came close to

**Enclosures**
Where land formerly farmed by a whole village as common land was fenced off by landowners and turned over to pasture of animals. Needed fewer agricultural workers.

**Laity**
The church congregation; strictly, any person not in the employ of the church.

Act of Uniformity: 1552

doing so. No Catholic could accept the 1552 Book of Common Prayer.

- Although Cranmer decided to retain the practice of the congregation kneeling at Communion, he had some sympathy with the objections of those who argued that kneeling implied some sort of Real Presence. Supplementary words – the Black Rubric – were added to the Book of Common Prayer to emphasise to the clergy that the act of kneeling implied no such thing.
- In place of the elaborate vestments of the Catholic priest, **ministers** were to wear a relatively simple white gown called a surplice when officiating in church.

What is particularly significant is that these religious changes, even when allied to continuing economic distress, did not lead to rebellion and disorder. This suggests that the Somerset reforms were seen by the laity as more traumatic. It is also possible that Northumberland was seen as a more formidable leader than Somerset and certainly not a man to countenance any form of rebellion. And, crucially, the absence of rebellion under Northumberland casts doubt on the traditional pro-crisis interpretation.

## The succession crisis

Early in 1553, Edward VI's health began to deteriorate. This placed Northumberland in a perilous position, since the accession of Mary would almost certainly mean his downfall and destruction. He was intimately associated with the Protestantism that Mary detested and was also blamed by Mary for the attempts made by Edward to force her to stop practising her Catholic faith.

Playing on Edward's hatred of Catholicism, Northumberland advised the dying King to overturn the 1544 Act of Succession through a 'Devise for the Succession'. This excluded both Mary and Elizabeth and vested the succession in the line of Henry VIII's youngest sister, Mary (through the heirs male of her daughter Frances, the Duchess of Suffolk). But, following the marriage of Frances' daughter Jane Grey to Northumberland's son Guildford Dudley in May 1553, a change was made: succession was to go to Jane. The stronger claim of the Scots line was ignored.

It is highly unlikely that Edward was persuaded against his will. The King summoned the judges and angrily demanded that they set aside their understandable doubts about the legality of the 'Devise': they duly submitted, and others fell into line. Cranmer later told Mary that he had agreed to sign the 'Devise' only after hearing their opinion. Parliament was to be called in September to give the 'Devise' the very necessary authority of statute, but, in the meantime, it was put into effect by **Letters Patent**. Northumberland allegedly had to bully several members of the council to sign them. Their reluctance was unsurprising, since Letters Patent lacked the legal authority of an Act of Parliament.

**Key terms**

**Minister**
The Protestant equivalent of the Catholic priest. Most Protestants preferred the former to the latter as 'priest' carried with it suggestions of a special status with special powers.

**Letters Patent**
A legal instrument used by the monarch to confer a title or post.

**Key dates**

Edward VI died: 1553

Lady Jane Grey proclaimed Queen: 1553

Mary I took the throne: 1553

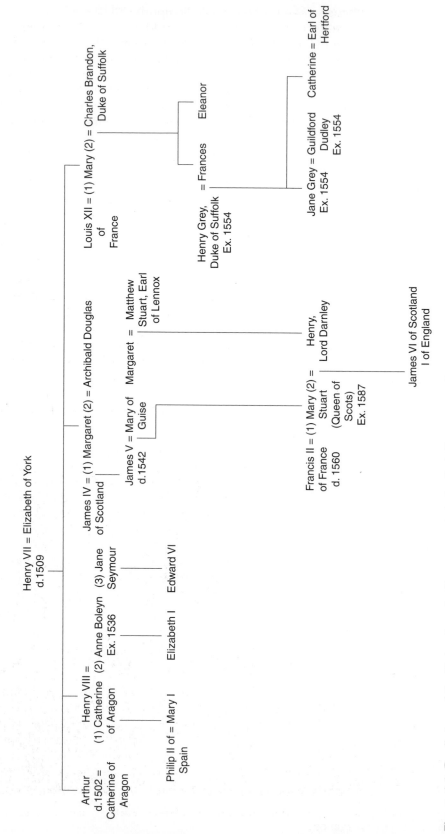

**Figure 1.1:** Family tree of the Tudor dynasty. Key: =, married; d., died; Ex., executed.

On 6 July 1553, Edward died. At first, it looked as if Northumberland was in a strong position. Most of the privy councillors, judges, 22 peers and the mayor and aldermen of London had given their assent to the 'Devise', and Queen Jane was proclaimed in London on 10 July. What he needed was to imprison Mary, and so he invited her to Greenwich to see her supposedly sick brother. On her way there, she was tipped off that Edward had died and hastily galloped away to her own manor at Kenninghall in Norfolk. There, she could rely on the support of Catholic gentry and, if needed, had an escape route to the continent via the port of Great Yarmouth. She then wrote to the council proclaiming her title to the crown and moved to the Howard stronghold of Framlingham in Suffolk.

It is possible that his failure to secure Mary's person was the key to Northumberland's downfall. He was obliged to leave London for Cambridge in pursuit of her, and the council as a whole noted that her revolt in East Anglia (and the strongly Catholic Thames Valley) was growing: her letter to the council claiming the throne arrived on 11 July. Several ships in the fleet sent to cut off Mary's escape route mutinied and declared for her. Northumberland's support on the council evaporated: on 19 July, the Catholic members of the council proclaimed Mary, and were joined by *politiques* such as Paget. Faced with widespread desertion from his armed forces, Northumberland surrendered in Cambridge on 20 July. He may have hoped that a strategic conversion to Catholicism might have saved his neck, but he was mistaken. On 22 August, he was beheaded on Tower Hill in London.

The execution of Northumberland, 22 August 1553 on Tower Hill in London. What evidence is there that this source is propaganda?

Proponents of the traditional interpretation of the period might argue that the succession crisis amounted to a rebellion, and, as such, represented yet another example of a structural crisis in which the authority of the monarch was under threat. This argument can be dismissed for the following reasons:

- The succession crisis developed out of the desperately unfortunate illness of a previously healthy and promising young King. It is therefore a crisis of circumstance, caused by abysmal luck.
- Edward's ability to impose a highly dubious 'Devise' on a reluctant élite demonstrates the innate strength of the monarchy.
- Dynastic loyalty was probably the key factor in Mary's success.

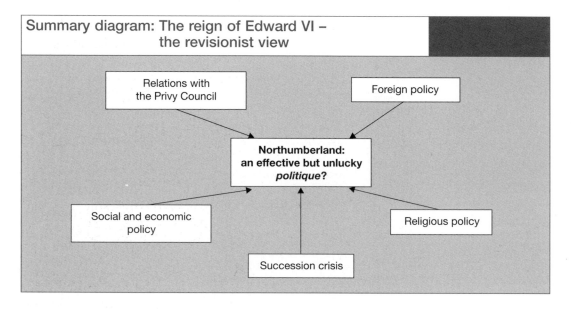

Summary diagram: The reign of Edward VI – the revisionist view

## 5 | The Reign of Mary I 1553–8: The Revisionist View

### The political effectiveness of Mary's government

Traditional historiography (see page 5) argued that the Marian government was conspicuous by its paralysis and sterility, and that the Privy Council was full of devout nonentities and too large and unwieldy to work effectively.

### The Privy Council

Mary had little formal training in the duties of a monarch. She recognised the need for advice, but the most experienced councillors either were Protestant or had served the Protestant cause and were therefore suspect in her eyes. Her most loyal co-religionists – who had served in her own household – were inexperienced and not of the highest rank (such as Sir Francis Englefield and Sir Robert Rochester). The one obvious exception was Gardiner, whom she duly made her Lord Chancellor.

Key question
What response might be made to Pollard's criticisms of the Marian Privy Council?

A portrait of Mary I painted by Anthonis Mor in 1554. Why is it important to know that the painting was probably commissioned by Philip II's family?

On the face of it, Pollard's traditional criticism about the size and make-up of the Privy Council, which allegedly encouraged debilitating factional squabbles, appears to be justified (see page 5). However, his criticisms can largely be dismissed. The Catholic backwoodsmen were nominal members and rarely attended. The council very quickly set up committees (exactly as had happened under Northumberland) dealing with the full range of governmental affairs (from the collection of debts on crown lands to the fleet): significantly, the casual members were excluded. Philip II, after his marriage and before his return to Spain in 1555, encouraged the setting up of an inner council of nine, including Gardiner and Nicholas Heath, the Archbishop of York, Sir William Petre, the Earls of Arundel and Pembroke, the very able Lord Treasurer, William Paulet, the Marquis of Winchester and that quintessential *politique*, Sir William Paget. In other words, this was not a council of pious incompetents. It was able to display some innovative approaches, including establishing a corporate seal for its business and negotiating for itself the terms of reconciliation with Rome. On the other hand, factional intrigue was not entirely absent. The impetus for the committee system appears to have come from Paget, who used it to check the influence of Gardiner (always a tricky customer).

## Parliament

The traditional, critical interpretation describes the Marian Parliaments as oppositional. The House of Commons, it is alleged, was quarrelsome and inclined to oppose all and every action of the Marian regime, particularly the Catholic religious settlement and the Spanish Match. However, this view is largely untenable. One needs to bear the following in mind:

**Key question**
What criticisms might be made of the traditional, critical interpretation of Mary's relations with Parliament?

- The frequency with which Parliaments were called and the amount of legislation passed were considerably greater than in the Edwardian period: hardly the sign of a crown and Parliament in conflict.
- Mary followed her father's lead in gaining parliamentary support for the most important matters of state, including the marriage treaty, the religious settlement and the conduct of the war with France.
- It is true that there was significant opposition to some of the potential implications of government policies. The main worry of both Houses of Parliament was over the church property acquired by the laity in the Reformation. In the third Parliament, neither House would proceed with the bill to reconcile England to Rome without an agreement confirming current ownership of former church land. Similarly, a bill confiscating the estates of Protestant exiles was rejected. The Lords and Commons, working together, curtailed the extent of Philip's powers and rejected the crown's proposal to bar Elizabeth from the succession. This opposition, however, cannot be seen as Protestant MPs and peers opposing a Catholic regime. Both Catholics and Protestants, for example, opposed the restitution of church land: they also worked together to limit Philip's powers.
- Parliament co-operated with the government in most religious matters and in social and economic legislation (such as the Retail Trades Act and the Woollen Cloth Act). Mary recognised that Parliament was generally prepared to compromise and was prepared to compromise herself (as over Philip's coronation, which she had longed for but Parliament would not grant).

## Social and economic policies

Let us briefly remind ourselves of some of the longer – and medium – term economic problems, against the background of the contemporary assumption that trade and economic life were generally no business of the government *per se*:

**Key question**
How accurate is the traditional claim that the social and economic policies of Mary's government were ineffective?

- population growth
- rise in prices
- **inflation** (caused by the above and by debasement of the coinage, although Northumberland had improved the situation somewhat)
- poverty and vagabondage

**Inflation**
Where money loses its value and prices rise.

Key term

- also, cloth exports faltered in the 1540s and 1550s due to saturation of the overseas markets.

These profound changes inevitably impacted on the economy as a whole. Some historians argue that they stimulated a movement away from pre-capitalist forms of enterprise to early **capitalism**:

- This was because the traditional assumptions about the way the economic life of town and village was shaped were called into question by the problems outlined above.
- Traditionally, towns regulated their economic activity through merchants and guilds of craftsmen who supervised apprenticeships and fixed prices and wages. This system simply could not respond to population pressure and price rises.
- Wage rates fell as competition for jobs grew due to the expanding population.
- This meant that there was a reservoir of cheap, available, mobile labour outside the traditional apprenticeship system: such labourers could very easily fall into poverty and vagabondage.
- Also, as the cloth market declined, manufacturers moved out of towns to escape the restrictions of the guild system. Husbandmen (farmworkers) might be able to supplement their agricultural work with textile trades (using family members) and relying on a new class of middlemen ('bodgers') to supply the raw material and sell the finished product.

These conditions were characteristic of the mid-Tudor period as a whole, but they were given a particular twist in Mary's reign due to two catastrophic harvest failures in 1555 and 1556 plus typhus and influenza epidemics of 1556 and 1558. Loss of life was high, and may even have relieved some of the population pressure.

## Actions of Mary's government

So, given the historiographical tradition alleging inertia and sterility, did the Marian government take any meaningful action to respond to the challenges facing economic life? Robert Tittler argues that the government did indeed take measures to attempt to cope with the painful structural changes and shorter term issues. These can be considered under the following headings:

- Improving international trade.
- Customs and the crown's finances.
- Government intervention in domestic commerce and industry.
- Poor relief, poverty and crime issues.

### Improving international trade

Improving international trade meant improving the wool trade, since England had little else to offer. This had begun to falter by mid-century. It was run through the twin **monopolies** of the Merchant Adventurers and the Merchants of the Staple in Calais: the former dealt with the sale of woollen cloth (the finished article) and the latter with the sale of wool itself. Mary's government made meaningful, if largely unsuccessful, attempts to protect the Adventurers against competition from the Hanseatic

**Key terms**

**Capitalism**
An economic system based on competition and an unrestricted market.

**Monopoly**
A licence granted by the crown that gave an individual or a group the sole right to produce or trade in a particular commodity.

League and to find a new home for the Staple once Calais had fallen to the French in 1557.

The Marian government continued with the Edwardian government's interest in developing trade links with Russia and the Baltic. The Muscovy Company was given the privileges of a charter in 1555. It imported useful naval supplies and sold herbs, wool and metalwork to Russians in return. Again building on the contacts made by Edwardian adventurers, useful footholds were established in Morocco and Guinea.

## Customs and the crown's finances

Asking Parliament for frequent subsidies always carried a certain political risk, and so Mary sensibly attempted to exploit one of the prerogative rights of the crown: customs duties.

Customs duties were ripe for reform. Hundreds of commodities were untaxed. Existing rates had fallen behind inflation. Northumberland's advisers had urged him to impose a new Book of Rates in 1552, and Mary adopted the recommendations in the new Book of Rates in 1558 (concentrating on increasing rates on non-essential goods to prevent hardship to the poor). She got it right – Elizabeth's government more or less kept to the Book of Rates throughout her long reign. Of course, new rates were of little use without efficient collection, and William Paulet, Marquis of Winchester, set up the office of Surveyor General of Customs, initially for the port of London, and with the intention of spreading its jurisdiction to the rest of the country. The brevity of Mary's reign meant that it could have no immediate impact.

Mary's government, like that of her predecessors, inevitably struggled to balance the books because the long-standing system of expecting the crown to fund the government from its own resources was inadequate for its needs. Mary was able to secure subsidies from Parliament in 1555, but still needed to ask for what was called a Privy Seal loan on top of this. Declaring war with France in June 1557 was fiscally risky, even though Philip was persuaded to pay £48,000 towards an expedition to the Netherlands. Mary did not return the church lands taken by the crown in the previous reign as she had promised, and was forced to raise loans on the Antwerp money-markets. Loades sees the Book of Rates as part of the battle to raise money for the war effort. Similarly, the government placed an increased duty ('imposition') on cloth that generated, by the 1560s, half the customs' revenue.

Also, the government planned a recoinage that fell foul of the problems of the final year of the reign (war, pestilence and famine) but which was adopted with great success by the Elizabethan government. Elizabeth also benefited from the personal interest Mary showed in the **Court of Wards and Liveries**. Mary prevented the Exchequer from taking over, and muddying the finances of, the Court of Wards and Liveries and insisted on the application of advanced methods of auditing and accounting. On balance, Loades judges that 'On the whole, Mary's financial management had been tight and effective.'

**Court of Wards and Liveries**
Responsible for administering the crown's feudal revenues.

Key term

The final point to be made on the crown finances is that, compared to fellow monarchs in France and the Empire, the English crown was far less in debt: after all, only Henry VII had really been able to balance the books – at considerable political cost.

### Government intervention in domestic commerce and industry

Generally speaking, the Marian government did indeed intervene; itself a sign of energy and commitment. It can hardly be blamed for coming down on the side of protecting the traditional industries rather than leaping into the dark and trying to encourage emerging capitalism by removing, rather than reinforcing, restrictions. The Retail Trades Act of 1554 protected merchants' monopolies and the Weavers' Act of 1553 and the Woollen Cloth Act of 1557 fined those who were making cloth outside the traditional jurisdictions of guilds and towns. Mary's government also responded positively to the appeal for help from towns which, as we noted earlier, were suffering from the winds of economic change. The Marian strategy was to grant twice as many requests for charters of incorporation as previous governments. This helped towns to raise revenue for poor relief and generally protect themselves against competition from other towns.

### Other poor relief, poverty and crime issues

We remember that the Marian years may well have experienced a more pressing need for relief than other governments. Certainly there is little suggestion of paralysis or inaction. In London Mary encouraged the development of five private charities (including the hospitals of St Bartholomew's and Bethlam) into a city-wide system of social welfare. Throughout the country the government took action against grain hoarders. In 1557, it experimented in Yorkshire with the system of using JPs as overseers of the poor (a strategy adopted by Elizabeth: see page 195).

Can we detect an improvement in the social and economic state of the country and its people in the short reign of Mary I? The answer is not really. But the problems were considerable. And there was no uprising based on social and economic issues like the Kett Rebellion, despite the real distress. It is true that Mary's rule increased the burden of crown debt (especially given the war with France), but Mary did encourage a climate of austerity at court fitting the times. Her reign is one of continuity with the past, but not inaction or complacency. Her government did plan for the future using traditional approaches, and her hated half-sister was the one to benefit.

### Religion and the Catholic restoration

Mary's past experiences undoubtedly affected her view of Protestantism. To her, it seemed to be a sham religion, used by factional enemies of her beloved mother, Catherine of Aragon, to secure the annulment that had brought so much misery on

**Key question**
What were the aims of Mary's religious policies, and how far did they succeed?

Catherine and Mary herself. Mary therefore assumed that there were very few true Protestants, and those who were true were a desperate minority, out to do Satan's work. In her view, all that she needed to do was to remove that hard core and provide the opportunity for the return of the Catholic practices her subjects enthusiastically awaited. We will need to assess how accurate this view was. In the first place, we should look at the state of religion at the start of her reign. Professor Loades has memorably commented on the reaction to a reintroduction of Catholicism: 'frequent enthusiasm, occasional resistance, and a large amount of unchronicled indifference'.

This may be so, but it has to be admitted that the attitude of the populace is notoriously difficult to uncover and therefore represents an area of major historiographical debate – a debate that covers the whole Reformation period. The very traditional stance was that the Protestant Reformation was largely an act of state; that is, one dictated by monarchs and successfully imposed on the people. This interpretation was amended by the massively influential work of A.G. Dickens. Dickens' *The English Reformation* (1964) suggested that the 'reformation from above' was complemented, even preceded, and, at times, opposed by a 'reformation from below' which relied on **anticlerical** feeling and an informed Protestantism. Dickens' thesis has been challenged by a number of historians, most of whom, like Eamon Duffy, J.J. Scarisbrick and Richard Rex, are Catholics. Along with Christopher Haigh, they argue that there is no evidence of widespread disillusion with the Catholic Church in England, and that the imposition of reformed ideas by the state (or factions within the government) was not welcomed. Scarisbrick sums up the issue by commenting, 'on the whole, English men and women did not want the Reformation and most of them were slow to accept it when it came'. This meant that Edwardian Protestantism was frequently resented, that iconoclasm in particular proceeded in the teeth of considerable local opposition and that local communities, aided and abetted by parish clergy and churchwardens, managed to conceal church property threatened with seizure by the authorities.

The overall impact of the revisionist work has been to suggest that widespread acceptance of Protestantism was certainly not a feature of Edwardian England, and that it was the second or even third decade of Elizabeth's reign before England was in any meaningful way Protestant (and even then with strong pockets of regionalised Catholic **recusancy**). The revisionist interpretation has received strong support from Ronald Hutton's 1987 work on churchwardens' accounts, which record parish responses to government instructions on changes to church ritual and ornamentation. Hutton concludes that: 'the evidence of churchwardens' accounts bears out the assertions of Dr Haigh and Professor Scarisbrick, that the great majority of the English and Welsh peoples did not want the Reformations of Henry, Edward and Elizabeth'.

**Anticlerical**
Opposition to the position and authority of the clergy.

**Recusancy**
The refusal to attend the services of the Church of England.

Key terms

This debate clearly impacts on our discussion of Marian religious policy, since her reinstituting Catholicism would arguably be more of a relief than a reimposition for most. In Marshall's *The Impact of the English Reformation* (1997), Dickens revisited the debate, and argued, not only that Protestantism was more widespread than Haigh and others alleged, but that Mary's rule did little or nothing to reawaken popular enthusiasm for Catholicism. In a memorable burst of rhetoric, he asks: 'Did the hapless Mary Tudor succeed in fusing **Spanish Inquisition** with Roman papacy in the popular mind?' This, of course, raises key questions: was Mary Tudor 'hapless' and did she really try to fill the popular mind in this way?

We should now consider Mary's religious policies in the light of this debate over their effectiveness and reception. What, then, were Mary's actions?

- On her accession, prominent Protestants were deprived of their livings. Six bishops and the two Archbishops were dismissed from their posts (four for having married).
- The Protestant church leaders, Cranmer, Hooper, Latimer and Ridley, were imprisoned.
- Protestant printing presses were closed down and foreign Protestants ordered to leave the realm.
- In October 1553, Mary's first Parliament repealed all the Edwardian religious legislation and restored the service in use at Henry VIII's death. Parliament refused, however, to pass a bill punishing those failing to attend church services. Nor would MPs agree to restore the property of the bishopric of Durham, given that it was now in lay hands.
- Mary detested the thought of married clergy, and so a quarter of the clergy were deprived of their livings. She refounded a number of monastic institutions in London (including Westminster Abbey).

Tittler sees 1554 as the pivotal year of Mary's religious policies. The Wyatt Rebellion of January of that year had demonstrated that Protestantism would not obligingly fade away, and so Mary decided to confront its former champions. In April, she forced Cranmer, Latimer and Ridley to take part in a disputation at Oxford. Cranmer partially **recanted**, but Ridley conducted his defence brilliantly even though he was deprived of books.

Mary's marriage with Philip II of Spain in July 1554 brought into England a number of **Dominicans** conspicuous for their experience in the fight against heresy: Juan de Villagarcia duly secured Cranmer's full recantation.

In November 1554, Reginald Pole (pronounced 'Pool') belatedly arrived as **cardinal legate**. Mary herself had obstructed his arrival. The problem was that Parliament would not pass legislation restoring to the church those lands seized largely through the dissolution of the monasteries and chantries and sold on to the aristocracy. She was aware that the Pope expected the restoration of land before Pole accepted England back into the Catholic fold. The monastic and church lands issue was left

## Key terms

**Spanish Inquisition**
The Spanish branch of the Holy Office, charged by popes with the uncovering of heresy. Methods might, with the participation of secular authority, include torture.

**Recant**
To withdraw former statements of belief.

**Dominicans**
A Catholic religious order devoted to preaching and combating heresy.

**Cardinal legate**
A top-ranking papal representative whose decisions could be overruled only by a pope.

deliberately unresolved, and so, in return for the abolition of all the Henrician religious legislation and the reinstating of the medieval heresy laws, Pole granted the country papal **absolution**. By January 1555 he had agreed to concede the lay ownership of church lands.

These initial manoeuvres suggest that Mary, far from being a politically dim religious zealot, was prepared to compromise over issues dear to her heart. She also recognised that church reform was necessary, and Pole shared her perspective. However, neither he nor Mary considered that a campaign of **evangelising** and mission to the laity was a priority. Pole did not make use of the new preaching order of the **Jesuits** to enthuse the laity with the spirit of **Counter-Reformation** Catholicism. His vision of the church was a clerical and hierarchical one: the laity would gain (in the end) from reform, but his first aim was to ensure that the bishops were of the right calibre. As MacCulloch has pointed out, both he and Mary are to be commended for the 13 appointments made to the bench of bishops. Gone were Henry's days when bishops were appointed primarily because they would be effective royal administrators: the Marian bishops were almost always theologians and prepared to obey Pole's demand that they remain in their dioceses and make their lifestyle appropriate to spiritual rather than **secular** lords. It is significant that these bishops refused to compromise when Elizabeth I came to the throne (see page 89).

Pole identified lack of **ecclesiastical** discipline and financial impoverishment as his chief priorities. His weapons were the bishops. He enjoined them to conduct rigorous visitations (inspections of churches in their dioceses) to improve the standard of the clergy and to audit accounts effectively. He sent them into battle as administrators, but not as evangelists. That, he felt, could wait until the clergy themselves were better disciplined and better trained. And so, the London Synod of 1555 issued 12 decrees. They included stern warnings against **pluralism**, but this fell foul of the simple fact that there was a chronic shortage of priests. Edwardian ordinations were not accepted, and the clergy who refused to discard their wives would not be re-employed. He was therefore forced to grant 200 **dispensations** for pluralism. He tried to help these hard-pressed clergy by commissioning a new version of the New Testament and a new book of **homilies**, but these were not implemented before the end of the reign.

In the view of Loades, the piety of the Marian church was not that of the Middle Ages, nor of the Counter-Reformation, but of the English **humanists** and reformers like Thomas More from the 1520s and early 1530s. There were no attempts to restore the great pilgrimage shrines of Canterbury or Walsingham. And, significantly, the crown did not entirely relinquish its ascendancy over the church despite the repeal of the Act of Supremacy. There were more references to the Queen's 'godly proceedings' than to the Pope, and Mary was quite prepared to refuse Pope Paul IV's demand that Pole (a former rival of his) return to Rome to face charges of heresy (in 1557).

## Key terms

**Absolution**
Releasing from sin.

**Evangelising**
Preaching God's message and the teaching of the Church.

**Jesuits**
A missionary religious order founded in 1534 and recognised officially by the Pope in 1540. Jesuits were characterised by a rigorous but emotional piety based on disciplining the will.

**Counter-Reformation**
Historians' term referring to the reform movement within the Catholic Church.

**Secular**
Non-spiritual.

**Ecclesiastical**
Of the church.

**Pluralism**
A priest owning more than one living and therefore being responsible for more than one parish.

**Dispensation**
Permission given to step outside the usual rules.

**Homilies**
Short sermon-like passages that could be read instead of preaching.

Key term

**Humanist**
Participant in the intellectual movement associated with the revival of the learning of classical Greece and Rome. Humanists looked towards a greater understanding of the Christian scriptures and were dismissive of what they saw as superstitious practices in the church.

## The persecution of Protestants

Between February 1555 and the end of her reign, Mary burned 300 Protestants. By comparison to burnings on the continent, it was not excessive: but it does seem to have backfired. Church leaders such as Cranmer, Latimer, Ridley, Rogers and Rowland Taylor all suffered the heretics' death, but the later victims were of humbler status: artisans, yeomen, labourers. The fact that Protestants of all classes were prepared to die for their faith exploded the argument that Protestantism was a convenient veil for political gain, and the creating of martyrs was, as ever, propaganda for the martyrs' own cause. Indeed, the Marian martyrs were the basis of John Foxe's *Acts and Monuments* of 1563: known popularly as *Foxe's Book of Martyrs*, the work defined English Protestant attitudes towards Catholics for centuries.

## Conclusion on the Marian religious policies

The return to Catholicism was probably not widely unpopular. Mary's strategies reflected her own religious upbringing and were, as one might expect of a monarch, characterised by top-down reform. The attempt to reinvigorate Catholicism was meaningful, but, as with all Mary's policies, it needed the time that, in the end, Mary did not have.

**Key question**
To what extent can Mary's foreign policies, including the Spanish Match, be seen as disastrous?

## The Spanish Match, Wyatt Rebellion and foreign policies

Mary's foreign policy had been generally viewed by Whiggish historians as an unmitigated disaster (see pages 5–6). She is blamed for insisting on a marriage that was deeply unpopular in England; this supposed lack of patriotism on her part was a mark of her identification with the ruling Habsburg family of Spain.

The martyrdom of Thomas Cranmer. An illustration to John Foxe's *Acts and Monuments*, 1570 edition. How might the burnings of Protestants affect attitudes towards Mary's rule?

The marriage with Philip II of Spain then led England into a war in the service of Spanish interests, which duly culminated in the loss of England's final outpost in France (Calais). The only honourable thing that Mary could do was to die, and she duly obliged. It has also been alleged that her marriage and the Habsburg alliance itself generated the Wyatt Rebellion, parliamentary protest and massive divisions in the Privy Council (between Paget, who was more or less in favour of the marriage and Gardiner, who was in favour of a marriage with Edward Courtenay).

On the other hand, Susan Doran argues that Mary's marriage was not as ill-conceived as this interpretation (or hindsight) suggests. There were, after all, few eligible candidates and contemporary (male) opinion found it difficult to contemplate a woman ruling alone. There was much to recommend the match with Philip. As Paget argued, it would provide England with an invaluable ally against Henry II of France who clearly had his beady eye on Calais and was assiduously building up links with Scotland. Commercial interests (particularly with the Netherlands) would benefit from a Habsburg alliance. However, one has to question whether such considerations were at the forefront of Mary's mind. The Habsburgs had ever been the staunchest friends of Catherine of Aragon and Mary in their unhappiest times.

Doran accepts that Mary's method of negotiating the Spanish Match was a mistake. She met with the Imperial ambassador in a **hugger-mugger** way rather than with Privy Council involvement. Mary announced her intentions to the council in October 1553. The clandestine negotiations had stimulated factional intrigue (Gardiner vs Paget). How serious this was is difficult to establish, but closeting herself with the Imperial ambassador, Renard, gave her councillors the feeling that, following the marriage, Mary would surround herself with Spaniards instead of Englishmen. Tittler comments that this was a typically Marian failure of public relations. Doran feels that the extent of antipathy towards the marriage is difficult to assess, but that there is a clue in the provisions of the marriage treaty – which strictly limited Philip's powers as king – and a comment made by Paget, who described 'the fears felt by the English that his Highness, if the Queen were to die without heirs, might try to make himself King of England'. Also, Philip had an evil reputation (the 'Black Legend') from his suppression of dissent in the Netherlands.

**Hugger-mugger**
Secretive.

**Key term**

## The marriage treaty, January 1554

The treaty explicitly stated that, if Mary were to die without an heir, Philip's title and rights would die with her. If, on the other hand, Mary produced a son, that child would inherit England, the Netherlands and Franche-Comté. If Philip's son by an earlier marriage were to die, then Mary's son would also inherit Spain. No Spaniard was to be appointed to any English office. Philip was to have the title of king, but none of the prerogatives or property that went with the title. Of course, one could argue that devising such an explicit and effective set of safeguards does demonstrate that the council could act quickly and effectively – and it may well be that the treaty was the fruit of co-operation between Paget and Gardiner. Philip himself commented to one of his aides that he did not consider the restrictions binding (not having been involved in the negotiations in any way), but it was as well that his comments were not reported to the Privy Council.

### The Wyatt Rebellion, January–February 1554

Key date

Wyatt Rebellion: 1554

There is an intimate connection between the proposed Spanish Match and a major conspiracy that was hatched with the aim of putting Elizabeth on the throne. The conspirators, who were generally prominent members of the Edwardian regime, including the Duke of Suffolk, Sir Peter Carew of Devon and Sir Thomas Wyatt of Kent, attempted to rouse local feeling against the Spanish Match and march on London. In the event, only Wyatt attracted enough support to make the attempt, but that attempt was genuinely dangerous given his proximity to the capital and the sympathy and support he collected on the way to London (and within the city itself). Here, Mary demonstrated an impressive resolve and an ability to communicate it: a speech at Guildhall roused her defenders, and Ludgate was held against Wyatt. His entry to the city was denied, and his followers fled.

The affair ended in the execution of Wyatt, Lady Jane Grey and Lord Guildford Dudley. Elizabeth herself was in danger, but no connection with Wyatt could be proved.

Although the overt motives for the rebellion were political, it would be unwise to dismiss the Protestant agenda. Tittler rightly points out that no major participant was Catholic, and that the only target for violence was the property of Bishop Gardiner.

The Wyatt Rebellion reveals a strength of Protestant feeling in the home counties and London which should not be disregarded. Mary is shown in a very positive light: astute; calm under pressure. However, the lack of response outside Kent and London is suggestive of the strength of loyalty to the Tudor regime and, perhaps, to traditional religion.

### The Habsburg–Valois war (Spain vs France)

We recall that Northumberland had sought to preserve reasonably friendly relations with France (despite the presence of Mary, Queen of Scots at the French court), while maintaining a wary approach to both Scotland and Charles V. This, of course, changed with the accession of Mary. Even so, Mary attempted (without success) to play the role of peace-broker by sponsoring negotiations between Spain and France at Gravelines. But the accession of the anti-Spanish Pope Paul IV proved to be the spark that ignited the conflict.

There is little doubt that Mary was happy to accept the advice of her councillors to keep out of the war. She was well aware of the danger to Calais, to her finances and to Scotland (and possibly Ireland) if she waged war with France. Unfortunately, the

French played right into Spanish hands. Henry II sheltered some English conspirators (the Dudleys), confiscated a merchant vessel and apparently sponsored a hare-brained Protestant landing in Scarborough by Thomas Stafford; more than enough to turn the council's thoughts to war. Nor was the country unprepared. With Philip's encouragement, the council had revitalised the navy (with 21 men-at-war available) until it was a genuinely formidable force. Its finances were under the care of the able Lord Treasurer, Winchester. And the administration had passed a crucial Militia Act which discarded the traditional and inefficient method of raising forces by feudal levy and placed the raising of troops under the Lord Lieutenants of the counties, towns and JPs: far more efficient. The final spur to war came when the Pope broke his alliance with France and so saved Mary the embarrassment of fighting against the Vicar of Christ. In June 1557, war was declared on France. As often in such cases, war with a long-standing foreign enemy united opponents and supporters of the regime – even the sons of the Duke of Northumberland fought for Mary. Parliament raised an ample subsidy.

At first, all went well. The Scots were contained, the English navy cleared French shipping out of the Channel and English forces participated in the capture of St Quentin (and were generously given the credit by Philip). Unfortunately, Philip then made a strategic mistake. He halted his forces for the winter, gave the French a breathing-space to recover and so allowed the French to make a surprise attack on Calais, whose garrison fought heroically for three weeks without help from Spain or England but duly capitulated. In purely economic terms, the loss of the Pale of Calais was not significant (the merchants of the Calais Staple were impoverished anyway), but the effect on morale was huge. And its loss gave Protestant apologists another stick with which to beat the Marian regime.

# 6 | Conclusion

Mary's was not a sterile regime. Dickens' attempt to link alleged political ineptitude with religious conservatism is, in the end, unconvincing. The Privy Council was neither inefficient nor naïf: nor was Marian Catholicism widely unpopular. The rule of Mary I was unproductive because, through no fault of its own, it lacked the one crucial ingredient: time. It had not undermined, or come close to undermining, the political system of king (or queen)-in-parliament by sabotaging relationships within the political nation. Its religious policies had not destroyed the unity of the kingdom or compromised central authority. Had Mary Tudor lived for 30 years, then one might be talking of a Marian, rather than an Elizabethan, Age.

The challenges facing Elizabeth on her accession in 1558, then, were considerable but they were not those which characterise a structural crisis. The mid-Tudor crises were real enough, but were crises of circumstance rather than of deep-seated fault-lines in the political, social and economic fabric of the country. It is true that

**Key question**
How far can Mary's government be seen as one without positive achievement?

the religious disunity generated by the English Reformation had the potential to destabilise regimes and, conceivably, monarchy itself. The religious conflicts in continental Europe were a case in point. But England was a far more centralised country than its continental neighbours, and its religious changes came, not from pressure below, but from the state itself. The government could generally rely on habitual acceptance of systems of authority and, in the end, possessed the coercive strength to smash persistent opposition.

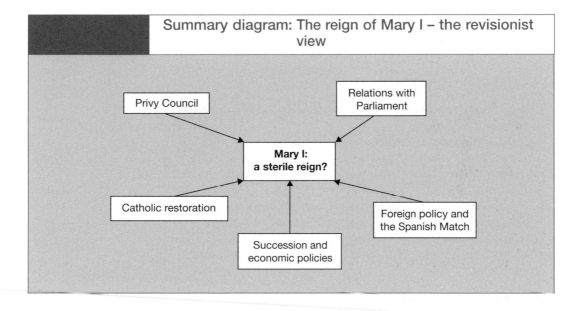

Summary diagram: The reign of Mary I – the revisionist view

## Study Guide: AS Questions

### In the style of OCR A

Assess the main problems that faced Elizabeth I at her accession in 1558. (50 marks)

---

*Exam tips*

An assessment of Elizabeth's problems in 1558 needs much more than a list or a series of descriptions. This kind of approach would score low marks only. An assessment requires you to evaluate the seriousness of each difficulty in respect of how easily Elizabeth dealt with each problem and decide whether any of the problems were inter-related. It is also important that you rank the problems in terms of their difficulty or seriousness. It is likely that you will discuss some of the following:

- English Catholics who were intent on maintaining their faith and supporting the Papacy.
- English Protestants who had been in exile during Mary's reign and returned with the aim of reforming the Church of England.
- Foreign problems: war with France, uncertain relations with Spain and Scotland, a desire to win over the Papacy.
- Mary, Queen of Scots, who as heir presumptive and a devout Catholic, was a serious rival to the English throne as long as Elizabeth remained unmarried and childless.
- Financial and economic problems: inherited debt, limited revenue, high war expenditure, limited overseas trade, narrow industrial base.
- Elizabeth's lack of administrative and political experience.

## In the style of OCR B

Why was England so divided over religion by 1558?      (25 marks)

---

*Exam tips*

*The page references are intended to take you straight to the material that will help you to answer the question.*

In this question you are asked to explain why different beliefs were held by English people at the time of Elizabeth I's accession to the throne. Also implicit is the need to explain why people held these beliefs so strongly that the country was divided over religious issues. You should show how these reasons are linked to one another and you should also evaluate your explanation, for example showing the role that these different factors played and assessing their relative importance in relation to the question.

   You might, for example, argue that most people's thinking was heavily influenced by the central role played by religion in all aspects of life, but that whether they subscribed to Catholic or Protestant beliefs was determined by a range of factors such as social and economic interactions, literacy levels and printed materials.

   You might further explain the role of government in introducing changes in the doctrines and allegiances of the English Church in the previous three decades (pages 3, 9–12, 16–17 and 25–9), showing that there were political and dynastic issues at stake for the ruling élite (pages 17–19) while the issue of land ownership might be more pressing for those who had benefited from the sale of monastic lands (page 22).

   What you should do:

- Plan your answer, starting with the different beliefs that were held then identifying reasons why each set of beliefs was held by a particular group of people.
- Continue your plan by grouping the reasons you have identified. You could group reasons why many people held strong religious beliefs, set against reasons why different sets of beliefs were held.
- Remember to go beyond the appeal of different forms of Christianity, explaining how people's motives might be influenced by political and economic concerns.
- Remember to consider the events in the previous few years that had helped to polarise people's beliefs.

What you should avoid:

- Describing the different sets of beliefs.
- Explaining a list of reasons in turn.

## Study Guide: A2 Question

### In the style of AQA

'The Duke of Northumberland's government was most strongly characterised by his ruthless ambition and determination to control the affairs of England.' Assess the validity of this view of Northumberland between 1549 and 1553.          (45 marks)

---

#### Exam tips

*The cross-references are intended to take you straight to the material that will help you answer the question.*

An A2 essay question will be more complex than those encountered for AS level and it will be necessary to analyse the question carefully before beginning. There are two premises to consider and support or challenge here: one that Northumberland was driven solely by ruthless ambition and lust for power, and the other that there was no other course but execution in 1553. It is possible to agree with one but not the other and it is, of course, possible to have shades of opinion too.

   You will need to refer to the material on pages 13–19 in order to remind yourself of Northumberland's actions and downfall and you should first decide what you are going to argue and secondly, draw up an essay plan. You will need to consider the motivation behind Northumberland's policies with regard to his:

- religious programme
- economic and social policies
- style of government and attitude to others, e.g. Somerset
- foreign policy decisions
- concern about the succession
- actions on Edward's death.

For all these points you should look not only for details that support the quotation, but also for those that can be used to argue against it. Do take care not to let the answer become simply a description of what historians have said about Northumberland. Although you will want to refer to historiographical interpretations, you should always try to reflect on the evidence on which such views are based and draw your own conclusions.

# 2

# Meeting the Challenge of Religion: The Elizabethan Religious Settlement

**POINTS TO CONSIDER**

Religious disunity was seen as a great evil and an enemy of political and social cohesion. The new Queen therefore had, through Parliament, to establish the form of religion to be taught in every church in the country. Mary's restored Catholicism was set aside in favour of a form of Protestantism. This chapter will therefore consider:

- The factors that shaped the settlement, including the religious beliefs of the Queen and the role of Parliament
- The way in which the settlement was established
- The nature of the settlement, including the teaching of the Church of England
- The Queen's treatment of the Church of England

**Key dates**

1559   Acts of Supremacy and Uniformity
             Book of Common Prayer
             Injunctions and Visitations
             Act of Exchange
1563   Parker drew up the Thirty-Nine articles
1566   Parker's *Advertisements* and the Vestiarian
             controversy
1571   Thirty-Nine Articles given parliamentary approval

## 1 | The Religious Beliefs of Elizabeth I

**Key question**
What does the evidence reveal about Elizabeth's personal religious beliefs?

No complete understanding of the Elizabethan religious settlement is possible without an awareness of the personal beliefs of Elizabeth I. Unfortunately she left no clear statement of her own religious views. Her opinions were shrouded in the obscurity of some of her utterances, in her constitutional incapacity for making decisions and in the distortions of those who reported her views.

On her religious upbringing, at least, we can be relatively clear. That upbringing would certainly predispose her towards Protestantism. Firstly, we must not fail to take into account the circumstances of her birth. The Church of Rome was not alone in denying the legality of Anne Boleyn's marriage to Henry VIII. But, given the fact that the legitimacy of her mother's marriage

'The Coronation portrait.' Shows Queen Elizabeth I crowned, wearing the cloth of gold which she wore at her coronation on 15 January 1559, which had previously been worn by Mary I. What messages does the portrait communicate about the new queen?

went hand in hand with the break with Rome, it is not difficult to see that Elizabeth would associate her own right to the throne with opposition to the Papacy. Also, her education was distinctly Protestant. The Boleyn faction was very interested in Luther's views on church reform. A few days before her arrest, Anne Boleyn had entrusted her like-minded chaplain, Matthew Parker (see page 40), with the spiritual welfare of her infant daughter. What use Parker was able to make of that trust is not clear, but Elizabeth's selection of Parker as her first Archbishop of Canterbury suggests the strong attachment and loyalty Elizabeth felt towards her Boleyn ties and to the issues which the Boleyns held dear. The evangelical (gospel-based) stance of the Boleyns was reinforced by Elizabeth's subsequent education when Queen Catherine Parr brought her back to court. Catherine was a convinced Protestant, and the education which Elizabeth and her half-brother Edward received reflected the Queen's convictions.

Any attempt to establish the precise nature of Elizabeth's Protestantism must be based upon inferences from her actions. These inferences will be drawn in Sections 2, 3, 4 and 5 of this chapter. As suggested earlier, her reported words are less easy to assess. We have a number of ambassadors' letters which appear to give precise information on her beliefs and intentions. Ambassadors, however, had a natural desire to present themselves to their monarchs as both incisive and effective. It is all too likely that the accuracy of their information suffered as much from this as from the Queen's undoubted mastery of the arts of evasion and ambiguity.

There is also a certain amount of anecdotal information. We have an account of the frosty reception given by the Queen to a New Year's gift from the Dean of St Paul's in 1561. The Dean, it seems, had left a prayer book by the Queen's place in the cathedral. The book contained elaborately engraved pictures of saints and martyrs:

> When she [the Queen] came to her place, she opened the book, and perused it, and saw the pictures; but frowned and blushed, and then shut it (of which several took notice) ... After Sermon ... applying herself to the Dean, thus she spoke to him:
>
> Q. Mr Dean, how came it to pass that a new Service-book was placed on my cushion?
>
> To which the Dean answered:
>
> D. May it please your Majesty, I caused it to be placed there.
>
> Then said the Queen:
>
> Q. Wherefore did you so?
> D. To present your majesty with a New year's gift.
> Q. You could never present me with a worse.
> D. Why so, Madam?
> Q. You know that I have an adversion to idolatry, to images and pictures of this kind.
> D. Wherein is the idolatry, may it please your Majesty?
> Q. In the cuts resembling Angels and Saints: nay, grosser absurdities, pictures resembling the Blessed Trinity.
> D. I meant no harm: nor did I think it would offend your majesty ...
> Q. You must needs be ignorant then. Have you forgot our Proclamation against images, pictures, and Romish relics in the Churches?

One imagines a stammering, red-faced and apologetic cleric who was left in no doubt as to the Queen's dislike for anything she considered too close to Roman Catholicism. By 'Romish' she meant Roman Catholic, and by Roman Catholic she meant superstition and the worship of false images in the place of God. Indeed, it is significant that Elizabeth's personal religious books – or, at least, those that have survived – are plain and unadorned. In Protestant fashion, there are few images. And in one book, The Litany, with certain other devout and godly meditations, there is a

## Profile: Matthew Parker 1504–75

1527 – Ordained a priest
1535 – Became chaplain to Anne Boleyn
1544 – Master of Corpus Christi College, Cambridge
1552 – Dean of Lincoln
1554 – Deprived of his clerical posts by Mary I. Went into hiding
1559 – Made Archbishop of Canterbury by Elizabeth I
1563 – Revised Cranmer's 42 Articles of Religion; reduced to 39
1566 – Published the *Advertisements* regulating the dress of the clergy
1571 – After further revision, the central doctrinal statement of the Church of England was issued: the Thirty-Nine Articles
1575 – Died

> **Key date**
> Thirty-Nine Articles given parliamentary approval: 1571

Matthew Parker was associated with the White Horse Tavern group of early Cambridge Protestants. His interests lay in early English church history and he was keen to demonstrate the independence of that church from Rome. With reluctance, he accepted the post of chaplain to Anne Boleyn: at her arrest in 1536, she asked him to take care of the Princess Elizabeth. He married in 1547 and was therefore doubly unacceptable to Mary Tudor. His moderation, respect for law and order and lack of interest in politics made him one of the few possible choices for Elizabeth's first Archbishop of Canterbury.

final prayer to God as 'the only ruler of all princes'. To link royal authority so closely to that of God was characteristic of Elizabeth I.

## 2 | Supremacy and Uniformity: The First Moves

> **Key question**
> Why was it wise for the Queen to adopt a moderate form of Protestantism?

It was vital for the new Queen to signal her religious intentions, not only to relieve dangerous uncertainty among her own subjects, but also to avoid turning the perilous international situation into a thorough-going disaster. What were her options? First, she could maintain the Catholicism of Mary Tudor. This would have its advantages, since it would preserve the alliance with Catholic Spain, whose help she desperately needed in the continuing conflict with France and Scotland. However, there is little doubt that Elizabeth's personal preference lay with Protestantism. Her surest supporters were Protestant, and she could not afford to abandon them. Also, failures in Marian propaganda and policy had enabled Protestants to link the burnings of martyrs with submission to Rome, and the policy of submission to Rome with subservience to Spain. Her second option would be to maintain the kind of Catholicism without the Pope which had seemed, at times, to suit her father. It could be argued that, since Elizabeth was the living symbol of Henry VIII's break with Rome, she would naturally feel an attraction for following in his footsteps. However, since those footsteps wavered and lurched theologically to suit their master's mood and political convenience, they would prove immensely difficult to pursue under the vastly different political and religious circumstances confronting Elizabeth.

Alternatively, Elizabeth might signal a moderate form of Protestantism. To do this would indeed prove politically sound at home in the short term, but a strident, Genevan-style reform would be another matter. The adoption of the model of John Calvin's reformed Church of Geneva would result in a wholesale destruction of all aspects of Catholicism. This in turn would create immense problems:

- It would presuppose the readiness of the country at large to accept the confusion of a further change of worship. Protestantism of the Calvinist type, with its emphasis on the sermon and the word of God, arguably required a literacy and education many did not possess.
- It would also remove church rituals which were often valued by communities because they fitted into the cycle of the seasons and the working year. Blessings at sowing time might be condemned as superstitious by contemporary Protestants, but nonetheless gave a sense of reassurance to the traditionally minded villager for whom the failure of a crop might mean something worse than hunger. After all, the **radical** Protestant reforms of Edward VI's time had themselves aroused resentment, and, as a consequence, disturbed local harmony. Second, in destroying the medieval system of church government through bishops, it might deprive the crown of the mechanism it used to maintain control over the church.
- This form of Protestantism would utterly alienate Philip II of Spain – Elizabeth's brother-in-law and potential suitor – to the extent of convincing him of the need to make common cause with the French against a woman who proclaimed her heresy from the rooftops.

Any sudden change of religious direction would also cause practical problems for the Queen. Since changes would have to be made by Act of Parliament, Elizabeth would have to bear in mind the attitude of the Catholic Marian bishops in the Upper House. If she wished for their co-operation, no radical Protestant approach would be possible.

The signals Elizabeth did make reveal not only her adherence to a milder form of Protestantism but also a considerable political astuteness. Apart from that Protestantism, she seems to have kept two principles firmly in mind as she entered into the stormy waters of a religious settlement:

- The first was the need to establish a national church which would seek to secure the religious conformity and attendance of as many of the Queen's subjects as possible. This desire to make the church at least acceptable to the majority rested on

**Key term**

**Radical**
Proposing or leading to rapid and highly significant change.

the assumption that no stable government could exist where subjects accepted the political rule of a monarch but rejected her religion in large numbers.

- The second principle reflected the need to perform a tricky balancing act to keep her likely (Protestant) supporters and her potential (Catholic) opponents, if not happy, then at least not alienated until political circumstances made her less unwilling to tread on sensitive consciences at home and abroad. This is why the first signs made by Elizabeth to her subjects and to foreign powers were cautious and not unduly strident.

Significantly, Elizabeth forbade the **elevation of the Host** at Mass in the Royal Chapel on Christmas Day, 1558. The officiating priest refused, and the Queen walked out. Similarly, in January 1559, she snubbed the monks of Mary's restored Abbey of Westminster when they approached her with their ceremonial tapers (candles): 'Away with these torches', she cried, 'We can see very well.' This was a very public snub, since it took place at the state opening of Parliament. The Protestants present would doubtless have been suitably encouraged. On the other hand, Elizabeth told the Spanish ambassador that she intended simply to restore the form of religion as practised in the conservative final years of Henry VIII's reign: a form which many Catholics had found acceptable. Such skilful – and inconsistent – manoeuvrings kept Protestants reasonably happy, but did not deprive Catholics of hope for the future.

**Elevation of the Host**
The Host is the wafer of bread consecrated by the priest which Catholics believe to be the body of Christ. The priest raised the Host as a sign of its transformation in essence from bread to body ('transubstantiation').

Key term

# 3 | Supremacy and Uniformity: The Parliament of 1559

**Key question**
What difficulties did the Queen face in passing Acts of Supremacy and Uniformity?

As Parliament assembled in January 1559, the international situation remained uncertain. Elizabeth could take comfort from the fact that Spanish interests were very much bound up with her retaining the throne. This was because her foremost rival to the English throne, Mary Stuart, might otherwise unite in her person the monarchies of France, England and Scotland against Spain. Since Mary was Queen of Scotland, wife of the Dauphin (heir to the French throne) and the most obvious Catholic candidate for the throne of England, this possibility – however alarming to Spain and the Protestant party in England – could not be ruled out. In the short term, Elizabeth might be somewhat reassured by the genuine desire of all three countries to end the war, which was represented by the negotiations taking place at Cateau-Cambrésis between France, Spain and England in February 1559.

## The Acts of Supremacy and Uniformity
In fact, the first three government bills presented to Parliament on the religious settlement were sufficiently radical to arouse determined opposition. One bill aimed to sever the connections with Rome re-established by Mary, and to endow the monarch with the title of Supreme Head of the Church of England, as last used by Edward VI. This was the Bill of Supremacy. The content

of the other two bills, which aimed to establish a uniform pattern of worship, is not known for certain, but it seems likely that they included the re-adoption of the second – and unmistakably Protestant – prayer book of Edward's reign. These Bills of Uniformity duly passed the House of Commons, but were rejected by the House of Lords. A second attempt was also wrecked by the Lords, who altered the bills beyond recognition and refused to repeal Mary's laws against heresy.

The Marian bishops in the Lords maintained an unwavering opposition to both bills. Their view was well explained in a speech to the House of Lords made by Bishop Scot of Chester in March 1559. Scot stated bluntly that Parliament had no right to meddle with matters of doctrine.

It had been expected that Parliament would be dissolved before Easter 1559. However, Elizabeth did not dissolve Parliament. The **Peace of Cateau-Cambrésis**, signed in April, had removed the French threat. With the spectre of invasion lifted, it may be that Elizabeth could afford to create some upset at home in pressing for a religious settlement more congenial to herself and her Protestant supporters. She had also learned that the Marian bishops were prepared to oppose any measure which tampered with Catholicism. It was therefore necessary to break the stranglehold of the Catholic bishops and nobility over the House of Lords. The government had considered arranging a disputation (debate) between Catholic and Protestant clergy even before the Lords had mangled the Acts of Supremacy and Uniformity. Aggressive propositions attacked the authority of the Pope, the spiritual value of the Mass and the use of Latin in public worship. When the Catholic representatives withdrew in anger, Elizabeth took the opportunity to arrest two of the departing bishops on a charge of disobedience to her authority. This reduced Catholic numbers in the Lords, gave the government a greater chance to push through openly Protestant measures and showed the Catholic laity in the Upper House that the government was determined to override opposition.

After the Easter recess, Parliament was therefore presented with new bills of supremacy and uniformity. In deference to the widely held view that a woman could not exercise spiritual authority over the church, the Queen did not claim her father's title of Supreme Head of the Church of England. Instead, the title 'Supreme Governor' was substituted. This allowed her apologists such as John Aylmer – a Protestant exile during Mary's reign and a future Bishop of London – the opportunity to accept that, whilst the New Testament clearly excluded a woman from performing a spiritual ministry, there was nothing to prevent a woman from acting as a kind of overseer to the church. Aylmer was, in fact, responding to the charge of his fellow Protestant John Knox (see page 155) that no woman had a right to hold any civil or religious power over men whatsoever. As we shall see, none of this theoretical limiting of her power had much effect on Elizabeth's own interpretation of her rights over the church. In particular, she expected obedience, and not instruction, from her bishops.

**Key term**

**Peace of Cateau-Cambrésis**
This treaty marked the end of the long struggle between France and Spain for the control of Italy. England had been Spain's ally against France in the Marian period, Although conflict between France and England was ended by the treaty, France did not relinquish Calais.

**Key date**

Acts of Supremacy and Uniformity: 1559

The Act of Supremacy also demanded that the clergy and royal officials swear on oath that they accepted the Queen's title. In addition, it sought to repeal the Marian laws on heresy, and to set up a Commission for Ecclesiastical Causes (the High Commission), which would itself have the right to judge on orthodox doctrine. The Marian bishops failed to muster enough **lay** support to block the passage of the bill: only one layman voted against it in the Lords. The uniformity bill had a considerably rougher ride through the Lords. Only the inexplicable absence of the Abbot of Westminster and the entirely explicable absence of the two bishops languishing in the Tower enabled the bill to pass.

## Act of Uniformity 1559

The new Act of Uniformity required the use of a **Book of Common Prayer** in all churches, and provided a system of punishment for those who failed to use it, or who publicly objected to it.

This 1559 book was based on the two Edwardian prayer books of 1549 and 1552. However, the Queen insisted on an important amendment to the 1552 book, which had included the so-called 'Black Rubric': a set of instructions to the clergy. This rubric, which had declared that kneeling at Communion must not be taken to imply that Christ was a **Real Presence** in the bread and wine, was now omitted. Also, the 1559 prayer book instructed the priest to say the words of both the 1549 and 1552 books when offering the bread and wine at Communion. This was a straight compromise. It was just possible for a Catholic to take the words to mean that Jesus was really present in the bread and wine, and a Protestant could dwell on those which implied that Communion was taken as a memorial and celebration only.

Elizabeth also removed insulting references to the Pope which had appeared in the 1552 book. The Queen's amendments demonstrate her concern to avoid the conflict which might have arisen if an Act of Uniformity adopted the kind of rigid theology which left many of her subjects outside the church. Since the Act included the obligation to attend church on Sundays and Holy Days under pain of a fine of one shilling for every absence, it was important to give potential opponents every opportunity to conform.

The Act also incorporated instructions on the ornaments of the church, which included the garments worn by ministers. The ornaments question was covered by clause 13:

> Provided always and be it enacted that such ornaments of the church and of the ministers thereof shall be retained and be in use as was in the Church of England by authority of Parliament in the second year of the reign of King Edward the Sixth until other order shall be therein taken by authority of the Queen's Majesty, with the advice of her commissioners … and also that if there shall happen any contempt or irreverence to be used in the ceremonies or rites of the Church by the misusing of the orders appointed in this book,

**Key date**

Book of Common Prayer: 1559

**Key terms**

**Lay**
From laity, meaning those who do not have official posts within the church.

**Book of Common Prayer**
Laid down the orders of church services, including morning and evening prayer, Communion, marriage, baptism, burial and other rites.

**Real Presence**
The teaching ('doctrine') that Christ was truly present in the bread and wine at Communion.

the Queen's Majesty may, by the like advice of the said commissioners … ordain and publish such further ceremonies or rites as may be most for the advancement of God's glory, the edifying of his church, and the due reverence of Christ's holy mysteries and sacraments.

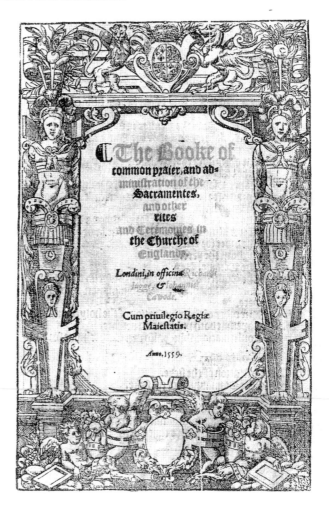

The first page of Morning Prayer, from a 1559 edition of the Book of Common Prayer. What evidence is there from this source that the Book of Common Prayer is Protestant?

## Summary diagram: Key features of the Acts of Supremacy and Uniformity

**Key features of the Acts of Supremacy and Uniformity**

**Act of Supremacy**
- Elizabeth adopted the title of Supreme Governor of the Church of England
- Oath imposed
- Marian heresy laws repealed

**Act of Uniformity**
- Imposed a Book of Common Prayer in English
- Compromise on the issue of Real Presence
- Black Rubric removed
- Obligation to attend church imposed
- Ornaments rubric

# 4 | Historical Interpretations of the Factors Shaping the Settlement

Key question
What is the Neale thesis, and what are its weaknesses?

The religious settlement of 1559 has provoked a major debate among historians on the issue of why it took the form it did. To assess the different interpretations, it is necessary to pose two questions. First, what are the values and assumptions of the historian in question? His or her world-view is likely to affect the way in which subject matter and evidence are selected and approached. Second, what method does the historian use in evaluating evidence? That method may well reflect the formal and informal academic training undergone.

Had this book been written in the early 1960s, it might well have followed the influential interpretation of Sir John Neale. In looking at the Elizabethan religious settlement of 1559, Neale stressed the role of Parliament – or rather, the House of Commons – and argued that the Queen had been forced by a well-organised and influential nucleus of Puritans within the Commons to move further in a Protestant direction than she had originally intended. He also argued that the Puritan faction, which he called 'The Puritan Choir', increasingly used the Commons to force the Queen into further reform of a Church of England which they felt was too close to the Church of Rome and too far from Calvin's Church in Geneva. This loyal but frustrated opposition also demanded the right to advise the Queen on foreign affairs and on the thorny question of her marriage. This led them to become increasingly jealous of the 'liberties' and 'privileges' which, they claimed, belonged to Parliament. In recent years, Neale's thesis has been subjected to extensive and effective attack. Neale has been accused of the kind of distortion of evidence that comes from allegedly identifying some form of 'progress' which happens to suit an historian's political standpoint. In this case, he identified an increase in the power of the House of Commons, and then read back through history to trace a line of development. This tendency to treat history as a series of 'Rises' – the Rise of Protestantism, the Rise of Parliament – has been labelled as the 'Whig' school of historical interpretation (see page 4), where the values of liberal democracy are imposed on the past to create a sense of inevitable progress.

Chapter 3 discusses Neale's claim that the House of Commons fell under Puritan influence and came to support demands for radical changes to the Elizabethan Church of England. For the moment, we need to look at that part of the Neale thesis which applies to the 1559 settlement. Was the Queen pushed into a more radical settlement than she had intended by an organised and disciplined group of Puritans, full to the brim of the latest reformed ideas picked up from their experience as exiles on the Continent? Did that group effectively control the House of Commons? The answer to both questions is no. The work of Norman Jones has demonstrated that there was no effective Puritan faction in the 1559 Parliament. Jones has calculated that there were no more than 25 MPs who could be considered

Calvinist or radically Protestant out of the 400 members of the Commons. Indeed, there were only four exiles among this 25. Nor were these so-called Puritans effectively led or organised. The dismantling of this part of the Neale thesis has two implications. The first is that the settlement itself, with its compromises and carefully contrived vagueness, represents more or less the wishes of the Queen herself. It is hard to overstate the importance of this conclusion, which not only forms the basis of the argument for the rest of this chapter, but also explains the determined way in which the Queen defended 'her' settlement. The second implication is that the major opposition in 1559 to such wishes came from the Catholic bishops and nobles in the House of Lords.

## 5 | The Settlement in Action

### The settlement and the bishops

**Key question**
Why did the Queen retain an episcopal system of church government?

**Key term**

**Episcopate**
The bishops.

The Queen might be Supreme Governor of the Church of England, but who was to be responsible for the detailed organisation, administration and supervision of the church and its clergy? There was never any doubt in Elizabeth's mind that the **episcopate** – the bishops – should retain that function. This section examines the reasons for this decision. It also discusses the way in which the Queen selected her bishops, and seeks to examine Elizabeth's treatment of her episcopate. This will, in turn, shed light on both the nature of the settlement and the attitude of the Queen towards the church.

Episcopacy was not the only possible system of church government. The most obvious alternative was that associated with Calvin's Geneva, where bishops had been discarded. The Genevan Church, whatever Calvin's personal influence might be, was not hierarchical in the sense of an episcopal church. The supervision of beliefs and standards of behaviour in Geneva was carried out by an organisation known as the Consistory, members of which included ministers (avoiding the use of the word 'priest') and men of considerable social standing known as lay elders. It was the Consistory, and the discipline it was able to impose, which gave Calvinism the cohesion it needed to develop from small and local beginnings into a major movement, spreading into many states. This pattern of organisation was precisely why the Queen would never consider such a system. How could she control a church which was based on decision-making by a number of people who were often remote from the centre of power? How was she to make her wishes known? How much easier it would be for her if she could use her bishops to control, not only her clergy, but also her subjects. After all, it was not just Calvin's church which claimed the right to deal with social behaviour: this had been a familiar duty of the church throughout the Middle Ages.

There were other advantages to the Queen in retaining bishops. Should it be advisable for reasons of foreign policy to minimise the differences between the Church of England and the continental Catholic Church, then the shared institution of episcopacy would help a great deal. Finally, we must not underestimate the importance that Elizabeth attached to tradition. After all, her father had never discarded bishops.

Granted that the Queen had decided to retain the episcopate, she had one immediate decision to make in 1559: which bishops? The Queen's first step was to encourage the Marian bishops to remain in office. However, their almost unanimous refusal to take the oath accepting the Act of Supremacy made this impossible. They were duly deprived of their offices, and the Queen turned to clergy of a Protestant persuasion: men who had been exiles during Mary Tudor's reign. In all probability the influence of the Queen's Secretary, William Cecil (see page 155), lay behind their appointments. These former exiles included Grindal (made Bishop of London), Cox (Ely), Jewel (Salisbury), Sandys (Worcester) and Young (Archbishop of York).

The Queen's manoeuvres here are not easy to interpret. It might be argued that the attempt to retain Catholic bishops reveals that Elizabeth was more interested in presenting an image of religious continuity than in securing full-blown Protestantism. This view generally complements our earlier argument that the Queen wished to emphasise as far as possible certain familiar and traditional elements to avoid confusion and disorder. On the other hand, the Elizabethan settlement as defined by the Acts of Supremacy and Uniformity was distinctively Protestant. It may be that the Queen was unrealistic in hoping that Catholic bishops could be persuaded to enforce a fundamentally Protestant settlement. She could hardly have expected them to be enthusiastic in spreading Protestantism, but was clearly prepared to forgo this in favour of her own interpretation of her political needs. The Queen, perhaps, was hoping that the Marian episcopate would fall into the mould of many of the bishops of her father's time: careerist clergy whose experience as royal officials gave them an in-built sense of loyalty to the monarch's demands and a willingness to make unpalatable compromises.

If we are right in arguing that Elizabeth's ideal bishop was first and foremost a loyal administrator, then it is clear why Elizabeth turned to the exiles only as second choices. Their recent experiences were not as crown servants, but as refugees whose religious ideals had forced them out of the country of their birth. How was the Queen to know whether men of this stamp would prove easy to control? How ready would they be to take on the traditional role of the bishop in political affairs? Indeed, some of them were clearly reluctant to accept a bishopric. There were no bishops in their favourite churches of Geneva, Zurich and Frankfurt. Most were strongly influenced by Calvinism, and would expect the theology of the Elizabethan Church to follow suit. And they would also anticipate further reform of the organisation and ritual of the church, where the Genevan model could be adapted to the needs of England. The Acts of Supremacy and Uniformity would be seen as a mere start to the reform process. The problem was that Elizabeth regarded it as the conclusion.

Key date

Act of Exchange:
1559

Key term

**Tithe**
A tenth part of the
fruits of the land or
of labour which by
law were to be given
to the church.

## Act of Exchange 1559

It is clear, therefore, that difficulties lay ahead for the new
bishops. The first such difficulty occurred before they took up
their offices. Under the 1559 Act of Exchange, the Queen was
given the right to exchange church property that she had in her
possession for temporal (non-spiritual) property in the possession
of the church. What it meant in practice was that things of limited
value, such as certain rectories, church buildings, rights to **tithe**,
were exchanged for castles and manors of considerable value. The
net result was that the church lost considerable wealth. It is also
important to note the attitude of some Protestant laymen to the
bishops. Quite simply, they did not like them: after all, some of
the Marian bishops had been truly energetic in seeking to burn
the heart out of Protestantism. To cut the wealth of bishops –
particularly in terms of church lands – would be an excellent
method of curtailing their power and influence.

The Act of Exchange also interfered with the way in which
bishops could deal with their lands. A bishop gained income from
renting out land just like any other landowner. However, the Act
prevented him from renting out land on leases lasting more than
21 years (except to the crown). This was partly an attempt to keep
the value of church land high, because long leases failed to take
account of rises in land value and inflation. This is not, however,
the action of a concerned administration worried about the
income of bishops. Instead, it saw church land as a useful
supplement to the Queen's patronage. If the Queen did not care
to use her own money or crown lands to reward her nobility and
gentry, then the bishops might be persuaded to grant favourable
leases to such laymen. It was therefore in her interest to make
sure that clerical land remained profitable. There was
considerable protest from the bishops-elect over both aspects of
the Act of Exchange. This kind of squabbling at the very birth of
the Elizabethan Church was unseemly and embarrassing to the
government, which backed away from demanding exchanges. But
the bishops were certainly subjected to pressure to grant leases to
the nobility on favourable terms. To refuse the demands of a
powerful nobleman who had the backing of Elizabeth was no light
matter. Few bishops cared to do so.

It would therefore seem reasonable to argue that Elizabeth
envisaged her bishops less as generals leading armies of
Protestant shock-troops and more as subservient civil servants
whose task it was to promote uniformity on the model approved
by her, and whose incomes might be tapped whenever the Queen
felt it necessary. Many bishops found this an uncomfortable role
at best. The following sections of this chapter provide further
supporting evidence of this interpretation. Chapter 3 discusses
the grave consequences when Archbishop Grindal rebelled
against that role and dared to remind Elizabeth that God was the
true master, not only of her church, but also of her soul.

## The Injunctions of 1559

This chapter has argued that Elizabeth sought to establish a basically Protestant settlement of religion, which nevertheless emphasised elements of continuity with the Catholic past in the interests of the stability of the crown. The Royal Injunctions of 1559 confirm this view. As a set of instructions aimed at establishing the detail of a pattern of worship (based on the framework of the Act of Uniformity), they inevitably attacked certain Catholic practices. But they did not destroy all links with tradition.

Under the Injunctions, the clergy were to observe and teach the **Royal Supremacy**, and to speak against the Pope's alleged usurpation of the right of the monarch to govern the church. The processions associated with the Catholic Church were almost entirely banned. Monuments to 'fake' miracles were to be destroyed, although the Injunctions stopped short of forbidding images in churches. Pilgrimages were, however, explicitly forbidden. **Recusants** were to be denounced to the Privy Council (the monarch's inner circle of advisers) or to local Justices of the Peace.

If a Protestant had been asked how England was to be made a truly Protestant country, he would have emphasised the crucial importance of preaching the word of God. However, the Injunctions placed very clear restrictions on such evangelising. No preaching was to take place without official permission, which meant that a licence had to be obtained from the authorities. This move meant that preaching would be restricted to those clergymen who held a master of arts degree. But these men were few and far between. Even in the university diocese of Oxford, considerably less than half the clergy held such a degree. So, the run-of-the-mill clergy were restricted to reading from books of prepared pastoral advice. They then had to try to get hold of their better-educated brethren to preach the legal minimum of sermons, which worked out at about 15 per year. This seemed pitiful to many Protestants: worse still, it was depriving the church's flock of the very words which might stir the most hardened and superstitious to seek salvation and obey the righteous demands of God. Why, then, did the Queen impose such restrictions?

- Most probably the answer is because she saw unlicensed and possibly unlearned preaching as disruptive of good religious and civil order. Soul-hungry preachers swarming into traditionalist Catholic areas would almost inevitably cause trouble and dissension. Such preachers rarely showed a great amount of tact. A violent verbal assault on a villager's faith – the faith his forefathers had accepted unquestioningly – was unlikely to result in anything other than strong (and possibly physical) opposition.
- The Queen had the dislike common to all sixteenth-century monarchs of seeing the lower orders gathered *en masse*. People attending open-air sermons were also people who might be

**Key question**
What do the Injunctions, Visitations, Crucifix and Vestiarian controversies suggest about the role of the Queen in shaping the religious settlement in the years after its inception?

Injunctions and Visitations: 1559

**Royal Supremacy**
The right of the monarch to govern the Church of England as imposed and enforced by the Act of Supremacy.

**Recusant**
Someone who refused to attend the services of the Church of England.

*Key date*

*Key terms*

swayed to criticism of her government. Elizabeth expected and demanded loyalty, but never took it for granted.

- Elizabeth's use of the bishops as the instruments of her personal authority over the church would be jeopardised by widespread and unlicensed preaching. How could bishops control and supervise large numbers of preachers? How could they be sure that preachers were not departing from the orthodox (standard and official) teaching of the church, and thus stimulating disunity?

**Injunction**
A royal proclamation on religious matters.

**Visitations**
Inspections of the churches and clergy in a diocese carried out by a bishop.

The **Injunctions** required that each parish church obtain a copy of the Bible in English and, significantly, a work by Erasmus, the *Paraphrases of the Gospels*. The latter is significant because Erasmus was no Protestant. His interest in reform and in translating the scriptures did not carry him out of the Catholic Church. The presence of a work by him in each church suggests once again the intention implicit within the Injunctions: namely, to minimise the distance being travelled from the traditional Catholic ways. Indeed, other Injunctions sought to promote continuity in worship and uniformity in practice. For example, the congregation was to bow at the name of Jesus, and to kneel at prayer. The clergy were ordered to wear distinctive clerical dress. In particular, they were to wear the garments specified in 1552 in the reign of Edward VI. These garments included the surplice: a white linen gown. As we shall see, its retention provoked controversy, since many Protestants saw it as all too similar to the garments worn by a Catholic priest when celebrating Mass.

On the issue of clerical marriage, the standard Protestant argument was that, since the minister did not have any special power granted by God, there was little need to separate him from other men. The marriage of clergy was therefore not only permissible, but also to be encouraged. It was a mark of Catholicism to demand celibacy as a sign of the special status of the priest. However, the Injunctions stopped well short of accepting the full Protestant position. Clergy could indeed marry, but only with the special permission of their bishop and two Justices of the Peace. This curious arrangement probably reflects the Queen's personal distaste for married clergy.

## The Visitations and the Crucifix controversy

We must distinguish between the moderate tone of some of the Injunctions and the result of the **Visitations** which were designed to enforce them. Since a number of visitors were aggressively Protestant, images, relics, altars and uniquely Catholic clerical clothing ('vestments') were simply destroyed. And, since visitors were also empowered to examine the beliefs of the clergy and to punish those who refused to subscribe to the Act of Supremacy, the Book of Common Prayer and the Injunctions themselves, some 400 clergy either resigned or were deprived of their positions between 1559 and 1564. At least half of the departing clergy were openly Catholic. Clearly, the bishops of the Grindal mould must have felt that the anticipated further reformation above and beyond the 1559 Acts was proceeding according to their wishes. But the Queen had other ideas. Most bishops were dismayed when Elizabeth, in 1559, demanded that each church should retain a crucifix – the cross with the crucified Christ – and that those crucifixes destroyed during the Visitations should be restored. This brought bishops such as Jewel and Sandys to the point of resignation, since they were being told to reinstate what they saw as an unequivocally Catholic ornament. The crisis was averted only when the Queen uncharacteristically backed down. However, she insisted that the crucifix remain in the Chapel Royal – where it would be seen by foreign ambassadors, who were then at liberty to stress the similarities between their own Catholic worship and that of the Protestant English Queen.

# 6 | Archbishop Parker and the Vestiarian Controversy

The issues underlying the dispute over the crucifix resurfaced in the so-called Vestiarian controversy. In January 1565, the Queen wrote to Archbishop Parker (see page 40) to demand that he used his authority to ensure that the rites and practices of the clergy did not deviate from the settlement of 1559. The Queen's desire to defend that settlement is a testimony to the importance she attached to it as an expression of her own wishes.

As Anne Boleyn's former chaplain and a man who had remained in the country throughout Mary's reign, Parker could be relied on to give full weight to the authority of the monarch, and was the obvious choice from Elizabeth's point of view as her Archbishop of Canterbury. He was quite prepared to impose uniformity on his clergy at the monarch's command. The Queen was particularly concerned over the widespread flouting of the requirement to wear vestments as specified in the Act of Uniformity. Several bishops had turned a blind eye to clergy who had refused to use the appropriate vestments, and Parker had no hesitation in calling them to order.

Parker published his *Advertisements* of 1566, in which he attempted to make a clear statement of exactly what was expected of the clergy in terms of doctrine, administration of prayer and the sacraments and, of course, clerical dress. Parker was clearly prepared to follow the Queen in requiring services to have an outward appearance of continuity with the past. Clergy were reminded that communicants were to receive bread and wine kneeling. The time-honoured font was to be used for baptism, rather than the more aggressively Protestant basin. But when it came to vestments, Parker showed a willingness to compromise. He decided that, rather than try to impose the full vestments as required by the 1559 settlement, he would settle for imposing the surplice only in parish church services. Dignitaries in cathedral and collegiate churches were expected to wear more elaborate vestments in addition. For outside wear, clergy were to have distinctive garb appropriate to their rank. In particular, Parker

**Key terms**

**Papistical**
A Protestant term, intended to be offensive, meaning 'Catholic-like'.

*Adiaphora*
A Greek term, meaning in this context 'things indifferent to salvation'; in other words, religious practices which might not in themselves be welcome, but which were not likely to affect one's destination in the after-life (heaven or hell).

**Key date**

Parker's *Advertisements* and the Vestiarian controversy: 1566

insisted on the traditional-looking square cap: only on long journeys could this be replaced by a hat. In March 1566, a curious fashion parade was held at his palace of Lambeth. The audience was the clergy of London, and on view were the correct vestments and outdoor wear. Of the 110 clergy present, 37 refused to accept clothing they judged to be **papistical**. They were duly suspended from their offices.

We do need to consider on what grounds the Archbishop felt justified in imposing such regulations, since he knew as well as any radical Puritan that there was nothing in the scriptures about apostles, disciples or anyone else for that matter wearing surplices and square hats. The argument employed was that it lay within the Queen's authority to impose a certain standard of dress for the sake of civil order. This was a familiar idea: laws already existed whose purpose was to prevent the wearing of inappropriate dress by persons of insufficient social status. The dress of the clergy was not, after all, an issue affecting the salvation of themselves or their flock. Here we see employed the idea of *adiaphora*, or 'things indifferent', which the monarch had the right to enforce. Helpfully, influential continental reformers such as Bullinger in Zurich were prepared to accept the concept of *adiaphora*, and even to warn zealous Puritans that they need not worry their consciences over the matter. But not all were ready to accept moderate advice.

Archbishop Parker urged the Queen to endorse the *Advertisements* officially, but she refused. It is tempting to argue that this shows the Queen's culpable lack of interest in the church, together with an almost malicious desire to force her bishops into confrontations and then refuse to back them up. However, we should remember that Parker was not precisely following the details on clerical dress as laid down in the Injunctions. It could be argued that the Queen was not prepared to support the bishops in imposing what she regarded as a breach of a settlement which she desired to be permanent.

There is little doubt that the Vestiarian controversy provoked intense debate about the validity of episcopacy as an institution. Calvin had been quite prepared to recognise the English bishops as part of a reformed church, but his successor in Geneva, Beza, disputed their necessity. It is no coincidence that, early in 1570, the Puritan minister and academic Thomas Cartwright used his position at Cambridge University to launch an attack on the system of episcopacy, which he condemned as unscriptural. Cartwright also suggested an alternative form of church government, which will be discussed in detail in Chapter 3.

# 7 | Elizabeth as Supreme Governor of the Church of England

So far, it has been suggested that the Queen viewed the religious settlement with her own political needs at the forefront of her mind. What is lacking is an assessment of the way in which she used her role as Supreme Governor. How well, in short, did she treat her church?

To answer this question, we should start by examining the theory of supreme governorship, and then look at how Elizabeth interpreted her governorship in practice. In 1562, Jewel wrote his *An Apology or Answer in Defence of the Church of England*. This piece of propaganda was written in response to Catholic taunts that the Church of England was nothing more than a mere parliamentary religion, whose lay head – the Queen – was, quite wrongly, able to decide on spiritual matters. Jewel's defence was two-fold:

**Key question**
What aims and attitudes lay behind Elizabeth's treatment of the Church of England?

- First, he cited Old Testament examples of monarchs who served God by watching over and protecting the faith, rebuking religious leaders where necessary and pointing out the errors of their ways.
- Second, he used passages from the book of Isaiah which referred to queens being the 'nursing mothers' of the faithful: the parent whose nurturing love and discipline were essential to the child's salvation.
- Jewel also assumed that the Queen's title did not permit her to interfere in purely doctrinal matters, which were the responsibility of the clergy.

We can take the various elements of Jewel's concept of the godly ruler, and see how far they apply to Elizabeth.

The Queen was rarely a protector of her church and more frequently exploited it, as in her use of the Act of Exchange for financial gain:

- The historian Felicity Heal has revealed how Elizabeth expected her bishops to provide church lands whenever she needed to reward courtiers and lacked the desire or resources to do so herself. With the exception of Cox and Sandys, few bishops stood up to her demands. The generation of bishops following the demise of the exiles seldom murmured at her financial exactions, which increased in the 1570s under the double stimulus of inflation and threat of foreign invasion.
- Nor would Elizabeth protect the church against the similar demands of influential nobles. In an era where land gave power and social status, her failure to defend the estates of her bishops did not assist their prestige.

**Key terms**

**Diocese**
The church territory, divided mainly into parishes, under the authority of a bishop.

**Predestination**
A Protestant doctrine associated particularly with John Calvin which stressed the power of God and the weakness of humankind. God, being all-powerful and all-knowing, had decided before a person's birth whether their fate would be salvation or damnation.

**Excommunicated**
To be completely isolated from the Christian community and denied access to all the services and rites of the church (including burial).

**Key dates**

Parker drew up the Thirty-Nine Articles: 1563

Thirty-Nine Articles given parliamentary approval: 1571

- There is plenty of other evidence to suggest that the Queen was only too ready to place her own financial interests before the justified needs of her bishops for security and lay respect. Her officials were rigorous in their taxation demands, and, with the bishops forced to take responsibility for the tax returns to the exchequer for their dioceses, many ended up in debt to the crown. This had not been an uncommon occurrence in the reigns of Edward VI and Mary. The difference is that, whereas her predecessors had been relatively sympathetic to the bishops, Elizabeth was not. The case of Bishop Parkhurst is a good example of the Queen's ruthlessness. Through no fault of his own, his **diocese** accumulated vast debts, which Elizabeth insisted on recovering. The result was that he had to leave his episcopal palace and live in retirement.

It is hard to avoid the conclusion that the Queen seldom acted as the 'nursing mother' of the church. At best, she was a very selfish parent, concerned with her own needs and authority and rarely responding to the needs of her offspring.

Did the Queen interfere in doctrinal matters? Indeed she did, but her involvement was generally of a negative type. Constantly at the back of her mind was the potential danger of allowing clerics to define doctrine in a rigid manner. What she could not afford politically was for numbers of people to be effectively excluded from the church by a particularly narrow set of articles of belief. In 1563, Archbishop Parker produced the Thirty-Nine Articles: a definitive statement of church doctrine. Some – but by no means all – articles reflected standard Calvinist ideas. Article 17, for example, spoke of the sweet comfort offered to the soul by the concept of **predestination**, where salvation was predetermined rather than attained through one's good deeds. Elizabeth had no role in the writing of the Thirty-Nine Articles, but, significantly, refused to allow them to be confirmed by Act of Parliament. This was not necessarily because she disapproved of most of the theology, but rather because the Articles included strongly worded condemnations of Catholic practices. She clearly felt that such attacks were likely to cause resentment among her Catholic subjects. However, once the Pope had **excommunicated** Elizabeth and sought her deposition in 1570, she allowed Parliament to confirm the Articles. Catholics were now identified as potential traitors and therefore did not need to be appeased.

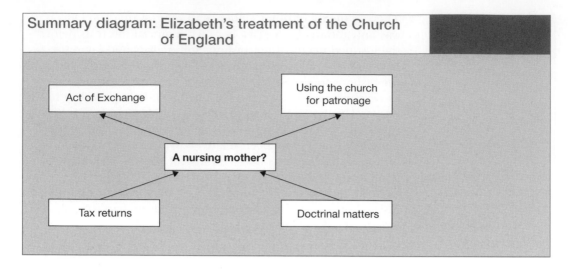

Summary diagram: Elizabeth's treatment of the Church of England

## 8 | Conclusion: The Elizabethan Religious Settlement

It is clear that the most important single factor in explaining the settlement is the Queen herself. That it was a Protestant settlement rather than a Catholic one reflected her religious views as well as those of her most loyal supporters. That the Church of England employed a Catholic-style **hierarchy**, retained certain practices reminiscent of Catholicism and was administered by a clergy whose appearance was also largely traditional, reflected Elizabeth's perception of her political needs. As we shall see in Chapter 4, Elizabeth intended to let Catholicism in England die out slowly in preference to stamping it out, which would have created discord and disunity.

It might be argued that the Elizabethan settlement of religion was largely **Erastian**. This means that it was intended primarily to serve the needs of the state, and to subordinate the clergy to secular authority. This is a useful argument up to a point. After all, the evidence in this chapter certainly tends to support the view that Elizabeth consistently used the church with political concerns uppermost in her mind. However, it would be a mistake to see this as simply Erastian, because what Elizabeth had in mind was less the needs of an abstraction like the state than the needs of Elizabeth I, Queen of England. Her own authority was to be jealously guarded through and against her bishops. Her financial needs were to be allayed by exploiting episcopal lands. And her fear of uncontrolled gatherings was to predominate over the needs of her church. Small wonder that she defended her settlement against change or development, since it was so much a part of herself. Her motto, after all, was 'Always the Same'.

**Key terms**

**Hierarchy**
An organisation with authority depending upon rank.

**Erastian**
Giving priority to serving the needs of the state.

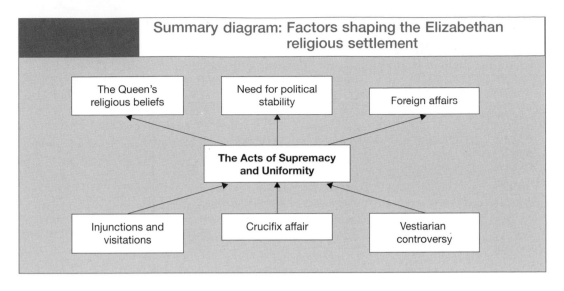

Summary diagram: Factors shaping the Elizabethan religious settlement

## Study Guide: AS Questions

### In the style of OCR A

Explain the motives behind Elizabeth's religious settlement of 1559. (50 marks)

> ### Exam tips
>
> There is a historiographical debate about how the religious settlement was reached but this does not form part of the AS requirement. Instead you should focus on assessing the different reasons behind the motives in question. Each motive of the interested parties (the Queen's objectives and the aims of her advisers, Privy Councillors, Parliament and clergy) should be explained rather than described, and a judgement reached. The main motives are likely to be:
>
> - Elizabeth's preference for a moderate Protestant church that combined elements of the Edwardian prayer book (preferably that of 1549) and certain traditional Catholic practices and ceremonies.
> - The Queen's desire that the church should determine the country's faith, and only when clerics failed to agree would she turn to Parliament.
> - Elizabeth's wish to rule a country at religious peace without confessional strife.
> - Elizabeth's desire not to alienate Catholic powers, especially Spain, France and the Papacy, aware that England was vulnerable to attack and her claim to the throne was disputed by Catholics.
> - The House of Commons' keenness to safeguard their recently acquired church property and restore Protestantism; the Lords' desire to preserve the Catholic church.
> - The Marian clergy's desire to retain the Catholic doctrine; the reformed clergy's hopes of a Protestant settlement.

## In the style of OCR B

Answer both parts of your chosen question.

**Key term**

*Via media*
Middle way between
Catholicism and
Protestantism.

**(a)** Why did Elizabeth want a *via media* in her religious
settlement?                                                    (25 marks)

**(b)** Why did Elizabeth's government experience difficulties in
passing the Acts of Supremacy and Uniformity through
Parliament?                                                   (25 marks)

---

### Exam tips

*The page references are intended to take you straight to the material
that will help you to answer the questions.*

**(a)** In this question you are asked to explain Elizabeth's intentions
and motives in relation to the church settlement. This implies
that your answer should start in the intentional mode of
explanation. However, you will also need to identify the beliefs
and attitudes that lay behind Elizabeth's intentions. Some of
these will be religious, but you should also consider the political
ideas such as *cuius regio eius religio* ('whoever rules, his is the
religion') that dominated at the time of Elizabeth's accession.
You should show how these different factors may be linked and
analyse the relationship between them. Having done this, you
should aim to evaluate the relative importance of the factors.

You might, for example, argue that Elizabeth's desire for a
middle way in religion was also driven by England's place in the
international situation of 1559 (pages 42–3) set against the
Queen's preference for a Protestant form of worship.

Equally you might argue that Elizabeth's main aim was to
avoid rebellion such as that during Edward and Mary's reigns
(Chapter 1, pages 8–12 and 31), perhaps showing how the
church settlement indicated a desire for monarchical control
through the episcopate (pages 48–9).

You might argue, on the grounds that Elizabeth was a
*politique*, that these practical considerations were more
important than Elizabeth's personal beliefs (pages 37–40). You
must, however, justify any such argument with supporting
evidence.

It is not necessary to argue that there is one overriding cause.
For example, you might argue that the circumstances in which
Elizabeth was brought up inclined her towards Protestant
doctrine, but nevertheless the degree of monarchical power that
could be exercised through the episcopate determined that the
church settlement retained a Catholic-style hierarchy, thus
creating a hybrid.

Above all, remember that the examiner will judge your
argument on its merits, not against an expected or required
answer.

What you should do:

- Plan your answer, starting with Elizabeth's motives in 1559.
- Consider the circumstances, both political and religious, in
which Elizabeth made her church settlement. This should

include what she might have learned from living through the reigns of her two siblings (see Chapter 1).

- Continue your plan by establishing the relationship between different factors.
- Remember to work out how Elizabeth would have seen the situation at the time and to consider the strengths of the church settlement from Elizabeth's point of view.

What you should avoid:

- Giving a lengthy account of what Elizabeth's personal beliefs may have been.
- Describing or explaining the church settlement without linking it to the question.
- Making assertions about the relative importance of factors.
- Using knowledge of what happened later to explain what Elizabeth did in 1559.

(b) This question asks you to explain what opposition there was in Parliament to the church settlement drawn up by the government. You may wish to distinguish between the reasons for difficulties with the Acts of Supremacy and Uniformity, bearing in mind their different functions. You should explain why certain MPs in the Commons and Lords opposed the original bill and how this was managed. Remember that the methods used by members of the government give an insight into the difficulties they identified in getting the legislation passed. Although an argument has been made for Protestant opposition, recent historians share the government's view that the main opposition came from the House of Lords, both from temporal and from spiritual peers.

What you should do:

- Identify a range of reasons why it was difficult to get the legislation passed.
- Categorise these reasons into beliefs that made for religious objections, causal factors such as the status of the opponents, and the motives of the opponents, such as preserving their own power.
- Plan your answer by looking for a logical chain of reasoning that explains the beliefs, motives and causal factors determining the voting of opponents of the legislation.
- Do not forget to take into account that the legislation floundered in the Lords, not the Commons.
- A comparison with the success of the new bills in the session of Parliament after Easter could help you to evaluate the relative importance of different factors.

What you should avoid:

- A lengthy description of the different historians' interpretations of this issue.
- A description of the ways in which the government set about steering the bills through Parliament.

## Study Guide: A2 Question

### In the style of AQA

How far was the Elizabethan religious settlement shaped by the attitude and beliefs of Queen Elizabeth I herself?        (45 marks)

---

*Exam tips*

*The cross-references are intended to take you straight to the material that will help you to answer the question.*

This question sounds deceptively straightforward, but it does require a full analysis of the various forces that shaped the Elizabethan religious settlement in order to assess how far Elizabeth personally made a difference. Note also that the question refers to attitude and beliefs. These are not the same and they will require separate treatment in the answer.

Broad factors are outlined in the summary diagram on page 57: the need for political stability and the impact of foreign affairs. You should be able to break down these two groupings to provide more precise reasons, for example, the need to appease the majority, the need for a national church, the avoidance of sudden change and the particular position of Spain, Rome and the changing international position. You should also consider the perceived dangers of Calvinism and the views of other leading churchmen, Parliament and prominent individuals and advisers. Balanced against such factors would be the personal religious preferences of the Queen and her political outlook. You should consider, for example, her determination to retain bishops, to keep both Protestants and Catholics 'on side' and to preserve continuity.

You will probably want to refer to historiography, but do remember that it is your personal and supported judgement that the examiner will want to see. Neale's views on the influence of the Commons have been largely discredited, so, while they are worth mentioning as a theory, it would be foolish to dwell too long on them.

# 3

# Meeting the Challenge of Religion: Elizabeth and the Puritans

**POINTS TO CONSIDER**

In Chapter 2, we discussed the Elizabethan religious settlement and its particular brand of Protestantism. In this chapter, we examine the ideas and impact of those Protestants who were, in varying degrees, dissatisfied with the settlement: the Puritans. The chapter is structured around the three types of Puritan (Conformist, Presbyterian and Separatist) and examines the nature and extent of the challenge the three types presented to the settlement itself. These issues are examined under the following headings:

- Puritanism and Presbyterianism in the 1570s
- The tragedy of Grindal
- Archbishop Whitgift and the Puritans
- Presbyterianism in the 1580s
- The *Martin Marprelate* tracts of 1588–9
- The Puritans under attack 1589–1603
- The Separatists
- 'Anglicanism'

**Key dates**

| | |
|---|---|
| 1570 | Cartwright's pro-Presbyterian lectures |
| 1571 | 'Alphabet' bills |
| 1572 | John Field's *Admonition to the Parliament* |
| | St Bartholomew's Day massacre |
| 1575 | Edmund Grindal made Archbishop of Canterbury |
| 1576 | Grindal refused the Queen's instruction to suppress prophesyings |
| 1577 | Grindal suspended as Archbishop of Canterbury |
| 1582 | Robert Browne published the Separatist *Treatise of Reformation without tarrying for any* |
| 1583 | Death of Grindal |
| | John Whitgift appointed Archbishop of Canterbury |
| | Three Articles |
| 1584 | Turner's pro-Presbyterian bill |
| 1587 | Cope's pro-Presbyterian bill |
| 1588 | *Martin Marprelate* tracts |
| 1593 | Richard Hooker's *Of the Laws of Ecclesiastical Polity* |
| 1595 | Lambeth Articles |

# 1 | Introduction

**Key question**
What are the similarities and differences between the three types of Puritan?

In Shakespeare's play *Twelfth Night*, the upper-class louts Sir Toby Belch and Sir Andrew Aguecheek have a discussion about a certain Malvolio. On hearing that Malvolio is 'sometimes a kind of Puritan', Sir Andrew comments: 'O! If I thought that, I'd beat him like a dog.' The same character remarks to Malvolio himself: 'Dost thou think, because thou art virtuous, there shall be no cakes and ale?' Aguecheek's attitude gives an insight into one meaning of the word 'Puritan', a nickname which became current from the 1560s. Shakespeare is not alone among playwrights in presenting Puritans as kill-joys: they also appear in plays by other writers as hypocrites with a strong line in sexual repression. This kind of invective is not restricted to writers who might have felt their livelihoods threatened. It also appears in a learned controversy in the 1570s between the future Archbishop of Canterbury, John Whitgift, and his Puritan opponent, Thomas Cartwright. For good measure, Whitgift also accused Puritans of being heretical in their obsession with 'purity' in their personal conduct, and divisive in their alleged refusal to associate with those who disagreed with them. Puritans, by this token, were dangerous opponents of all lawful authority.

'Puritanism', then, is a term that historians must use with considerable care. Any word originating in abuse is as likely to tell you as much – or as little – about the abuser as it does about the abused. Moreover, since the term was applied so widely and incautiously in the sixteenth century, the historian must take particular care both to define Puritanism and then to outline crucial differences of viewpoint among those who would, however reluctantly, accept that the name 'Puritan' applied to them. Obviously, Puritans had certain shared values and ideas, but this does not necessarily mean that Puritanism was a unified movement. Elizabethan Puritanism cannot be handled in a meaningful way unless a preliminary attempt is made to work out what Puritans had in common and what divided them. Only then can we deal with the questions that have been of particular interest to historians: namely, 'How strong was Puritanism?', 'How greatly did it influence the Elizabethan Church of England?' and 'How much of a challenge did it represent to the Elizabethan religious settlement?'

## Common ground

Our first task, then, is to establish what Puritans had in common. In this book, the term 'Puritanism' was introduced on page 46 in the course of a discussion of Neale's supposed 'Puritan Choir'. In this context, it meant Protestants who were influenced by the 'godly society' of Calvin's Geneva and who wished to push the Elizabethan religious settlement as far as possible in that direction. This is a useful starting point. In theology, a Puritan would certainly be Calvinist. He would also be strongly anti-Catholic, and so would wish to remove everything from the church that was reminiscent of Catholicism. For the greater glory of God, he would wish to control social behaviour. This **discipline** was necessary because Puritans viewed humankind as being sinful and weak. Life on earth was not for frivolity, for enjoyment or for the display of wealth, but for the fulfilment of God's commands. Finally, a Puritan would place great emphasis on the preaching of God's word. In this most vital of tasks, ministers (Puritans did not use the word 'priest') were expected to explain to their congregations what God demanded of His people.

It is helpful to identify three different types of Puritan who accepted the central assumptions of Puritanism but whose differences were no less real:

- Conformist Puritan
- Presbyterian
- Separatist.

**Discipline**
As in 'godly discipline': the control of social and moral behaviour in accordance with the correct interpretation of the gospel.

Key term

## Conformist, Presbyterian and Separatist

We should identify the 'Conformist' as a Puritan who certainly accepted the major aspects of the wider Puritan position, but who was prepared to compromise on what he saw as less essential elements. Calvinist theology, the centrality of preaching and the importance of 'discipline' were at the heart of the Conformist's Protestantism. However, he was also prepared to give due weight to other factors. He recognised that there were aspects of the Elizabethan religious settlement that were distasteful to his conscience, yet he was prepared to bite on the bullet in the interests of the national church, of uniformity and of loyalty to the Queen. The Catholic-style hierarchy and clerical dress of the Church of England might be offensive, but they were bearable.

Puritanism and the Elizabethan Church of England were not necessarily mutually exclusive. It was possible to be a Puritan and to work within the church. It was also possible to rise to the very top of the hierarchy, and yet retain those central assumptions of Puritanism. But what was possible was not always easy. This will become clear when we examine the career of Edmund Grindal as Archbishop of Canterbury in Section 3. Conformists frequently found the compromises hard to swallow, especially when they discovered that Elizabeth had no intention of moving beyond the letter of the Acts of Uniformity and Supremacy. But to argue that all Puritans were out to subvert or destroy Elizabeth's Church of England would be a travesty. We cannot count the number of Conformist Puritans, but we know they were there. This chapter will discuss a number of incidents which amounted to confrontation between Puritans and the bishops when the latter chose or were forced to insist on the full observation of the settlement. What is significant is the readiness of many Puritan clergy to accept compromises when offered, rather than to follow some of their fellows into opposition to the Elizabethan Church of England.

To Presbyterians, such compromise was unacceptable. The church was, in their eyes, fatally flawed because it employed a Catholic-style hierarchy of archbishops and bishops. Where in the

Bible, they asked rhetorically, were these titles and offices to be found? Opponents might argue that the Bible gave no clear indication of the structure of the church anyway. But the Presbyterians denied this. They felt that the system used by the Apostles could be identified from the New Testament. To fail to use it was nothing less than a rejection of the authority of scripture. Presbyterians argued that God required a church organisation based on the government of each congregation by ministers and lay elders.

Indeed, the term 'Presbyterianism' is derived from the word 'presbyter', meaning 'elder'. It was claimed that this system was particularly effective in imposing the discipline which was central to Puritanism. Ministers and elders could lead the congregation into a godly way of life through, for example, counselling, through criticism – both mutual and personal – and through spiritual punishments such as excommunication. Presbyterians could point to Geneva and say that this system of discipline worked. Where else in the world did such courtesy, such good order and such godliness prevail?

All this does not mean that congregations were to be independent of each other. To the Presbyterians, such independence would lead to chaos. Instead, they demanded a national system whereby individual congregations sent representatives to regional and national meetings (or **synods**). The uniform doctrine and discipline decided there would then be taken back to, and imposed on, the local churches. What need, therefore, for bishops and archbishops? They stemmed from man, and man was corrupt. But presbyters, it was claimed, derived from God. Who would argue for the corruptness of God?

If Presbyterianism sought to discard the authority of bishops and archbishops over the church, where did it leave the authority of the monarch? The short answer is, somewhat uncertain and exposed. It is difficult to see how the Queen, for example, could effectively control a church organised in this manner. In fact, such a system separated the church from secular authority in a radical way. Major landowners – especially since the Henrician Reformation – had become used to exercising the right to appoint clergymen of their choosing to churches on their own lands. This right had been inherited along with land bought at the time of the dissolution of the monasteries. But the Presbyterian system gave the right of appointment to the elders, with or without advice from the synods.

Presbyterianism, then, was uncompromisingly a national system. But some Puritans refused to accept any form of ecclesiastical authority which failed to coincide with their individual understanding of scripture. This led logically to the independent congregation of the Separatists, where a group formed its own church, not on the basis of the need for national or even regional unity, but on the basis of a doctrine agreed by the members of a single congregation. Discipline could still be imposed, because members marked their agreement by entering

**Key term**

**Synods**
Regional or national decision-making meetings of church representatives.

into a contract, a **covenant**, which bound them to that shared interpretation. This kind of church frequently looked for a role model to the persecutions of early Christians at the time when true believers were in a minority. There were also plenty of biblical passages to show that believers should expect such persecution. This was probably just as well, because Separatists were bound to be persecuted. Those in authority assumed that Separatism was the first step towards the overthrow of all established order. It seemed to break down traditional loyalties to social as well as to religious superiors.

Three major types of Puritan within the England of Elizabeth have been identified: the Conformist, the Presbyterian and the Separatist. However, one must not assume that these three types are rigid in the sense that Puritans were unable to move between or in and out of these varying attitudes towards the church. Nor would the Protestant who found the Elizabethan religious settlement very much to his taste necessarily be antagonistic to all manifestations of Puritanism.

**Key terms**

**Covenant**
An agreement whereby a church member agreed to conform to church discipline.

**Apostolic Church**
Made up of the first Christian churches, founded by the earliest followers of Christ.

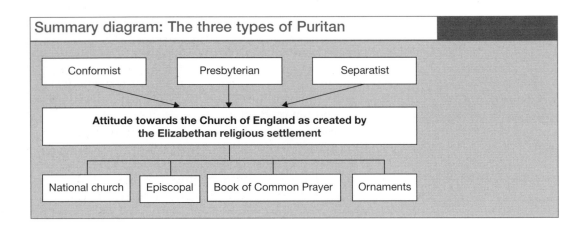

Summary diagram: The three types of Puritan

Conformist — Presbyterian — Separatist

Attitude towards the Church of England as created by the Elizabethan religious settlement

National church | Episcopal | Book of Common Prayer | Ornaments

# 2 | Puritanism and Presbyterianism in the 1570s

In dealing with the growth of early Presbyterianism it is important to recognise that the development of the movement cannot be traced just to one individual or just to one incident. This is not to deny the importance of a theorist such as **Thomas Cartwright**, whose lectures at Cambridge University represented the first influential public demand for a Presbyterian system. But it is also necessary to understand that Presbyterian ideas became attractive to some Puritans when they felt themselves to be the victims of persecution at the hands of bishops.

## Thomas Cartwright

In Cartwright's spring lectures of 1570 he contrasted the hierarchy and discipline of the Church of England with that of the **Apostolic Church**. Needless to say, the former was found wanting. In particular, Cartwright called for the abolition of the

**Key question**
What was the nature of the complaints about the Elizabethan Church of England made by Cartwright and Field?

**Key figure**

**Thomas Cartwright 1535–1603**
Professor of Divinity at Cambridge University, he was deprived of his position in 1570 for preaching against the hierarchy of the Church of England.

titles and offices of archbishops, bishops, deans and archdeacons. He also argued that the minister should be elected by his congregation. In effect, Cartwright was suggesting full-scale Presbyterianism. A system of this type left little or no place for Elizabeth's Supreme Governorship. No doubt this is why Cartwright's lectures skirted the issue of the Queen's authority over the church. They did, however, cost Cartwright his professorial chair. He left for Geneva where he could see a system in operation which bore a distinct resemblance to his vision of the Apostolic Church.

There is, however, no evidence that a Presbyterian movement developed as a result of Cartwright's lectures. Indeed, it is clear that other centres of radical Puritanism were inclined to accept – albeit reluctantly – the authority of the traditional hierarchy. But this conformism was not the result of carefully considered compromise. Instead, it depended on the local bishop not asking awkward questions about how far Puritan ministers were conforming to the Act of Uniformity. However, the activities of some Puritans did suggest to the bishops the need to conduct such checks. In particular, there was considerable episcopal resentment when Puritan tactics in Parliament led – unintentionally – to the loss of important reforming legislation.

In the session of 1571, the bishops had hoped to see certain bills (known as the 'Alphabet' bills) pass through Parliament to curb the evils of ministers holding more than one parish living, or failing to reside in their own parish (abuses known as 'pluralism' and 'absenteeism'). But the Puritan MP William Strickland had tried to yoke that legislation to a Prayer Book Bill of his own devising. This bill attempted to do away with certain practices reminiscent of Catholicism, such as the use of the surplice and kneeling at Communion. All it achieved, however, was the Queen's indignation. In her view, Parliament had no right to tamper with the religious settlement. She simply vetoed most of the Alphabet bills.

The bishops, not unnaturally, were inclined to blame Puritans for the loss of useful reforms. Their response was to increase pressure on Puritans to conform. To do this, use was made of Convocation's right to grant or renew the licences without which no clergyman could preach. Licences were not to be renewed unless the minister gave full and unconditional subscription to the Thirty-Nine Articles. On top of this, certain influential Puritan ministers were summoned before the Ecclesiastical Commissioners and told they must subscribe, not only to the Articles, but also to the Book of Common Prayer and to the surplice.

## John Field

Among those summoned was the young clergyman John Field, a man who was to play a central role in the attempt to organise a Presbyterian church system for England. It is significant that Field did his best to respond with some form of compromise: a sign that he was not, at this stage, out to reject the authority or role of

### Key dates

Cartwright's pro-Presbyterian lectures: 1570

'Alphabet' bills: 1571

John Field's *Admonition to the Parliament*: 1572

the episcopate. He offered a qualified subscription to the Articles and Prayer Book and, although he could not bring himself to wear the surplice, he promised not to condemn those who did. But his offer was rejected. Early in 1572, he was forbidden to preach.

Field's response to this ban reflects his bitterness. In 1572 he co-wrote and published manifestos which were nothing less than a public attack on the institution of episcopacy. The first of the two *Admonitions to the Parliament* accused the bishops of being enemies of true Christianity. Presbyterianism was advanced as the only form of church government and discipline to be supported by scripture. The extract below claims that only ministers, elders and deacons can secure true Christian discipline over social and moral behaviour:

> May it therefore please your wisdoms to understand, we in England are so far off from having a church rightly reformed, according to the prescript of God's word that as yet we are not come to the outward face of the same ... Let us now come to the ... part, which concerneth ecclesiastical discipline. The officers that have to deal in this charge are chiefly three: ministers ... elders; and deacons. Concerning elders, not only their office but their name is out of this English church utterly removed. Instead ... the pope has brought in, and we yet maintain, the lordship of one man over many churches ... The final end of this discipline is the reforming of the disordered and to bring them to repentance and to bridle such as would offend. The chiefest part and last punishment of this discipline is excommunication, by the consent of the church determined ... In the primitive church it was in many men's hands; now alone one excommunicateth ... now it is pronounced for every light trifle. Then excommunication was greatly regarded and feared; now, because it is a money matter, no whit at all esteemed.

Attached to this *Admonition* was Field's *A View of Popish Abuses yet remaining in the English Church*. Field clearly intended to pull no punches. This work listed the articles to which the author and others had been instructed to subscribe. The first was that the Book of Common Prayer contained nothing 'repugnant to' the word of God. Field commented:

> We must needs say as followeth, that this book is an unperfect book, culled and picked out of that popish dunghill, the Mass book full of all abominations ... By the word of God, it [the minister's office] is an office of preaching, they make it an office of reading: Christ said go preach, they in mockery give them the Bible, and authority to preach, and yet suffer them not, except that they have new licences ... In this book we are enjoined to receive the Communion kneeling, which ... has in it a show of popish idolatry ... The public baptism, that also is full of childish and superstitious toys ... they do superstitiously and wickedly institute a new sacrament, which is proper to Christ only, marking the child in the forehead with a cross.

**Key terms**

**Marian exiles**
Those Protestants who fled to Protestant centres such as Zurich and Geneva on the accession of the Catholic Mary I in 1553.

**Translation**
In church terminology, the transfer of a bishop from one bishopric to another.

**Key dates**

St Bartholomew's Day massacre: 1572

Edmund Grindal made Archbishop of Canterbury: 1575

**Key question**

Why did the Queen demand that Grindal suppressed prophesyings, and why did he refuse?

Field spent a year in prison as a result of his literary efforts. The vehemence of his opinions and the savagery of his attack on the bishops appalled many Puritans, including the older generation represented by the **Marian exiles**.

The impact on Parliament was slight. The House of Commons, rather than follow the lead of the *Admonition*, preferred to adopt a deferential approach. The Commons tended to present petitions to the Queen rather than introduce bills which would simply be vetoed. Archbishop Parker took the opportunity to use the subscription weapon against as many Puritans as he saw fit, but there were a number of reasons why the hierarchy of the church and the Puritans were by no means irreconcilable enemies:

- All Protestants were united in horror at the St Bartholomew's Day massacre of Huguenots (French Protestants) in Paris in 1572.
- The Puritans were not without friends in very high places. Robert Dudley, Earl of Leicester – the Queen's favourite – and his brother, the Earl of Warwick, were well known as patrons to many a godly preacher.
- The **translation** of Edmund Grindal from the Archbishopric of York to that of Canterbury in 1575 meant that a known and respected reformer was at the helm. Could episcopalian government forge an alliance with Puritans and deflect attention away from Presbyterianism?

## 3 | The Tragedy of Grindal

### Archbishop Grindal and the 'prophesyings'

Chapter 2 included a brief account of the sorry end of Grindal's effective career as Archbishop, brought about when the Queen suspended him following his refusal to stop the so-called 'prophesyings'. This episode must be looked at in greater detail, since it helps us to answer important questions. Was the Queen correct in seeing these meetings as a threat to her authority? Why was the issue so important to Grindal that he was prepared to sacrifice his position? Seeking an answer to these questions provides insight, not only into the nature of Grindal's relationship with Puritanism, but also into the extent to which Puritanism was revolutionary.

There is evidence to suggest that, at the start of Grindal's episcopal career, he took on the role of bishop only after considerable heart-searching. Like many other Marian exiles, Grindal had kept up a correspondence with influential continental reformers. An exchange of letters with Peter Martyr in Zurich reveals that Grindal had accepted that his elevation as Bishop of London would involve him in some regrettable compromises. He argued, however, that compromise was permissible so long as it did not affect the salvation of those in the minister's care. Grindal, it should be recalled, did not care for the use of the surplice. But he was prepared to accept the right of the Queen to enforce it because it was no handicap to the

## Profile: Edmund Grindal c.1519–83

|        |                                                          |
| ------ | -------------------------------------------------------- |
|        | – Educated at Cambridge University                       |
| 1538   | – Fellow of Pembroke Hall                                |
| 1550   | – Chaplain to Bishop Ridley                              |
| 1551   | – Chaplain to Edward VI                                  |
| 1553   | – On Mary's accession, fled abroad to Strasbourg         |
| 1559   | – Bishop of London                                       |
| 1570   | – Archbishop of York                                     |
| 1575   | – Archbishop of Canterbury                               |
| 1577   | – Suspended and placed under house arrest by the Queen   |

Grindal's academic career at Cambridge was a glittering one. He was chosen in 1549 as one of the four disputants in a debate held before Edward VI's visitors (inspectors) on the Catholic doctrine of transubstantiation. In exile at Strasbourg in Mary's reign, he worked (without much success) to repair the rifts in the English exile community between those who wished to base the church on the Edwardian Prayer Book and those who wished for a more Genevan model. He also contributed material to Foxe's *Book of Martyrs* (see page 29). On his return to England in 1559, he was promoted rapidly, but his effective career as Archbishop of Canterbury was a very brief one: he refused to obey the Queen's instructions to suppress '**prophesyings**', which he supported as vital for improving the quality of the church's ministers. He was duly suspended.

> **Prophesyings** Meetings of ministers and other interested parties in which ministers honed their preaching skills in front of a critical audience.
>
> Key term

teaching of true doctrine. The concept of *adiaphora*, or matters external to salvation, was therefore of great value to him as he strove to reconcile his role as bishop and archbishop in a national church with his role as a guide for souls.

Grindal's willingness to accept the right of the Queen to demand uniformity over minor matters should not, therefore, be seen as weakness or pliability. Instead, he represents the position of the 'Conformist' Puritans. But, as we shall see, this was not an easy position to maintain. When he saw his central principles threatened – the principles shared by all Puritans – Grindal stood fast. The prophesyings storm should be put into the context of Grindal's undoubted interest in clerical education and his view of the vital importance of securing effective preachers. Grindal expended much time and effort both in enquiring into the learning of candidates for the ministry and also in conducting visitations of the clergy within his archdiocese. The problem for him was that he saw the Queen's demand that he crush prophesyings as an attack on a necessary tool in improving the effectiveness of the very preaching ministry on which the evangelising of England depended. It has already been noted that this commitment to preaching was a characteristic of Puritanism.

How far were prophesyings a threat to the 1559 settlement? The term itself seems to imply the wild and unbridled enthusiasm of would-be visionaries and prophets. In fact, these meetings were

**Orthodoxy**
The official teaching of the church.

gatherings of clergy where preachers could practise their skills and obtain an assessment of their performance and **orthodoxy** from their colleagues. The 'exercise' was performed under the supervision of a moderator, who was usually a respected practitioner in the art of preaching. Its value to the inexperienced or ill-educated clergyman was enormous. As Professor Collinson has pointed out, prophesyings were seen as the 'universities of the poor ministers'. After all, did not the Royal Injunctions of 1559 require non-graduate ministers to study the scriptures and other works? The 'exercise' generally started with two or three sermons on the same text preached in front of a mixed clerical and lay audience. After the sermons came a conference from which laymen were excluded. Preachers were here given the opinion of the moderator and others on their sermons.

The effect of such regular fortnightly or monthly exercises was bound to improve the morale of the clergy as well as their professional expertise. This is why many prophesyings had taken place with the full support of the bishops, who had appointed moderators, instructed them to enforce attendance and published orders of the proceedings. This also serves as a reminder that, while prophesyings would indeed appeal to Puritans of all types, non-Puritans were not unaware of their value. Prophesyings were certainly not a uniquely Presbyterian weapon, whatever vague similarity the meeting might have to a synod. Very possibly the Queen thought otherwise. Local meetings lacking in the firm and consistent direction provided by bishops may have implied, in her mind, lack of uniformity, and lack of uniformity was a threat both to the Supreme Governorship and to the stability of the realm. As Chapter 2 revealed, the Queen was generally hostile to evangelism which would, in the short term, provoke resentment from those who were more conservative in religious matters. And resentment was a potent disturber of the peace.

It would seem, perhaps, that the Queen had little real cause to fear prophesyings as a factor stimulating disunity. On the other hand, it is true that some prophesyings did appear to reflect Separatist tendencies. Goings-on of this sort at Southam in Warwickshire came to the ear of the Queen, and Leicester, along with Burghley and Walsingham, attempted to defuse the situation. They warned Grindal of the need to make sure that the local bishop was fully aware of what was taking place. However, it is clear that Grindal, for one, felt that the value of prophesyings considerably outweighed their potential dangers. When, in 1576, the Queen demanded that Grindal suppress all prophesyings and restrict the number of preachers to three or four per shire, his response was to canvass the opinion of his fellow bishops on the value of godly exercises. Out of 15 bishops, 10 approved with various degrees of qualification. Only one saw them as a threat to the episcopate. Grindal's resulting letter to the Queen defended prophesyings, discussed ways of making sure they were rigorously controlled and, in the end, implied that Elizabeth must be aware of the need to please God rather than herself. This is an extract from Grindal's letter:

Grindal refused the Queen's instruction to suppress prophesyings: 1576

The speeches which it hath pleased you to deliver unto me, when I last attended on your highness, concerning abridging the number of preachers, and the utter suppression of all learned exercises and conferences among the ministers of the church … have exceedingly dismayed and discomforted me … Howsoever report hath been made to your majesty concerning these exercises, yet I and others of your bishops … having found by experience that these profits and commodities following hath ensued of them:

I.   The ministers of the church are more skilful and ready in the scriptures, and apter to teach their flocks. …
III.  Some afore suspected in doctrine are brought hereby to open confession of the truth.
IV.  Ignorant ministers are driven to study, if not for conscience yet for shame and fear of discipline.
V.   The opinion of laymen touching the idleness of the clergy is hereby removed.

And now being sorry, that I have been so long and tedious to your majesty, I will draw to an end, most humbly praying the same well to consider these two short petitions following. The first is, that you would refer all these ecclesiastical matters … unto the bishops and divines of your realm. … For indeed they are things to be judged, as an ancient father writeth: 'In the church, or a synod, not in a palace.' … Remember, madam, that you are a mortal creature. 'Look not only … upon the purple and princely array … .' Is it not dust and ashes?

Flattery, it seems, was not a weapon in Grindal's armoury. Uncompromising, almost threatening, in the way it reminded Elizabeth of the accountability of her actions before God, this was not a letter seeking to advise, but one informing the Queen, not only of her duty, but also of the limits of her power. There were precedents in the history of the early church for bishops lecturing their monarchs, but Elizabeth was too angry to care to refresh her memory on ecclesiastical history. Grindal, it seems, would accept little help in the storm that followed. His friends in the Privy Council tried to find some sort of compromise between the Archbishop and the enraged Queen, but Grindal would not budge. The Queen gave instructions for ways to be found of depriving Grindal of his office, but there was, as Burghley remarked, no precedent for the removal of an archbishop in these circumstances. Grindal was under virtual house arrest in his palace at Lambeth, and was suspended from his duties. There followed five years in which Grindal could do nothing for the church on whose behalf he had made such a courageous, if ill-advised, stand. Only his death in 1583 brought the sorry tale to an end. As for the prophesyings, Elizabeth wrote directly to the bishops:

**Key dates**

Grindal suspended as Archbishop of Canterbury: 1577

Death of Grindal: 1583

Right reverent father in God, we greet you well. We hear to our great grief that in sundry parts of our realm there are no small number of persons ... which, contrary to our laws established for the public divine service of Almighty God and the administration of His holy sacraments within this Church of England, do daily devise, imagine, propound and put into execution sundry new rites and forms ... as well by procuring unlawful assemblies of a great number of our people out of their ordinary parishes ... which manner of invasions they in some places call prophesying and in some other places exercises ... we will and straitly charge you that you ... charge the same forthwith to cease. ... And in these things we charge you to he so careful and vigilant, as by your negligence, if we shall hear of any person attempting to offend ... without your correction or information to us, we be not forced to make some example or reformation of you, according to your deserts.

The result of the Queen's action was indeed a clampdown on prophesyings, but there were ways and means of ministers getting together to hear and discuss sermons without calling them prophesyings. If, for example, there was one 'lecture' rather than a number of sermons, then this still left the clergy the opportunity to meet together to discuss it. Some larger towns appointed their own lecturer, or clergy found market days ideal for hearing the sermons of visiting rural ministers. Of course, this kind of meeting appealed to the converted, and therefore lacked the capacity of the prophesyings to improve clerical education in general.

Grindal's fate demonstrates the difficulties facing the 'Conformist' Puritan. The concept of *adiaphora* was sufficient to permit Conformists to accept with a reasonably good grace the rituals and **ornaments** of the Church of England. But when the Queen's actions threatened their most central assumptions, then they were in trouble. It was a matter for individual conscience how far each Conformist was prepared to compromise further. Grindal had clearly reached the sticking point. One problem was that both parties in a compromise are usually expected to give a little ground. However, the Queen had no intention of deviating from her stance in the interests of anything at all, let alone of compromising. It is hard to escape the conclusion that the Queen's rigidity created avoidable problems. Conformist Puritans were, like prophesyings, no real threat to the Elizabethan religious settlement if sympathetically handled.

## Archbishop Whitgift and the Puritans

Following Grindal's death in 1583 the Queen appointed John Whitgift as his successor. He was a man with little or no sympathy for Puritanism in any form. It was convenient for the Queen that Whitgift also had a particularly well-developed sense of the importance of authority and uniformity. In his first major sermon as Archbishop, he called upon all parties who were discontented with the Elizabethan settlement – Catholics and Puritans alike – to obey their superiors. By superiors, he meant the bishops and the Queen.

## Profile: John Whitgift c.1530–1604

|      | – | Educated at Cambridge University |
|------|---|----------------------------------|
| 1560 | – | Ordained |
| 1567 | – | Regius Professor of Divinity |
| 1571 | – | Dean of Lincoln |
| 1577 | – | Bishop of Worcester |
| 1583 | – | Archbishop of Canterbury |
|      | – | Drew up the Three Articles |
| 1586 | – | Privy Councillor |
| 1595 | – | Drew up the Lambeth Articles defending Calvinist doctrine |

Whitgift was born in Lincolnshire; he matriculated from Queen's College, Cambridge, in 1549. He served as chaplain to Richard Cox, the Bishop of Ely. When in positions of authority at Cambridge he was instrumental in depriving Thomas Cartwright of fellowship and professorship. Although Calvinist in doctrine, Whitgift had no sympathy for Puritan aims in church organisation.

In examining Whitgift's career as Archbishop, it is important to consider two questions:

- What was the effect of Whitgift's attack on Puritanism?
- What conclusions can be reached on the strength of Puritanism in this latter part of the Queen's reign?

**Key dates**

John Whitgift appointed Archbishop of Canterbury: 1583

Three Articles: 1583

### The Three Articles of 1583

Whitgift's harsh and uncompromising approach is revealed in his attempt to impose his Three Articles of 1583 on all ministers.

- The first article required the minister to accept the Royal Supremacy.
- The second required him to agree that the Book of Common Prayer and the **Ordinal** contained nothing contrary to the word of God. The Ordinal dealt with the ordination of bishops as well as ministers. Anyone accepting it would therefore also be accepting episcopacy as the right and proper system of church government.
- Thirdly, the subscriber had to acknowledge that the Thirty-Nine Articles were similarly agreeable to the word of God.

Whitgift would accept nothing but complete and unreserved subscription. There were to be no deals, no turning of blind eyes to Puritans of uneasy conscience. The Archbishop's severity is also revealed in his instructions on how the Articles were to be administered. Clergy under suspicion were forced to take an oath that they would answer all questions truthfully. But they were not told beforehand what the questions would be. This was known as an *ex officio* oath, and was borrowed from civil law: its use in church courts was without precedent. A minister might therefore be faced with a question such as 'Do you use the Book of Common Prayer without alteration?' and be forced to reply yea or

**Key terms**

**Ordinal**
The book containing the regulations for becoming a minister or bishop.

*Ex officio* **oath**
A legally binding promise to respond truthfully to whatever question was asked, but without prior knowledge of the question.

nay. Small wonder that such inflexibility and aggression caused uproar. Within the dioceses covered by the province of Canterbury, at least 300 ministers were suspended for refusing to subscribe. The Privy Council, bombarded with protests from sympathetic gentry, advised Whitgift to accept a modified subscription. Whitgift followed this advice, and most of the recalcitrant ministers duly subscribed.

### The Classical movement

What was the effect of Whitgift's aggressive pressure for uniformity? It seems reasonable to argue that he unwittingly gave stimulus to the case for Presbyterianism. After all, being persecuted by an archbishop was hardly likely to arouse enthusiasm for episcopacy among Puritan ministers. There is, however, some difficulty in finding evidence to support this argument. One would need to establish the relative strengths of Presbyterianism before and after the arrival of Whitgift as Archbishop. But how?

**Key term**

**Classical movement**
A series of meetings, mainly or entirely of Protestant clergy, for study and prayer.

- One might argue that establishing the number of *classes* might help, since these were meetings of clergy which ignored diocesan boundaries and were not set up by bishops. Historians refer to these meetings as the **Classical movement**. The name derives from the term *classis* (plural *classes*), meaning a regional meeting to which the local congregation sent its representatives for discussion of such issues as discipline.
- But danger lies in assuming that these *classes* were Cartwright-style Presbyterian synods. Not all those who took part in *classes* were committed Presbyterians. Often, these meetings were informal arenas for study and prayer, rather than the synods in embryo. Presbyterianism demands a major role for lay elders, yet these meetings were usually attended only by the clergy.

**Key question**
Why, by the end of the 1580s, was the Puritan challenge apparently over?

## 4 | Presbyterianism in the 1580s

No doubt John Field hoped that the *classes* would respond to the resentment caused by Whitgift by stimulating the growth and expansion of Presbyterianism. But noisy propaganda from the likes of Field does not prove that Whitgift's Articles caused an influx of recruits to the Presbyterian position. Field, not for the last time, underestimated the desire of ministers to avoid radical positions and unseemly conflict. Field's message was simple: clergy should not offer any form of subscription to the Articles, conditional or otherwise. But what alternative did the ministers have if they wished to maintain their profession and to have influence over their parishioners? If Whitgift had really pushed clergy into opposition and Presbyterianism, why then did so few refuse to subscribe to the modified Articles? 'Conformist' Puritans, in the main, continued to conform.

**Key dates**

Turner's pro-Presbyterian bill: 1584

Cope's pro-Presbyterian bill: 1587

Field did seek to exploit wider resentment at Whitgift's behaviour. He launched a national survey to establish grievances against the bishops, in the hope that forthcoming parliaments could be influenced thereby to pass pro-Presbyterian legislation.

However, despite the best efforts of Field and his sympathisers, the 1584 election was by no means a Puritan triumph. As the historian MacCulloch has pointed out, even the supposed heartlands of Puritan influence like Essex failed to return the hoped-for godly MPs. Nevertheless, the Presbyterians did their best to sway Parliament. Secret presses issued manifestos, and a bill was introduced by Dr Peter Turner in 1584 which would have set up a national Presbyterian system. But the Queen could and did come up with her standard veto, using the powerful **oratory** of Sir Christopher Hatton to forbid the House to discuss religious matters.

**Oratory**
Persuasive speech.

Key term

## The Parliament of 1586–7

In the Parliament of 1586–7, the Presbyterians tried again. Excitement over Leicester's Netherlands expedition (see pages 129–30) and the Babington Plot (see pages 161–2), together with the publication of the results of some of Field's surveys, may have contributed to the return of a larger number of MPs sympathetic to Puritanism in general (although not necessarily to Presbyterianism). Perhaps we are at last getting close to Professor Neale's elusive 'Puritan Choir' (see page 46). One of their number, Anthony Cope, offered for discussion 'a bill and a book' in February 1587. The bill proposed doing away with the Book of Common Prayer and replacing it with a version of the Genevan Prayer Book which incorporated a fully Presbyterian system of church government. Cope and some supporters were despatched to the Tower on Elizabeth's instructions, and government spokesmen brought their guns to bear on a bill and book which, in any case, had little or no chance of passing through Parliament with or without government intervention.

- As Christopher Hatton pointed out, a system of church organisation like that envisaged by Cope would threaten the influence of landowners over church livings.
- Even Sir Walter Mildmay, the founder of Emmanuel College, Cambridge – an institution dedicated to the training of Puritan ministers – had nothing good to say about this proposal.
- The fact that the House of Commons had given leave for Cope's bill to be read proves merely that MPs were prepared to listen to Puritan grievances. This in turn may suggest sympathy with Puritanism in some form, or it may simply reflect a dislike of the bishops as rivals in provincial affairs. The House of Commons certainly had little or no sympathy for Presbyterianism itself.

As a result of the failure of his parliamentary campaign, Field had come to the inescapable conclusion that the Presbyterian revolution could not be imposed from above. Instead, he turned his efforts to a slower, clandestine reform from below, using the style and organisation associated with the continental Calvinist Churches. One pressing need was for a book of discipline. This might provide the basis of a uniform church organisation which, if accepted by the *classes*, could undermine the Ordinal and the Book of Common Prayer. The Presbyterian theorist Walter

Travers was largely responsible for such a work, his *Church Discipline* of 1587. But this could only have had a significant effect if a genuine, national framework of *classes* had also existed. As we discovered earlier, it did not. And the efforts of Field and others of a similar mind tended to obscure the fact that there was no general agreement on the exact organisation of a Presbyterian Church. This explains why Travers's book was not uniformly welcomed even by those sympathetic to Presbyterianism.

Nor must it be forgotten that Puritanism itself – Presbyterian or otherwise – was not a nationwide phenomenon. The research of Professor Collinson has revealed that there were whole areas in the country where Puritanism in any form had failed to make a meaningful impact. These areas included the traditional Catholic strongholds of the north, Wales, the West Midlands and parts of the West Country.

### The *Martin Marprelate* tracts of 1588–9

**Key date**

*Martin Marprelate* tracts: 1588

The *Martin Marprelate* tracts were Puritan pamphlets, but were anything but scholarly or theological. They were outrageous, satirical and bitter attacks on the hierarchy of the church. A rough modern equivalent of the title would be 'Martin bishop-smasher', and the tracts were certainly an exciting read. But they presented a most unsavoury picture of the writer. Were Puritans, then, the violent, sarcastic, offensive, hot-headed, foul-mouthed and destructive individuals as suggested by the style of Martin Marprelate himself? Martin, for example, called Whitgift 'The Pope of London', complained of his 'crazed brains' and claimed that, to be a true Martinist, one should be 'neither a papist, atheist, traitor nor lord bishop'. Thomas Cartwright, among others, was quick to disassociate himself from the tracts.

So, what damage was done to the Puritan cause by Martin? First, his timing was unfortunate. In the year of the Spanish Armada, when God seemed to have favoured the English and their church and when unity against a powerful enemy was vital, Martin could easily be accused of being a seditious traitor. Had he forgotten that his Queen was commonly seen as the defender of Protestantism throughout Europe? Second, the effectiveness of his secret printing organisation alarmed even those members of the Privy Council who sympathised with the Puritan position.

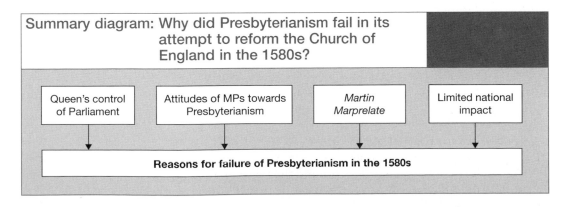

Summary diagram: Why did Presbyterianism fail in its attempt to reform the Church of England in the 1580s?

Queen's control of Parliament

Attitudes of MPs towards Presbyterianism

*Martin Marprelate*

Limited national impact

**Reasons for failure of Presbyterianism in the 1580s**

# 5 | The Puritans Under Attack 1589–1603

By the end of the 1580s, Puritanism had lost not only John Field, but also its most important patrons. Death had carried away Leicester, Mildmay and Walsingham. In the absence of such defenders, a major and official onslaught against the Puritans was launched: an onslaught which crushed the remnants of Elizabethan Presbyterianism. Richard Bancroft, chaplain to Sir Christopher Hatton, set the tone with a sermon at Paul's Cross, the open-air pulpit outside St Paul's Cathedral in London which was used to put across pro-government propaganda. Bancroft explicitly linked Puritans with Separatists and so-called 'sectaries', such as the much-abused **Anabaptists**, and gave the whole picture some credibility with a cunningly vague tinge of conspiracy theory. Puritans were allegedly linked to certain powerful men of position and influence. Indeed, government voices were keen to suggest that Puritanism was a vehicle for Presbyterianism, and Presbyterianism a signpost on the road to Separatism. Bancroft was as efficient in uncovering secret organisations as he was at slandering them. A widespread examination of ministers in the winter of 1589–90 laid bare what existed of the Classical movement. Ringleaders were arrested, including Thomas Cartwright. What frightened these men was not so much their appearance before the Court of High Commission as their subsequent examination before the Court in Star Chamber. Star Chamber was the court for traitors. With remarkably bad timing, a few extremist Puritans proclaimed a deranged individual named William Hacket as the new Messiah, and followed up this announcement with another deposing the Queen. For this, Hacket lost his life in July 1591, and Cartwright and his fellow Presbyterians any chance of retrieving their influence and credibility. When they finally emerged from prison, they had little fight left in them. Nor had Elizabethan Presbyterianism.

**Anabaptists**
A Protestant Separatist movement from Switzerland and Germany that grew up in the first years of the Lutheran Reformation. Some Anabaptists preached extreme political and religious views, including the abolition of private property.

Key term

## The Separatists
### Robert Browne

The most important group of Separatists made its appearance in the 1580s under Robert Browne and Robert Harrison. The group is generally known as the 'Brownists': indeed, the term was used by the government to describe all Separatists. After a spell of imprisonment following the setting up of Separatist congregations in Norwich, Browne left the country and settled in the Netherlands. There, in 1582, he wrote his *Treatise of Reformation without tarrying for any*. The title is revealing, as Browne argued that the Christian should set about reformation without waiting for the permission or guidance of anyone in authority. He further claimed that the Church of England was so corrupt and riddled with papist superstition that the true Christian must shun it at all costs. To distribute works by Browne or Harrison was made a criminal offence for which death was the punishment. In 1583, John Copping and Elias Thacker were hanged for such activities.

**Key question**
Why was the government able to crush Separatism?

Robert Browne published the Separatist *Treatise of Reformation without tarrying for any*: 1582

Key date

### Henry Barrow and John Greenwood

By 1584, Browne was back in England, having quarrelled with his Dutch congregation. He submitted to Whitgift, and was ordained in the Church of England seven years later. But new leaders for the London Separatists were forthcoming in the persons of Henry Barrow and John Greenwood. Barrow and Greenwood were imprisoned for a number of years, but were able to arrange to have several of their works published abroad. In 1593, in the middle of attempting to get a bill against sectaries through Parliament, the government executed the two of them. The title of this measure, passed in the same year, reveals very clearly the link made in the government's mind between refusal to attend divine service in the Church of England and simple disloyalty: 'An Act to retain the Queen's subjects in obedience.' The Act gave the Separatists a number of unpalatable choices. They could either conform or leave the country for good. Should they continue to worship as Separatists, then the death penalty would be invoked.

### Weakness of Separatism

Throughout Elizabeth's reign, Separatists were numerically insignificant. But the government treated them with all possible harshness as potential traitors. The Separatists' denial that church and nation were identical was seen as nothing more than disloyalty under another name.

The Separatists had no powerful supporters to protect them against the government, since their ideas on autonomous congregations and rejection of a national church sabotaged the authority of the monarch and the rest of the political élite.

Separatism can barely be called a 'movement', since it inevitably lacked the unity a national church, or a would-be national church, would encourage.

<table>
<tr><td>

**Key question**
What is 'Anglicanism'?

</td></tr>
<tr><td>

**Key date**
Richard Hooker's *Of the Laws of Ecclesiastical Polity*: 1593

</td></tr>
</table>

### 'Anglicanism'

Of greater long-term significance than the Elizabethan Separatists themselves was a work in defence of the Church of England which was rushed through the presses in time for the debate on the 1593 bill against the 'seditious sectaries' (traitors and Separatists). This was Richard Hooker's *Of the Laws of Ecclesiastical Polity*. It was a monumental defence of the position often called 'Anglicanism'. This is a term which has been avoided in the course of this book so far. It is only right to point out that some historians use it to describe the Elizabethan Church of England throughout the reign. We might prefer to use it to describe a particular theological position rather than the church as a whole. This permits us to appreciate that there were elements within Hooker's 'Anglicanism' which were deeply disturbing to many of the Church of England's most loyal advocates. In defending his church against Presbyterians and Separatists, Hooker emphasised the value of tradition and continuity. The Church of England was not, therefore, the result of Henrician, Edwardian or Elizabethan reformation, but a body whose development could be traced from medieval times and beyond. This meant that the Roman Catholic Church of the Middle Ages was indeed part of the True Church (as ordained by God) – and that the sixteenth-century Church of Rome remained so, despite its errors. This is hardly a position which the likes of Grindal or Whitgift would find comfortable. Significantly, Hooker allotted a relatively minor role to preaching in the scheme of salvation. Using the argument from tradition, Hooker stressed the prime importance of the **Eucharist** in worship. Worship itself was the most important route to salvation, and preaching was just one of a number of ways for the soul to worship its maker.

**Eucharist**
The bread and wine offered to the congregation in the Communion service.

Key term

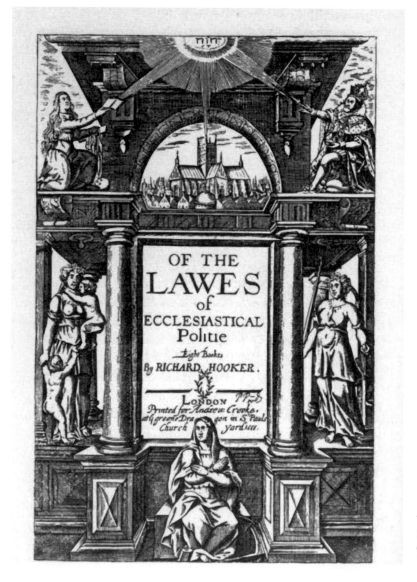

Title page of Richard Hooker's *Of the Laws of Ecclesiastical Polity* 1593–7.

What is extraordinary is that, as MacCulloch has pointed out, Hooker's huge work should mention Calvin only nine times. On three of those occasions, Hooker disagreed with him. And full of significance for the future is Hooker's use of the concept of *via media*. This translates as the 'middle way' supposedly trodden by the English church between the alleged excesses of Calvinist Protestantism on the one hand and the different excesses of Roman Catholicism on the other. Also of great future import was a concept which blends with Hooker's arguments but which was not employed by him. This was the defence of episcopacy as an institution demanded by the law of God (***jure divino***). This case was argued by, among others, Richard Bancroft. The *jure divino* argument is some distance from the viewpoint of Whitgift, who had argued that the scriptures contained no precise system of government for the church. Had a specific system been necessary to salvation, then it would have been made crystal clear.

While Hooker largely ignored Calvinism, other writers had the audacity to attack ideas central to Calvinist theology. This, of course, meant attacking much of the theology of the Church of England. In the 1580s and 1590s, some university scholars blended ideas on the importance of sacraments, of tradition and of *jure divino* episcopacy with an attack on the theory of predestination. A major row broke out in Cambridge in 1595 when one of the university chaplains, William Barrett, attacked that theory and, for good measure, Calvin himself. Despite the intervention of influential sympathisers such as the court preacher and Master of Pembroke College Lancelot Andrewes, Barrett's Cambridge career was in ruins. Whitgift himself entered the fray, and drew up the Lambeth Articles of 1595. These restated the centrality of Calvinist theories of salvation to the doctrine of the Church of England. Significantly, the Queen refused to grant these articles official backing on the grounds that Whitgift had been so rash as to pronounce on true doctrine without consulting his Supreme Governor.

The new theology of Anglicanism was to prove nothing short of explosive in the future. When voiced by such men as William Laud, Charles I's Archbishop of Canterbury, it became an important cause of the conflict known as the English Civil War. Its attack on Calvinism, its appeal to the importance of tradition, its lack of emphasis on preaching and its claims for episcopal power would make the position of the Conformist Puritan impossible, and stimulate the very Presbyterianism which Elizabeth had so effectively crushed.

**Key term**

*Jure divino*
A Latin phrase meaning 'by the law of God'.

**Key date**

Lambeth Articles: 1595

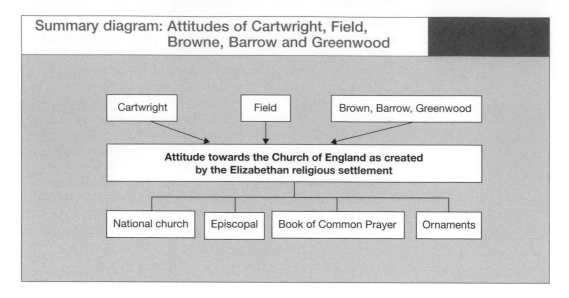

Summary diagram: Attitudes of Cartwright, Field, Browne, Barrow and Greenwood

# 6 | Conclusion: Elizabeth and the Puritans

Any attempt to argue that Puritanism was a 'threat' to the Elizabethan Church of England must consider the need to define the three types of Puritan and the nature of the threat presented by the three types to the Church of England:

- Conformist Puritans were prepared to work within the church in the hope of gradual reform and therefore cannot be seen as a threat as such.
- Presbyterians were supportive of a national church, but it would not be an episcopalian (bishop-led) church. Nor would it be a church which the monarch, in the absence of bishops, would find easy to manipulate.
- Separatists in theory represented the greatest threat, since they denied that a national church was possible at all.

The extent of the threat represented by the three groups was as follows:

- Conformist Puritans represented little threat. The case of Grindal was instructive, in that he did not move into opposition despite the severity of his treatment by the Queen.
- Presbyterians. The monarch could and did employ formidable powers to suppress that perceived threat. These powers were such that the Presbyterians had little chance of success: therefore, the Presbyterian threat was no real threat at all, despite the noisome gnashing of teeth practised by both sides. Take the case of Parliament and Presbyterian efforts to manipulate it. Elizabeth was able to quash such efforts by voicing disapproval, forbidding the discussion of religious questions and imprisoning the hot-heads. She had further powers – including the proroguing (suspension) or dissolving of Parliament – on which she never needed to call. In addition,

Key question
How far was Puritanism a threat to the Elizabethan Church of England?

there is little evidence that Parliament was at all supportive of the Presbyterian position. It threatened too many established interests of the ruling classes, including the right of patronage to church livings. Moreover, Presbyterianism was too much of a leap in the dark to appeal to those whose power rested on stability and social control. And it cut down to size the position of the secular lord, who was a member of a church, and not a ruler of it. All this does not mean that Puritanism in its broader sense was without support amongst the ruling classes. Calls for further reform of the church and a demand for effective preaching could and did find support in the highest ranks of the government itself. But to identify the House of Commons with the Puritan interest is mistaken. Puritan voices were listened to with particular attention when MPs felt that the country was under some sort of threat from anti-Protestant elements, be it Catholics at home or Catholics abroad. A reasonably sympathetic MP could rely on the Puritans for some splendid and forthright name-calling: one could enjoy their gift for invective without incurring the wrath of the Queen by actually supporting their demands.

- Separatists were not a threat in practice. They were too few in number, too addicted to bickering with each other and totally devoid of élite support. In addition, the Queen could and did employ savage penalties against them.

Historians who argue that Puritans posed a major threat to the established church find it difficult to accept that they made a positive and vital contribution towards it. Even though the Puritan minister, pursuing his godly course, might be treated with suspicion by the hierarchy of the church, his work did much to spread enthusiasm for the Protestant way among those who were not content to sneer and name call, but were, instead, prepared to listen. And Calvinism, it must be remembered, lay at the heart of the doctrine of the Church of England. It is true that Puritans failed to change the organisation and hierarchy of the church. The Thirty-Nine Articles remained, and ministers had to wear surplices and conduct services in the prescribed manner. But what the historian cannot measure is the influence of the Puritan minister in his parish or the Puritan gentleman in his hall: an influence perhaps deeper and more lasting than some of the rituals to which they accommodated themselves.

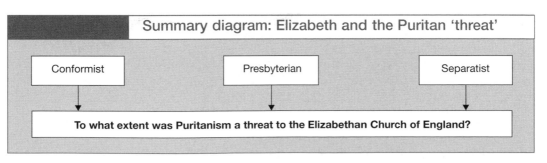

Summary diagram: Elizabeth and the Puritan 'threat'

Conformist → Presbyterian → Separatist →

**To what extent was Puritanism a threat to the Elizabethan Church of England?**

## Study Guide: AS Questions

### In the style of OCR A

How successfully did Elizabeth tackle the Puritan challenge to her religious settlement by 1589?                              (50 marks)

---

### Exam tips

A question that asks 'How successfully … ?' requires an assessment of the challenge. Although it will be necessary to describe the different elements of the Puritan movement before 1589, such descriptions should be brief and relevant to the task of identifying the nature and extent of its challenge and how far this was effectively controlled by the crown. Similarly, the different ways in which Elizabeth countered the challenge, through Parliament, the Privy Council, Convocation, the Court of High Commission and her archbishops, need to be assessed rather than described.

You need to have a good understanding of the condition of Puritanism and the state of the Church of England in 1589. Do resist the temptation to write about the Catholic challenge although you might make a passing comparison by way of an evaluation. You might conclude that the Puritan challenge was never as serious as contemporaries believed but that Elizabeth's success in containing it was by no means inevitable.

## In the style of OCR B

Answer **both** parts of your chosen question.

**(a)** Why did Puritans want to change the Elizabethan religious settlement? (25 marks)

**(b)** Why was Puritanism perceived to be a threat to stability in Elizabethan England? (25 marks)

---

### Exam tips

*The page references are intended to take you straight to the material that will help you to answer the questions.*

**(a)** This question focuses on the motives of Puritans. These are likely to be concerned principally with religious beliefs, about both doctrine and the organisational hierarchy of the established church. However, to explain their ideas solely in terms of religious beliefs would be too simplistic. Certainly Puritan ideas about doctrine and church organisation were derived from the Bible, but the influence of reformers such as Calvin and the experience of exile during Mary's reign built on this.

You might, for example, argue that the remaining Catholic elements in the Elizabethan church were the main reason the Puritans wanted to change the religious settlement, as they regarded the church as only partly reformed. However, without the influence of Calvinism in continental Europe, Puritans would not have pushed so strongly for further reform.

You might also refer to groupings within the Privy Council and the role they played in supporting Puritans in their bid for further reform. The motives here might be considered to be founded less on religious beliefs and more on self-interest.

What you should do:

- In your planning, identify a range of factors that may be used to explain Puritan demands.
- Refine your plan by organising your factors into those which were most significant and those on which the main factors depend.
- While you may focus mainly on an empathetic explanation, including the beliefs of the Church of England set against those of the Puritans, do not forget to look at the wider context in which these ideas developed.

What you should avoid:

- Questioning the acceptability of the term 'Puritan': this is a valid point, but not one that will move your argument forward.
- Descriptions of the different kinds of Puritans identified by historians (unless you are using these to organise different points in your essay).

**(b)** The key to explaining the threat to stability lies in an understanding of how religious division might undermine stability in the sixteenth century and also to understanding the fragility of government control in this period.

You should make sure that you understand and can explain why and how religious division and discord could cause rebellion (Chapter 1, the Western Rebellion, pages 11–12, and the Wyatt Rebellion, pages 29–30). You might consider ideas about government and how the crown kept control through the nobility and gentry (see Chapters 1 and 7). You should aim to show how these ideas combined together made the authorities fear what too much Puritan influence in the church might lead to. You should also ensure that you can explain how Puritan ideas conflicted with those of the Church of England and why they would be unlikely to appeal to the majority.

You might argue, for example, that if the church structure were further reformed along Puritan lines, the crown would lose the significant control (Chapter 2, pages 48–9) that it exercised via bishops. Therefore the existing governmental structures can be used to explain why Puritans were seen as a threat. You might therefore argue that it was not so much the Puritans' ideas, but a fear of change and a reluctance to relinquish such important figures of authority that determined that Puritans were regarded as a threat to stability.

What you should do:

- Identify the Puritan ideas that might be perceived to threaten political and religious stability.
- Identify the theory and methods of government that would be destabilised if Puritan practices were adopted.
- Plan an answer that shows how these ideas and methods were incompatible in the context of the second half of the sixteenth century in England.

What you should avoid:

- Describing what the Puritans wanted to change.
- Writing an account of the Puritan campaign in Parliament and the way the government countered it.

## Study Guide: A2 Question

### In the style of AQA

How successfully did Elizabeth I meet the challenge posed by the Puritans in the years c.1570–1603?                    (45 marks)

---

*Exam tips*

This is a broad and basic question, but that does not mean that it is easy to plan an answer! First, it would be difficult to answer this question without showing an awareness of the different types of Puritans that existed at this time. You will probably want to point out that not all Puritans posed a challenge (or at least not the same type of challenge) and you will certainly need to state what you consider those challenges to be.

You also need to pay attention to the given dates. The starting date, c.1570, coincides with Cartwright's spring lectures and the beginnings of a demand for a Presbyterian system, but you may wish to argue that the real challenge only came after 1589 when separatism became a bigger issue. Although the question is focused on Elizabeth I, you might also like to consider whether the policies adopted were actually hers or whether, for example, Whitgift was the driving force from 1583.

Finally, the question asks you to assess 'success'. To do so, you need premises to judge against, which means a consideration of the aims of those involved and also a consideration of the broader implications of the Elizabethan policies for the stability and prosperity of England. These are separate issues and one line of argument (although it is not the only possible one) would be that Elizabeth was successful in meeting her own aims but that in doing so, she actually created more problems.

---

# 4 Meeting the Challenge of Religion: Elizabeth and the Catholics

**POINTS TO CONSIDER**

The issues discussed in this chapter are not uniquely religious ones. We have noted in previous chapters that religion and politics were seen by contemporaries as two sides of the same coin, and Catholicism posed a potential challenge to Elizabeth in a number of ways. Given that those adhering to the traditional religion heavily outnumbered Protestants, and that Catholics might be first to dispute Elizabeth's claim to the throne, the potential for strife was considerable. Elizabeth also found herself faced with the aggressive anti-Catholicism of her most loyal supporters and key members of the Privy Council. As we shall see, Elizabeth's approach was dictated by her view of her political needs; an interpretation which complements our earlier comments on the Elizabethan religious settlement and the Puritans.

The chapter is structured chronologically around the various challenges posed by Catholicism:

- Catholicism and the Elizabethan religious settlement
- Mary, Queen of Scots, the revolt of the Northern Earls and papal excommunication
- The arrival of the missionary priests
- Conflict within the Catholic community

We also examine a key historiographical debate on the strength of Catholicism throughout the reign.

## Key dates

1540   Ignatius Loyola founded the Society of Jesus
1568   Mary Stuart fled to England
        William Allen founded the seminary at Douai
1569   Norfolk–Mary Stuart marriage plot
        Revolt of the Northern Earls
1570   Pope Pius V issued Papal Bull *Regnans in Excelsis* excommunicating Elizabeth
1571   Ridolfi plot discovered
        Treason Acts
1574   First missionary priests arrived in England from Douai
1580   First Jesuits (Campion and Parsons) arrived in England

1581   Act 'to retain the Queen's Majesty's subjects in their due obedience'

1585   Act 'against Jesuits, seminary priests and such other like disobedient persons'

1588   Defeat of the Spanish Armada

1598   George Blackwell appointed Archpriest

**Key question**
What principles underpinned official policy towards the Catholics early in Elizabeth's reign?

# 1 | 1559–68: The Government Treads with Caution?

## The Queen's aims in tackling Catholicism

It was not in Elizabeth's interest to pursue an aggressively anti-Catholic policy which would disturb domestic and foreign tranquillity.

Equally, it was not in her interests, having adopted a basically Protestant settlement, to grant some form of religious toleration to those who wished to adhere to the old faith. It was an assumption of government that the religion of the country should follow the religion of its prince. To permit religious division was seen as issuing an invitation to civil war.

- First of all, what could be done about the clergy? In Chapter 2, it was explained that virtually all the Marian bishops refused to accept the government's legislative changes over matters of doctrine (see page 48). Their deprivation, rather than their execution, resulted.
- As for the parish priests, it was their responsibility to put the new service and prayer book into effect. And most of these priests were not, of course, Protestants. As it happened, very few clergy refused the Oath of Supremacy when it was tendered to them in the summer of 1559: perhaps up to 300 in all.
- We cannot assume that this means that the clergy were fully committed to the doctrine of the Elizabethan settlement. For commitment, however, the Queen was quite prepared to wait. In any case, it was not possible to replace existing clergy with enthusiastic and trained Protestants. Such men were simply not available in any number.
- What the Queen could realistically hope for was the longer term effect on staunch Catholics of attending Church of England services. Habit – doing what your neighbours did – might safely achieve over the years what aggression and punishment might never secure. Indeed, the next generation, baptised, married and buried according to the rites of the Church of England, would hopefully come to regard Catholicism as something un-English and unnatural.

## The Act of Uniformity and Catholics

This means, of course, that the Catholic laity was expected to conform outwardly. The Act of Uniformity specified that:

- A shilling fine was levied for each failure to attend church on Sundays and other designated days.
- Refusal to take the Oath of Supremacy meant that those holding government offices of any type would lose their positions.
- A person upholding the Pope as rightful head of the church – either in writing or in speech – lost property for the first offence, all goods and his liberty for the second offence, and was executed for the third.
- A layman who attempted to persuade any priest to deviate from the order and doctrine of the 1559 Book of Common Prayer was similarly subject to increasing penalties. For, say, persuading a priest to perform a Catholic Mass, the fine was 100 marks (there were three marks in a pound), increasing to 400 marks and then life imprisonment along with forfeiture of goods for second and third offences, respectively.
- Penalties were imposed on **clerics** who did not follow the required usages of the Book of Common Prayer. In particular, it made it clear that nothing was to be added to the words said in the delivery of Holy Communion. This would therefore prevent the cleric from using the familiar Catholic words to imply the Real Presence of Christ in the bread and wine. In fact, the Act avoided altogether the use of the word 'priest', preferring 'pastor', 'minister' or 'vicar'. This duly underlines the distinction between the Catholic priest and Church of England pastor.
- Penalty for failure to follow the specified rites was six months' imprisonment with loss of a year's income in the first instance. A second offence carried one year's imprisonment, and a further offence life imprisonment.

Perhaps we should conclude that these penalties were by no means excessively harsh. They would not create martyrs. On the other hand, the fines imposed for attempting to maintain a system of worship outside the Church of England were sufficiently stiff to encourage Catholic gentry to conform outwardly.

## The persistence of tradition

It would be a mistake to assume that the demands of the Act of Uniformity were carried out to the letter. What really matters is what happened in practice, and this is particularly difficult to assess. There is evidence from regional studies to show that conservative clergy, while operating within the Church of England, nonetheless made it clear that the old ways were the right road to salvation. And the churchwardens who were empowered to impose the shilling fine for non-attendance were often disinclined to do so. Because of this, the fact that there were very few prosecutions in the church courts for persistent absenteeism tells us little. It certainly does not tell us that there was little absenteeism. Nor, of course, should we assume that failure to attend church was a sign of committed Catholicism. A dislike of new ways, a hankering after the 'good old days', a conviction that what was good enough for one's forefathers was good enough for oneself: all these are potent reasons for non-attendance, and none has much to do with theology. The attractions of continuity are obvious. Christopher Haigh and Eamon Duffy catalogued problems with clergy who continued to use Latin, raised the bread and wine as if 'elevating the host', kept the old altar in its traditional position in the east of the church and so on.

## Parliament and anti-Catholicism

The cautious policy towards Catholicism should be identified with the Queen herself. The Protestant members of the political nation, as represented by Parliament, were much less reluctant to raise the cry of heresy against Catholicism. At the opening of the Parliament of 1563, Dean Nowell of St Paul's is reported to have said:

> The Queen's majesty of her own nature is wholly given to **clemency** and mercy ... [but] clemency ought not to be given to the wolves to kill and devour, as they do the lambs ... For by the scriptures, murderers, breakers of the holy day, and maintainers of false religion ought to die by the sword.

**Key term**

**Clemency**
Leniency.

No doubt the Dean was satisfied by the legislation of this Parliament. The Oath of Supremacy was to be demanded of a much wider group. Schoolmasters, lawyers, court officials and MPs were all required to subscribe. More to the point, a second refusal of the oath carried the death penalty. Any priest found guilty of saying Mass, and any laymen who had requested a Mass, were also to suffer death. Attendance at Mass carried a 100 mark fine. But, once again, we must not assume that the existence of a law guaranteed its enforcement. The Queen instructed Archbishop Parker not to demand subscription to the oath a second time if it had been refused the first. This meant that the death penalty could not be invoked. Nor were there any executions for the saying of Mass before 1577, when the international climate had changed completely.

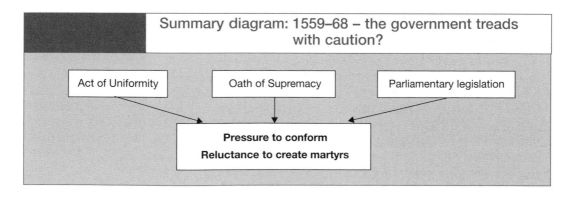

Summary diagram: 1559–68 – the government treads with caution?

Act of Uniformity — Oath of Supremacy — Parliamentary legislation

**Pressure to conform**
**Reluctance to create martyrs**

## 2 | The Attitude of the Pope

**Key question**
Why did the Pope not act against Elizabeth in the first years of her reign?

It might be argued that leniency is the luxury of a monarch who does not feel under threat. Chapter 2 demonstrated how ruthless Elizabeth could be in the defence of her own interests. For the first decade of her reign, the Queen felt reasonably secure from the possibility of a crusade against her on religious grounds by her Catholic fellow monarchs. The friendship – even protection – of Philip II of Spain gave her little reason to make a link between Catholicism among her subjects and the Catholicism of a foreign enemy. Indeed, the Pope himself, for a number of years, carefully avoided a stance opposing Elizabeth.

Pope Pius IV may well have anticipated that Elizabethan England might be encouraged to return to the Catholic fold. He even hoped that Elizabeth might send representatives to the Council of Trent in 1559. This Council, first convened in 1545, was intended to spearhead reform in the Catholic Church in the face of the many challenges of the century. What was not immediately obvious was the extent to which it would be under papal control. Previous General Councils of the Church had explicitly challenged papal authority. Elizabeth, it seems, genuinely contemplated sending representatives, until it became clear that the Pope had, by the end of 1560, firmly established his authority over the Council of Trent. Despite the non-appearance of English representatives at the Council, the Pope continued to work constructively for contacts with England. It is also significant that the Pope failed to instruct Catholics to shun Church of England services – including Communion – until 1562, and only then in response to a direct enquiry from English Catholics. In fact, English Catholic exiles requested the Council of Trent to excommunicate Elizabeth in 1563. It was a mark of the Pope's increasing frustration that he agreed to do so, and a mark of the desire of Philip II to retain English friendship that he persuaded Pius IV not to carry out his intention at that time.

## 3 | The Revolt of the Northern Earls (or 'Northern Rebellion') 1569

**Key question**
What does the course and failure of the revolt of the Northern Earls suggest about Catholic attitudes towards Elizabeth?

### The arrival of Mary, Queen of Scots in England

We have argued that Elizabeth's lenient treatment of English Catholics reflected her view that they represented little threat in the context of a fairly secure international and domestic political climate. If this is an accurate assessment of her motives, it is to be expected that the treatment of her Catholic subjects would have become increasingly harsh as that climate deteriorated from the mid-1560s onwards. Such is indeed the case.

**Key dates**
Revolt of the Northern Earls: 1569

Mary Stuart fled to England: 1568

One of the most significant reasons for that deterioration was the flight from Scotland and arrival in England of Mary Stuart, Queen of Scots, in 1568. A full discussion of the Mary Stuart question can be found on pages 159–63. For the moment, it is sufficient to note that Mary had appeared, at various times, to unite in one person all the worst nightmares of English foreign policy: a rival and Catholic contender for Elizabeth's throne and a focus for the traditional anti-English alliance of Scotland and France. It is at this point that Mary Stuart becomes one of the factors which explain a major change in the Elizabethan government's attitude towards the Catholics. We can use 1568 as a convenient point from which to chart the implications of that change.

The presence of Mary Stuart in England therefore brought into the open the unresolved problems and dangers facing Elizabeth. The problem which most exercised her Council and Parliament was that of the succession. The Parliament of 1566–7 had insisted that time be allocated for the succession issue to be debated. But this was a matter on which the Queen would brook no interference. In an impressive display of temper, tantrum, threats and abuse, she chose to interpret anxiety about the matter and requests for her to marry as opposition.

## The Norfolk marriage plot

**Key date**

Norfolk–Mary Stuart marriage plot: 1569

Mary's arrival in England reopened the issue. An attractive proposition to one faction at court was a projected marriage between Mary and the greatest of the English nobles, Thomas Howard, Duke of Norfolk. Such a marriage might have the effect of inducing Elizabeth to accept Mary as her heir. This would have two further implications.

- First, the possibility of a Catholic succession would be materially advanced. The Duke of Norfolk himself might attend Protestant services, but few were unaware that his sympathies were Catholic.
- Second, the marriage could be used as a lever to force out of office the Secretary of State, William Cecil. Cecil's sympathies were most definitely not with the Catholics. He saw Spain as the head of a conspiracy to destroy Protestantism throughout Europe. The English Catholics were pawns in the Spanish game.

The anti-Cecil and 'semi-Catholic' party at court (to use historian John Guy's term) was backed by certain northern nobles whose Catholicism was unquestionable. The Earl of Northumberland had reconverted to Rome in 1567 and, together with the Earl of Westmorland, had moved beyond the stage of factional intrigue at court and into treason. The two earls had been in touch with Rome and with Spain in the hope of obtaining military backing for the cause of Norfolk and Mary. Their only hope of emerging unscathed was to shelter behind the Duke and pray for his success, but Norfolk's plan was brought to a shuddering halt when the Queen heard rumours of the proposed marriage. The royal veto promptly descended, and Norfolk, after the tensest of hesitations, threw himself on the Queen's mercy and his allies to the dogs. He got away with a brief spell in the Tower. Westmorland and Northumberland were unlikely to be so lucky. When Elizabeth summoned them to court, they came out in rebellion.

## Profile: Thomas Howard, Duke of Norfolk 1536–72

| | |
|---|---|
| 1554 | – Inherited the dukedom from his grandfather. Created Earl Marshal |
| 1562 | – Privy Councillor |
| 1568 | – Headed commission to enquire into Scottish affairs after the arrival of Mary, Queen of Scots in England. Schemed to marry Mary, Queen of Scots |
| 1569–70 | – Links to Revolt of the Northern Earls: imprisoned. Implicated in the Ridolfi Plot |
| 1572 | – Executed |

Although he was educated by John Foxe and was adamant that he remained a Protestant throughout his life, Norfolk was suspected of having Catholic sympathies. This made him, in the eyes of English Catholic nobles alienated by Elizabeth's regime, a likely candidate for marriage to Mary, Queen of Scots once Mary had fled to England in 1568. Norfolk, already resentful at the rise of Elizabeth's favourite Robert Dudley, appears to have been seduced by the vision of himself in the role. He was arguably fortunate to escape with his life given his links with the revolt of the Northern Earls, but could not resist further plotting with Mary in mind. The Ridolfi plot of 1571 (see page 160) cost him his head.

> **Key date**
>
> Ridolfi plot discovered: 1571

## The rebellion starts

Religion, then, provided the justification for the rebellion. After the failure of the rebellion and his subsequent arrest, Northumberland stated that the main aim of the uprising had been to reform religion and to establish and safeguard the position of Mary Stuart as heir to the throne. However, we should add that this religious dissent had been fuelled by increasing isolation from the centres of political power. Northumberland felt slighted at not being given some role in the custody of Mary Stuart. Both earls were well aware that Elizabeth had sought to weaken their control over the north, where the crown's authority was traditionally overshadowed by the influence of the great landowners.

As for the rebellion itself, the earls marched on Durham, ejected the Protestant Communion table from the cathedral and restored the Catholic Mass. It may be that the intention was to rescue and release Mary from her custody in Tutbury. However, support from the staunch Catholic gentry was not forthcoming. In particular, Lancashire and Cheshire – strongholds of the old faith – failed to join in. The major problem for the rebels was geography. Their power was limited to the North Riding of Yorkshire. To venture towards the centre of government in the south without the prospect of support there would be foolhardy in the extreme. With the approach of a large royal army, Northumberland and Westmorland fled across the border into Scotland.

---

**Summary diagram: The revolt of the Northern Earls**

**Revolt of the Northern Earls**

**Aims of the rebels**
- Norfolk marriage plot
- Mary Queen of Scots
- Anti-Cecil factionalism

**Reasons for failure**
- Lack of support from Catholic gentry
- Distance from London
- Norfolk's loss of nerve

---

**Key question**
Why did *Regnans in Excelsis* fail to stimulate Catholics to rebel against the Queen?

**Key date**

Pope Pius V issued Papal Bull *Regnans in Excelsis* excommunicating Elizabeth: 1570

**Key terms**

**Papal Bull**
A document containing a pope's explicit instructions which the faithful were to obey.

**Usurp**
To take power to which one is not entitled.

**Heretics**
Those who do not accept the teaching of the church.

# 4 | Papal Excommunication 1570

The most significant element in the short-lived rebellion of the northern earls was the reaction it called forth from the Pope. On 22 February 1570, to encourage the rebels and to try to whip up support for them from other English Catholics, Pius V issued a **Papal Bull**: *Regnans in Excelsis*. By this, Elizabeth was excommunicated (see page 96):

> The number of the ungodly has so much grown in power that there is no place left in the world which they have not tried to corrupt with their most wicked doctrines; and among others, Elizabeth, the pretended queen of England ... has assisted in this. ... This very woman, having seized the crown and monstrously **usurped** the place of supreme head of the church in all England ... she has followed and embraced the errors of the **heretics**. She has removed the royal Council, composed of the nobility of England, and has filled it with obscure men, being heretics. ... We, seeing impieties and crimes multiplied ... do out of the fullness of our apostolic power declare the foresaid Elizabeth to be a heretic ... moreover we declare her to be deprived of her pretended title to the aforesaid crown.

## Pope Pius V

Pius V – who had become Pope in 1566 – was not a man to be governed by considerations of mere politics. When his early hopes for Elizabeth's conversion evaporated, he began to consider excommunicating her. In March 1569, he had consulted the Duke of Alva – Philip II's military commander in the Netherlands – on the possibility of a joint invasion of England by France and Spain. Alva was unenthusiastic; perhaps, he suggested, the Pope might confer the kingdom on some Catholic nobleman who would marry Mary. No doubt Alva was concerned that Mary Stuart ruling alone would mean an England wedded to Mary's beloved France: a dangerous alliance indeed for Spain to face. The Pope sent Nicholas Morton, an English Catholic exile based in Rome, to gauge the reaction of Catholic nobles to any excommunication of Elizabeth. Morton would seem to have

Pope Pius V issuing the Bull of Excommunication against Elizabeth I in 1570.

reported that such a move would be welcomed. Hot on the heels of this report came news of the rebellion of the Northern Earls and a letter from Northumberland and Westmorland asking for papal support. Hence the Bull *Regnans in Excelsis*.

## The terms of the Papal Bull *Regnans in Excelsis*

The Bull was uncompromising. If Catholics continued to obey the Queen, then they too incurred the sentence of excommunication. This would deprive them of all the resources of the Catholic Church in their fight to avoid the pains of hell. If they did obey the Bull, then this would bring on them the pains of a traitor's death. *Regnans in Excelsis* should, therefore, have concentrated the mind of the Catholic community wonderfully. The time for compromise and evasion had, it seems, gone for ever. To the historian, an examination of the impact of the Bull should shed light on some vital issues. How far did Catholics respond to the call for rebellion? What does the episode tell us about their attitude towards papal authority?

## The impact of the Bull

As far as the rebellion of the Northern Earls was concerned, the Bull was an irrelevance. Westmorland and Northumberland had fled before it appeared. What is much more significant is that the Bull was virtually ignored by its intended audience. The English Catholics did not want to know. In fact, since little effort was made to publish and publicise the Bull, they might plausibly have argued that they actually did not know.

This singular lack of response suggests that few English Catholics accepted unconditionally papal claims to fullness of authority over all earthly matters (such as the legitimacy of a monarch's title). These claims were not new, and neither was resistance to them. Traditionally, even the most orthodox of Catholic kings of England had expected their subjects to follow them in their attempts to limit papal involvement in anything affecting the power or wealth of the crown. On top of this was the issue of simple, straightforward loyalty. The landowner of Elizabethan England, Catholic or Protestant, had a very well-developed sense of hierarchy and status. This was based on landed property. Rights of inheritance were, he felt, the only protection against the **anarchy** and upheaval which lay beneath the surface of a violent society. To refuse loyalty to Elizabeth, only surviving child of Henry VIII, was therefore contrary to landowners' instincts for self-preservation. It would be difficult for them to claim the protection of laws of inheritance for themselves and to deny it to the crown.

Perhaps the most important impact of the Papal Bull was the parliamentary legislation intended to neutralise it. The 1571 Treason Acts made it a treasonable offence to deny that Elizabeth was the lawful queen. In addition, it was made clear that anyone using *Regnans in Excelsis* or any other Bull to convert or reconvert a person to Catholicism was guilty of the same offence. However, it is significant that the Queen, once again, refused to allow hardline anti-Catholics to heap further repressive legislation on to their adversaries. Bishop Sandys' bill to increase penalties for those who refused to attend Church of England services ('recusants') was vetoed by Elizabeth, despite its successful passage through Parliament.

**Key term**

**Anarchy**
Lawlessness, rejection of authority.

**Key date**

Treason Acts: 1571

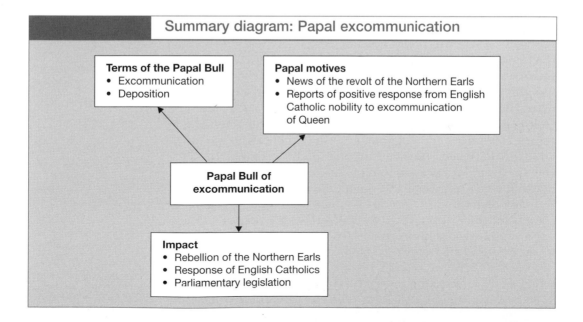

## Summary diagram: Papal excommunication

**Terms of the Papal Bull**
- Excommunication
- Deposition

**Papal motives**
- News of the revolt of the Northern Earls
- Reports of positive response from English Catholic nobility to excommunication of Queen

**Papal Bull of excommunication**

**Impact**
- Rebellion of the Northern Earls
- Response of English Catholics
- Parliamentary legislation

# 5 | The Arrival of the Missionary Priests

Setting aside the perennial problem of Mary and the worries of incidents like the Ridolfi plot (see page 160), the government had considerable cause for comfort in the immediate aftermath of the excommunication. After all, the signs suggested that Catholics were remaining loyal to the Queen. The rebellion of the Northern Earls had failed to attract much Catholic support. It is doubtful whether the Bull brought many Catholics who had previously conformed to the Church of England (known as 'church-papists') into open recusancy. Indeed, if the government had felt troubled by such recusants, why release from prison in 1574 a number of important Marian clergy?

And so, after the initial flurry when the Bull of excommunication first appeared, Elizabeth's government settled down to its former attitude: Catholicism would wither away with the passing of time. What made its attitude change was a new threat: the arrival in England of **missionary priests** from continental Europe. These were priests whose aim was to rekindle Catholic ardour and to convert heretics to the true faith.

## The Douai seminary

The missionary priests mainly came from the seminary (or college) of Douai in the Netherlands. Douai was founded by William Allen in 1568. Its aim was to provide a Catholic education for Englishmen and, subsequently, to train priests for missions to England. William Allen had followed a promising academic career at Oxford during the reign of Mary I. He resigned early in Elizabeth's reign on religious grounds and joined other Catholic exiles in Louvain in the Spanish Netherlands, where the university provided a focus and a base for many distinguished English Catholic scholars. The priests trained at Douai were particularly well equipped for the English mission. They were left in no doubt as to the alleged evils of the heretics, but they were also taught to recognise the sinfulness of Catholics past and present which had encouraged the temporary triumph of Protestantism. The priests were able to meet the Protestants on their own ground through in-depth study of the Bible and training in effective preaching. Added to this was the emphasis placed on **confession**. The confessing of sins to a priest was, of course, a purely Catholic practice, but it had much potential as a vehicle for stiffening the faith of English Catholics who might otherwise have been prepared to conform to the Elizabethan church. Its importance was that the priest was in a position to transmit God's forgiveness. It is not difficult to imagine the response of an English Catholic who might not have been able to confess for some years. Faced by a priest whose personal holiness was as impressive as his learning, the moment of confession could easily arouse a sense of reborn faith and a commitment to proclaim, rather than to hide, one's faith.

The first four Douai priests arrived in England in 1574. By 1580, about 100 more had come. The impact of these priests –

**Key question**
What was the impact of the missionary priests?

**Key terms**

**Missionary priests** Catholic priests sent to England from the continent to win back souls for the Roman Catholic Church.

**Confession** The practice of acknowledging sins to a priest in the hope of God's forgiveness.

**Key dates**

William Allen founded the seminary at Douai: 1568

First missionary priests arrived in England from Douai: 1574

**Key term**

**Secular priests**
Catholic priests who
are not also
members of the
Society of Jesus or
other religious
orders.

usually referred to as '**secular priests**' because they were not members of a particular religious order – is difficult to assess. The problem is that any judgement about their impact depends much on one's opinion of the state of English Catholicism at the time. Were the missionary priests rescuing the dying embers of a church, or simply fanning the flame of a slow-burning but still-strong faith? The major historiographical debate on the continuity of Catholicism in England is discussed in detail on pages 105–7.

### The response of the government to the arrival of the Douai priests

- The response of the government to the Douai priests was initially to press for greater use of existing machinery for identifying and punishing recusants. But sending out such policy directives to sometimes unwilling local representatives of central authority was not the most effective method for dealing with what was seen as a serious threat.
- In 1577, bishops were instructed to provide the government with the numbers of recusants within their dioceses.
- In the same year, the missionary priest Cuthbert Mayne was executed under the existing legislation of 1571 for bringing into the country a Papal Bull. Two more priests were executed the next year for denying the Royal Supremacy.

**Key question**
Why did the
government pass
harsh legislation
against missionary
priests?

## Missionary priests and politics

The death of Mayne gives us insight into an important new theme. Under examination, he had unhesitatingly admitted that he would have supported any Catholic prince who invaded England to restore the Catholic faith. It was small wonder, then, that the members of the Privy Council should be certain that their identification of Catholicism with treason had been confirmed by the activities of the missions. Despite Mayne's words, the link between missionary priests and rebellion may not be so clear-cut. It is true, for example, that the missionary priests were instructed not to involve themselves in matters of politics. But it should be remembered that there was automatically a political dimension to any religious activity in late sixteenth-century England. Whether they liked it or not, the missionary priests were deeply involved in politics. After all, if religious matters were entirely separate from power politics, why was the Pope at this time strenuously seeking to secure an invasion of England?

Pius V's successor, Gregory XIII, had followed the standard pattern of papal policy towards Elizabeth. Initial hopes for her conversion were soon dashed, to be replaced by attempts to persuade a generally reluctant King of Spain to sponsor an invasion of England. William Allen himself was invited to Rome in 1576 to advise the Pope on the possibility of an invasion from the Spanish Netherlands under the governor, Don John of Austria. In 1579, another English exile, Nicholas Sander, was encouraged by the Pope to stir up trouble for Elizabeth in Ireland through a small-scale invasion. Sander's tiny force of 80 men was supplemented by the thousand or so Spanish sent by Philip II, but nothing of significance had been achieved by the time the rebellion was over in 1581. It did, however, make still more implausible – or unrealistic – the claim of the new wave of missionary priests in the 1580s that they were uninterested in political matters.

## The Jesuit missions, 1580 onwards

This second wave of Catholic missionary activity in England owed much to the impetus provided by English members of the Society of Jesus (Jesuits). It is important to know something of the background to the Jesuits in order to understand their effectiveness as missionaries. The order had been founded by the Spaniard Ignatius Loyola in 1540. Its main purpose was to undertake missionary activity. Loyola had not intended the order as an anti-Protestant weapon, having a much wider concept of its role. This is why Jesuits sought to convert non-Christians in parts of the world where Christianity had previously been unknown. However, as a force to re-awaken loyalty to the Catholic Church, to encourage recusancy, and, crucially, to attract converts from the various forms of Protestantism, the Jesuits were unrivalled. If there was one thing which made the Jesuit priest so effective, it was his use of Loyola's devotional technique known as the Spiritual Exercises. This involved meditation on the actual experiences, sensual and emotional, of Jesus himself. Under the guidance of a Jesuit, a layman would often find that such meditation led to a profound outpouring of religious feeling and emotion, which in turn led to a new commitment and a desire to lead as perfect a life as possible. Not all laymen would be able to maintain that commitment. Yet the technique of the Spiritual Exercises was a powerful tool, and earned the Jesuits much success, much support and considerable jealousy from fellow workers in the field.

The first Jesuits to arrive in England were Edmund Campion and Robert Parsons (or Persons) in 1580. Parsons set about building up an organisation based on safe houses, which the previous missionary priests had lacked. Wandering individuals without clear destinations in mind were likely to be detected quickly. After all, wandering about was not an acceptable practice in Elizabethan England. Vagrancy laws, deep-set localism and suspicion of foreigners made a stranger without a discernible purpose vulnerable in the extreme. A network of safe houses meant, of course, that the priests had to rely on the gentry class for protection. Even then, detection rates were high. Campion himself was captured in a hiding-hole in a Berkshire manor house in the summer of 1581. He was well known to the Queen and members of the government from his Church of England days at Oxford University. He was even offered a senior post in the Church of England if he would turn back to Protestantism. He

**Key dates**

Ignatius Loyola founded the Society of Jesus: 1540

First Jesuits (Campion and Parsons) arrived in England: 1580

## Profile: Robert Parsons (or Persons) 1546–1610

1562 – Studied at St Mary's Hall, Oxford
1568 – Fellow of Balliol College, Oxford
1574 – Obliged to resign fellowship due to religious views and personal quarrels
1575 – Joined the Society of Jesus in Rome
1580 – Accompanied by fellow Jesuit Edmund Campion on mission to England
1581 – Campion captured; Parsons fled abroad
1588 – Rector of English College in Rome (briefly). Subsequently founded seminaries in Spain
1596 – Involved in Archpriest Controversy on return to Rome

Parsons was an able propagandist whose willingness to contemplate and encourage a Spanish invasion of England was unlikely to appeal to the many English Catholics who wished to maintain a political loyalty to the Queen. His harsh treatment of the so-called Appellants, who journeyed from England to Rome in protest at what they saw as a pro-Jesuit appointment of an Archpriest to lead Catholicism in England, did nothing to heal divisions within the Catholic community.

refused, and was tortured in a vain attempt to extract important information on his contacts. Nor was he humiliated, as intended, in a series of public debates with Protestant theologians, despite being allowed no access to the scriptures and commentaries by way of preparation. At his trial, he denied that he was anything other than a loyal subject of the Queen. He suffered the traitor's death of hanging, drawing and quartering in December 1581.

### Parliament's responses to the missions

Once again, Members of Parliament came up with bills that demonstrated their concern about a Catholicism which would not fade away in a convenient manner. Once again, it was probably the Queen who moderated their severity. One bill would have enforced the death penalty for the first offence of saying Mass. Another bill attempted to make the taking of Communion, rather than simple church attendance, the criterion of conformity. This was clearly intended to smoke out those conformists who were really recusants at heart. But the bill which was passed to become the 1581 'Act to retain the Queen's Majesty's subjects in their due obedience' was not quite so harsh, although it was certainly not lenient. Its clauses reveal the extent to which it was a response to the perceived threat of the missionary priests. The penalty for saying Mass was fixed at a swingeing 200 marks and a year's imprisonment. Penalties for recusancy were substantially increased. Failure to attend church – taking Communion was not required – would carry a fine of £20 per month.

**Key dates**

Act 'to retain the Queen's Majesty's subjects in their due obedience': 1581

Act 'against Jesuits, seminary priests and such other like disobedient persons': 1585

However, within three years the Queen had agreed to an Act which recognised the threat posed both by the missionary priests and by the increasing tension abroad. The arrest of Francis Throckmorton in 1583 exposed plans for an invasion of England by French Catholic forces, with Spain and the Pope as the paymasters and Allen and Parsons as the instigators. The assassination of the Protestant leader William of Orange in July 1584 re-awoke the fear of a similar fate befalling Elizabeth. On top of this, the Spanish commander, Parma, appeared to be all too close to finally subjugating the Netherlands. What better base than the Netherlands ports for a Spanish invasion? What better preparation than to riddle England with allegedly traitorous priests seeking to turn Her Majesty's subjects from their allegiance? Hence the 1585 Act 'Against Jesuits, seminary priests and such other like disobedient persons'. Any Catholic priest ordained since the beginning of Elizabeth's reign was to leave the country within 40 days. Presence in England thereafter would be high treason. Anyone receiving or protecting such traitors also put themselves in danger of the death penalty. The significance of this Act is that it made things very simple for a government committed to the proposition that militant Catholicism was treason. There was no longer any need to prove that a priest had acted or spoken in a treasonable manner: merely his presence in the country was enough to damn him. According to the historian Philip Hughes, of the 146 Catholics put to death between 1585 and 1603, 123 were indicted (accused and charged) under this Act, rather than under the earlier Acts. The Throckmorton and Babington plots of 1585 and 1586 (see pages 161–2) further compromised the reputation of Catholics in general, and further justified the government's stance.

Fortunately for the recusants, the arrival in England of the Jesuits Garnet and Southwell offset some of the long-term effects of the plots. In particular, Garnet, who quickly became Superior of the English Jesuits, was able to streamline the system of dispatching incoming priests to live with staunch Catholic gentry. Their movements might be constrained, but they would at least be as safe as possible in an unsafe time.

## 6 | The Missionary Priests and the Threat of Invasion from Spain

The 1580s represented a worsening international situation for Elizabeth, as Philip II of Spain became increasingly convinced of the need to invade England. Pope Sixtus V did not like the way Philip II treated the Spanish Catholic Church as if it were his personal property, and needed some convincing that a Spanish invasion of England was a practical possibility. However, he bowed to Spanish requests for financial assistance and, again in response to Philip's demand, made William Allen a cardinal (in 1587). Allen's attitude to the intended onslaught on England is revealing. In his 1584 pamphlet *True, Sincere and Modest Defense of English Catholics … wherein is declared how unjustly the protestants do*

**Key question**
Why did English Catholics generally ignore the Allen/Parsons call to support the projected Spanish invasion?

Defeat of the Spanish Armada: 1588

Key date

*charge the English Catholics with treason*, he argued that Catholics, both priests and laymen, continued to be loyal to the Queen despite the Bull of excommunication. He did not deny that the Pope had the right to depose a monarch, but he pointed out that the Pope had not declared the Bull to be in force. The implication was that the possibility of his so doing was not only hypothetical, but also remote. However, in 1588, with the Spanish fleet (the Armada) ready, Allen prepared *An Admonition to the Nobility and People of England* which was intended to be distributed once the Armada landed in England. Of Elizabeth, he wrote:

> … an incestuous bastard, begotten and born in sin. … Fight not, for God's love, fight not, in that quarrel, in which if you die, you are sure to be damned. … Match not yourselves against the Highest: this is the day no doubt of her fall. … Forsake her therefore betime, that you be not inwrapped in her sins, punishment and damnation.

Robert Parsons joined Allen in urging English Catholics to turn against Elizabeth. The call was not heeded. Allen's *Declaration of the sentence and deposition of Elizabeth the usurper* (1588) had urged Catholics to arms to fight on the Spanish side. However, a secular priest named Wright wrote a response that typified the position of the English Catholics. Spain, argued Wright, had launched an attack for political reasons. It was therefore entirely in order for English Catholics to defend their Queen and country against such aggression.

## Catholic divisions: Appellants vs Jesuits

**Key question**
What does the Archpriest Controversy reveal about divisions in the Catholic community?

The issue of loyalty to the Queen was one which created tension within the ranks of English Catholics. The more uncompromising stance of the Jesuits in particular annoyed some laymen and secular priests who, like Wright, were keen to stress practical loyalty to the Queen. More particularly, a sense of rivalry developed between a number of secular priests and the Jesuits. The former maintained a strong attachment to the traditional hierarchical systems of the church. The Jesuits seemed to cut across such systems. And what was particularly disconcerting was that they were trespassing on the pastoral work of the secular clergy. Most of these seculars felt that the proper place for religious orders was outside the world and inside the **cloister**. This is symptomatic of the way in which the seculars emphasised the continuity between themselves and the traditional, pre-Reformation Church in England.

**Key date**

George Blackwell appointed Archpriest: 1598

**Key terms**

**Cloister**
Part of the interior of a monastery or, in this sense, the monastery itself.

**Archpriest Controversy**
A dispute over the appointment of George Blackwell as an Archpriest with authority over the mission to England.

The so-called **Archpriest Controversy** was the fruit of these attitudes. The difficulty arose when it became necessary to appoint someone to assume authority over the English mission. One obvious candidate, William Allen, had died in 1594. It was Robert Parsons whose solution was accepted in Rome. This was to appoint an archpriest, whose task would include some supervision of the secular clergy. In 1598, George Blackwell was appointed to this position. However, some priests found the whole arrangement distasteful. First, it offended the traditionalists as the office of archpriest was entirely novel. Second, it was felt that Blackwell was simply a Jesuit appointee, who would naturally favour the society in each and every action. Blackwell's formal instructions gave some support to this view. They praised the efforts of the Jesuits, and encouraged Blackwell to work closely with them, but ignored the work of the majority of the missionary priests who were, of course, seculars. There is little doubt that some priests were highly antagonistic towards what they saw as an élitist, secretive, arrogant and pro-Spanish organisation.

One group decided to appeal to Rome against the appointment, arguing that Blackwell had, in any case, been appointed merely by the Cardinal Protector of England and not by the Pope himself. Two priests, William Bishop and Robert Charnock, were sent to Rome on the behalf of these objectors. The Pope was out of Rome, and the two found themselves in the hands of Robert Parsons, who made sure they were not given the chance to see the Pope when he returned. They were subjected to what amounted to a trial and thrown out of Rome without a papal audience. This did not prevent the anti-Jesuit '**Appellants**' from continuing to appeal to Rome. A bitter pamphlet war between Jesuits and Appellants ensued. One significant contribution came from the Appellant William Watson, who argued that the Queen had been mild and gracious towards Catholics. He also argued that loyalty to the Pope did not include supporting the enemies of England. The Jesuits, he complained, conspicuously failed to display that loyalty. Arguments of this sort pleased the government: indeed, there is evidence that the Appellants were given access to printers who would normally refuse to handle Catholic material. By 1602, the Appellants had won at least part of their case in Rome. Pope Clement VIII instructed the arrogant and insensitive Blackwell not to exceed his powers, to take on three of the Appellants as assistants and to refrain from consulting with the Jesuits.

This was not enough for some Appellants. First of all, the Archpriest remained. Secondly – and worse – so did the Jesuits. Thirdly, they hankered after some form of religious toleration from the Queen which would enable a traditional, episcopal hierarchy to be re-introduced. The government was happy to exploit these differences to drive a wedge between the Appellants and the Jesuits, but it was not prepared to allow two religions to co-exist within the realm. Religious toleration was out of the question.

**Appellants**
Anti-Jesuit missionary priests who appealed to the Pope against the appointment of George Blackwell as Archpriest.

Key term

Summary diagram: The missionary priests

## 7 | Key Debate: The Strength of Catholicism

How strong was Catholicism over the period of Elizabeth's reign?

### Dickens's View

As was suggested in Chapter 1, the question of how strong Catholicism was in the reign of Elizabeth I has generated much debate among historians. A.G. Dickens's magisterial *The English Reformation*, first published in 1964, argued that the Reformation as a whole was neither the product of a rejection of traditional Catholicism at the local level nor an imposed settlement by the monarch. Instead, it was a combination of the two, and was fuelled by the ideas of increasingly numerous Protestants.

This view has clear implications for his view on the strength of Catholicism in Elizabeth's reign. Dickens had, after all, argued that traditional Catholicism was weak enough to be rejected by many in the reigns of Henry VIII and Edward VI. But he did accept that there is evidence of strong support for Catholicism in some areas by the middle of Elizabeth's reign. He therefore attributed this strength of support to the activities of the missionary priests. This is known as the 'discontinuity thesis', since he denied that there was significant continuity between the Catholicism of the pre-Reformation Church and the Catholicism of the mid-1580s.

### The Revisionists

Christopher Haigh has led the attack by so-called 'revisionist' historians on most elements of the Dickens thesis. Haigh, in *The English Reformation Revised* (1987), argued for a continuity in English Catholicism which was neither severed by the Elizabethan settlement nor in inexorable decline. His evidence came largely from regional studies (such as his own work on Tudor Lancashire). In his view, the Catholic clergy from Mary's reign (the 'Marian clergy') not only were effective in maintaining Catholicism but also forged meaningful links with the missionary priests themselves.

However, the Catholic historian John Bossy upheld the discontinuity thesis. Bossy argued that Catholicism was more or less dead until saved (at a cost) by the missionary priests. The cost was its transformation from a mass religion to a **seigneurial religion**: in other words, to a religion where priests served the needs of gentry households which increasingly withdrew from wider society. In Bossy's view, the Marian clergy had been sadly ineffective and were trapped by a nostalgia for a vanished, pre-Reformation Catholic England.

Haigh has made some interesting points about the origins of this 'discontinuity' thesis. He has argued that its first appearance was in the writings of the missionary priests themselves, who would, quite naturally, stress the contribution made by their own orders to the salvation of Catholicism. The temptation would be for these writers to play down the continuity of Catholic worship and the role of the former Marian clergy. This would make the success of the missions more remarkable, and therefore inspire greater devotion among the readers. A good example is the autobiography of John Gerard, a Jesuit who spent 18 years in England. Gerard speaks of his use of the Spiritual Exercises on a Catholic gentleman who had just inherited a fine estate from his father:

> His thoughts were very far from Christian perfection. … As he kept at a distance from the seminary priests he was not disturbed by the authorities. … The persecution at that time [1589] was directed chiefly against the seminary priests and on the whole was unconcerned with the old men ordained before Elizabeth came to the throne. It was a distinction similar to that made nowadays between secular priests and Jesuits, for today the persecution is much fiercer against us. … As I was saying, this gentleman lived peacefully with his family on his estate. … His eyes were blind to the snares of Satan. … But, in spite of this, he found himself ensnared in the toils of grace. He walked straight into the net, was trapped and showed no wish to escape. … The way, I think, to go about making converts in these parts is to bring the gentry over first, and then their servants.

Haigh does not wish to deny the importance of the missionary priests. After all, the former Marian clergy were dying out and needed to be replaced. Catholicism could not operate without priests. However, Haigh does feel justified in pointing out that the missionary priests failed to exploit the survivalist Catholicism of the remoter areas of England and Wales, such as the North and West Ridings of Yorkshire, south and west Lancashire, Herefordshire and south Wales. For reasons of proximity to their ports of entry, for the congenial company of people of their own social class, and primarily for reasons of safety, the missionary priests tended to be based in gentry households, more often than not in the south-east of England. This area was the prime stronghold of Protestantism. Since the priests were mainly concerned with securing and intensifying the devotion of existing

Catholics rather than converting heretics *en masse*, it was an area in which their services were of limited value. Meanwhile, recusancy among the common people of, say, Lancashire or Yorkshire faded due to the inadequate supply of priests. By the end of Elizabeth's reign, the pattern had been set for the future: a future in which Catholicism would become the preserve of a small minority of the upper class until well into the nineteenth century.

The dust has not settled on the discontinuity versus continuity argument (see box). But we might add that it is unwise to impose too rigid a pattern on the impact of the missionary priests. If we read accounts such as that of Gerard, we get the impression that the Catholic gentry were happy to follow the clerical lead. This is unlikely to have been the case. The missionary priests often found the Catholic gentry unresponsive to their **clericalism**, and it is ironic that the priests were obliged to rely on gentry who disliked clerical pretensions to authority. As Michael Questier has suggested, some Catholic gentry and nobility showed 'sheer hatred' for the Jesuits, and some Jesuits reciprocated. Parsons himself claimed that it was the **anticlericalism** of great men that led to the kingdom falling into heresy.

**Key terms**

**Clericalism**
Belief in the authority of the priesthood over the laity.

**Anticlericalism**
Dislike of clerical claims to authority.

| Continuity thesis | Discontinuity thesis |
|---|---|
| The argument that Catholicism remained strong until the third decade of Elizabeth's reign and that the Marian priesthood was generally effective in serving the needs of the laity (until its members started dying out and pressure for conformity grew). | The argument that Catholicism withered relatively quickly following the accession of Elizabeth, given the indifferent quality and lack of numbers of the Marian priests. It was saved by the missionary priests, but turned into a religion of the gentry household and their servants and tenants rather than a religion of parish church and people. |

## 8 | Conclusion: Elizabeth and the Catholics

The Protestant Queen Elizabeth I was bound to see Catholicism as a threat, both to what she genuinely felt to be true religion, and also to her throne. Her Protestant privy councillors felt likewise. That sense of threat was compounded by deteriorating relations with Catholic Spain, by the presence of Mary Stuart and by the Queen's childlessness. It was also compounded by the fact that, in many areas of the country, Protestantism was, at best, unwelcome at the start of the Queen's reign.

By the end of Elizabeth's reign, Catholicism in England was withering. It was increasingly the preserve of a minority of gentry. Its mass base was dwindling, even in areas remote from the seat of government and Protestant evangelising. From her point of view, the Queen's policies must be judged successful. Apart from the Revolt of the Northern Earls, she faced no major uprising in support of Catholicism. The various plots surrounding Mary Stuart were worrying, but could be used by the government to argue that Catholicism was the religious veneer given to treason.

The Queen refused to adopt policies of unmitigated harshness towards Catholicism. We have no way of knowing what the effect would have been had Elizabeth allowed her privy councillors and bishops to attempt to stamp out Catholicism with aggressive and punitive legislation from the first days of her reign. It is at least likely that opposition would have been stimulated. Martyrdom is an aid to the persecuted, not to the persecutor. Her religious settlement encouraged conformity through penalties for recusancy which were worth avoiding but by no means excessively harsh: time and usage would cut the ties binding her people to traditional Catholicism.

The threat of Spanish invasion and the activities of the missionary priests forced the Queen into accepting the severe legislation of the 1580s, but she could by this time rely on her greatest ally: the political and largely instinctive loyalty felt by most Catholic gentry towards their Protestant Queen. The Appellant/Jesuit rivalry was itself stimulated by this issue of political loyalty. The Queen had the good sense not to jeopardise it.

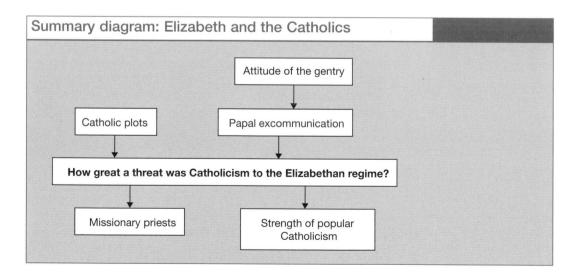

Summary diagram: Elizabeth and the Catholics

Attitude of the gentry

Catholic plots

Papal excommunication

How great a threat was Catholicism to the Elizabethan regime?

Missionary priests

Strength of popular Catholicism

## Study Guide: AS Questions

### In the style of OCR A

How serious was the threat posed by Roman Catholics to the Elizabethan church and state?  (50 marks)

---

*Exam tips*

An evaluation of the seriousness of the threat lies at the heart of this question. Avoid describing the Catholic plots, the activities of missionaries and Jesuits, and the Rebellion of the Northern Earls. Instead, these Catholic challenges should be assessed. Which episode presented the greatest threat to the Queen's life and to the church? Did any of them come close to achieving their objective? How far was the threat exaggerated by the mainly Protestant council and Parliament? Did Elizabeth and her advisers manage Mary, Queen of Scots' presence in England effectively?

It will be essential to distinguish between Roman Catholics and English Catholics: the former stayed loyal to the Pope and a minority engaged in treasonable activities. The English Catholics formed the majority and were loyal to the Queen. Although many became recusants after 1570, they never presented a threat to either the Queen's person or her church.

## In the style of OCR B

Answer **both** parts of your chosen question.

(a) Why was there no Catholic uprising until 1569?   (25 marks)

(b) Why had the Catholic threat largely disappeared
    by 1603?                                          (25 marks)

---

### Exam tips

*The page references are intended to take you straight to the material that will help you to answer the questions.*

**(a)** In this question you are asked to explain why Catholics did not take action and rise in rebellion. The failure of papal and other Roman Catholic leadership, the lack of a figurehead until the arrival of Mary, Queen of Scots in England and the light touch imposition of the Act of Uniformity all played a part. Your task is to show how these and other factors combined and to analyse the role each factor played. The factors causing the 1569 rebellion could be used to test your explanation by identifying what was different in 1569 compared with the first decade of the reign.

You might, for example, argue that initially Catholics had little reason to rebel in many parts of the country as existing priests were retained and services carried on with minimal change (pages 89–91). You might argue that this policy was only possible because of the lack of papal action against Elizabeth (page 92). Changes in papal attitude, with the promise to excommunicate Elizabeth, together with the arrival in England of Mary, Queen of Scots, who, from an hereditary point of view should be Elizabeth's heir, combined to change the situation.

You might argue that factional divisions among the nobility (pages 92–3) were less important as these had existed previously; while they contributed to the Northern Rebellion, they did not help to prevent rebellion earlier in the reign.

What you should do:

- Identify a range of reasons that explain why the Catholics did not have sufficient motive to rebel in the first decade of Elizabeth's reign.
- Organise and categorise these causes in order to ensure that you include analysis of your explanation.
- Devise a means of testing your evaluation of the causes, perhaps using a comparison between the reasons for rebellion in 1569 and those preventing an earlier rebellion.

What you should avoid:

- Describing Catholic opposition to and dissatisfaction with the religious settlement.
- Explanation of the rebellion of the Northern Earls for any purpose other than comparative evaluation.

**(b)** The implication here is that the Catholic threat had virtually disappeared by 1603 and this should be accepted or you will become distracted from answering the question. In seeking to explain why the Catholic threat had disappeared you are looking for an explanation of why a belief system had lost its appeal in general and also why those who retained their religious belief in Catholicism had ceased to present a political threat.

You might, for example, argue that the missionary priests had failed to maintain a significant number within the Catholic faith because of their tactics and location, while the Spanish threat had undermined Catholicism from a political point of view.

You might, for example, argue that the execution of Mary, Queen of Scots had removed the hope of a Catholic succession, and that this, combined with the growing familiarity with and broad interpretation of the Book of Common Prayer, had encouraged acceptance of the Church of England.

What you should do:

- Focus on reasons why Catholicism tended to die out.
- Organise reasons in groups focusing on ideas, attitudes and beliefs, the motives of those who abandoned Catholicism and the circumstances and events that made it more difficult to retain the Catholic faith.
- Remember to analyse the reasons, showing the role they play in the explanation.
- Evaluate the reasons, arguing the relative importance of factors. Remember that these may vary, for example according to which social class is being discussed.

What you should avoid:

- Describing the debate among historians about the effectiveness of missionary priests.
- Describing the imprisonment, trial and execution of Mary, Queen of Scots, or the details of all the plots against Elizabeth that involved her.

## Study Guide: A2 Question

### In the style of AQA

'The English Catholics were never able to challenge the Elizabethan religious settlement because they were too divided among themselves.' Assess the validity of this view with reference to the years 1559–1603. (45 marks)

---

### Exam tips

This question invites a balanced consideration of the reasons why the Catholics were unable to mount an effective challenge to the Elizabethan religious settlement. 'Division' will need to be explained as one of these factors and you will probably want to consider:

- the division between the 'active' Catholics who tried to challenge (e.g. the northern earls) and the 'quiet majority' who wanted a peaceful life
- the division between the gentry and the lower classes
- the geographical division; particularly after the arrival of the missionary priests who mainly operated in the south
- the division between the 'English' gentry and the foreigners.

You will need to balance the importance of these divisions against other factors, such as:

- Elizabeth's skill in handling the settlement (cautious but clear and sufficiently lenient not to create a united Catholic reaction?).
- The fear of being branded a traitor (particularly after the 1571 Treason Acts and remember to mention the position of Mary, Queen of Scots which might be regarded as a hindrance rather than a help to the Catholic cause).
- The attitude of the Pope and other Catholic nations (especially Spain).

Clearly the extent of the 'challenge' changed over time and you will need to show that you understand this, but try to avoid simply 'going through' the events of the reign in a chronological fashion. Looking at issues, as suggested above, will help you to write analytically and support a judgement.

# Meeting the Challenge of Foreign Affairs: Elizabeth, France and Spain

**POINTS TO CONSIDER**

This chapter examines the foreign policy challenges facing Elizabeth by considering the following:

- The fundamental aims and objectives of foreign policy, concentrating on France and Spain
- The assumptions which underpinned those aims and objectives
- Foreign policy in the first two years of the reign (1558–9)

France and Spain are discussed separately as we evaluate the effectiveness of Elizabethan foreign policy in comparison to those aims and objectives (and identify any changes in aims).

**Key dates**

| | |
|---|---|
| 1559 | Death of French King Henry II: accession of Francis II and Mary Stuart |
| 1560 | Treaty of Edinburgh: French troops withdrew from Scotland |
| | Death of Francis II |
| 1562 | Treaty of Hampton Court with the Huguenots |
| | Le Havre occupied by English troops |
| 1564 | Treaty of Troyes ended English armed hostilities with France |
| 1566 | Major rebellion against Spain in the Netherlands |
| 1568 | England seized Philip II's Genoese bullion |
| 1569 | Suspension of trade between Spain and England |
| 1570 | Pius V excommunicated Elizabeth I |
| 1572 | St Bartholomew's Day massacre |
| | First stage of the Elizabeth–Alençon marriage negotiations |
| | Treaty of Blois |
| 1573 | Treaty of Nymegen: trade resumed between Spain and England |
| 1576 | Sack of Antwerp |
| | Pacification of Ghent |
| 1577 | Perpetual Edict: Spanish army temporarily withdrew from the Netherlands |
| 1578 | Parma's victory at the battle of Gembloux |

1581    Elizabeth funded Anjou to intervene against Spain
            in the Netherlands
1585    Treaty of Nonsuch: Elizabeth sent troops under
            Leicester to the Netherlands
1588    Defeat of the Armada
1589    Accession of Henry IV of France
            English troops sent to Normandy
1593    Henry IV converted to Catholicism
1596    Elizabeth concluded triple alliance with Dutch and
            French against Spain
1598    Death of Philip II

## 1 | Aims and Objectives in Foreign Policy

An assessment of foreign policy must involve a discussion of its
success or failure. And success and failure can be judged only in
terms of the aims of the policy. But it is as well to recognise that
there existed no blueprint of precise aims in Elizabethan foreign
policy. England was too much of a second-rate power on the
European stage – militarily and economically – to have the luxury
of undertaking forward-planning in its affairs with its neighbours.
This suggests that the only meaningful 'aims' which can be
identified are very broad, generalised and common to many
periods of history:

- The first is that the government should prevent the country
  from being either invaded or controlled by a foreign power.
- The second is that the government should make sure that
  relations between states led to a furtherance of English
  interests. Such interests might be simply economic, or might
  less simply reflect England's international prestige. However,
  the problem is that, although most sixteenth-century monarchs
  would pay lip-service to the idea of foreign policy being
  conducted in the best interests of the country, what they really
  meant was that it should be in the best interests of themselves.

**Dukes of Burgundy**
Although the
French lands of the
Duchy of Burgundy
had been annexed
by the French crown
in the fifteenth
century, the title
and its Netherlands
lands were
inherited by the
Habsburgs.

Key term

## 2 | Assumptions on Foreign Policy

The most basic assumption at the time was that England's
'natural' enemy was France. It was felt that France would
constantly seek to exploit England's troubled relations with
Scotland. The objective of English foreign policy would therefore
be to curb the French by cultivating the traditional alliance with
the **Dukes of Burgundy**. It was particularly convenient that the
House of Burgundy should rule over the 17 Netherlands
provinces, because most of the export trade of England, which
was woollen cloth, was sold in the Netherlands' commercial centre
of Antwerp. So, a major objective of English policy was that the
Netherlands should retain their traditional independence. This
was based on the looseness of the links between the provinces and
their strong sense of separate identity, factors which would work

**Key question**
Why, and in what
way, were traditional
assumptions about
the Anglo-Burgundian
alliance subject to
challenge?

against the Netherlands being assimilated into the great monarchies of France or Spain.

However, for Elizabeth, the situation was complicated by the fact that the Burgundian ruler of the Netherlands was none other than the King of Spain. It was undeniably awkward that Philip was a devout Catholic and that Elizabeth had established a markedly Protestant regime. On the other hand, Philip had, it seemed, every desire to keep the traditional Anglo-Burgundian alliance for the same reasons as Elizabeth: it was a bulwark against French ambitions.

- But what if Philip should turn against England, using the Netherlands both as an economic weapon and as a convenient springboard for the invasion of a heretical kingdom?
- And what if the worst possible happened: a Catholic alliance between Spain and France against England, with the Netherlands the key to English defeat? After all, England was the most powerful Protestant power in Europe. It is scarcely surprising that Spain and France should increasingly see Elizabeth as the centre of an international Protestant conspiracy.
- It is even less surprising that English Protestants should similarly see growing links between Spain and France as evidence of a Catholic alliance aimed at smashing heresy once and for all throughout Europe. This theory was held most firmly by those of Puritan sympathy. There is evidence that, as the 1570s progressed, an increasing number of Elizabeth's councillors sought to discard completely the old ideas about Anglo-Burgundian alliances in favour of a very new objective: a Protestant alliance system to counter the supposed Catholic threat. The reasons for this major transformation will be discussed fully on pages 119–23 and 129–31.

**Key term**

**Royal prerogative**
Decisions which, by right, should be made by the monarch alone.

One assumption remained valid throughout the reign, and nowhere more so than in the mind of Elizabeth: the **royal prerogative** of the monarch to decide foreign policy. Councillors offered advice, and that was all. This kind of blunt statement of principle may, however, be misleading. Although councillors were frequently in disagreement, they expected the monarch to be at least responsive to their advice and show that she valued their views. After all, some advice was offered from deep personal conviction, some from the feeling that the safety of the country was at stake and some from the selfish but no less important motives of personal status and profit. It would have been politically unwise for Elizabeth to have made arbitrary decisions which took no account of the opinions of influential and wealthy men.

## Marriage and foreign policy

The issue of Elizabeth's possible marriage provides some insight into both the limitations and the reality of the influence of the councillor. Marriage, in fact, was an important weapon in the foreign policy armoury. One problem, however, with this weapon was that it could be fired only once. The usual assumption was that firing was necessary.

Elizabeth's talk about the virtues of the unmarried state was, at the start of the reign, taken by her councillors as maidenly but impractical in political terms.

The most serious candidate in 1559 was probably the Archduke Charles, younger son of the Austrian branch of the Habsburgs. A match between Elizabeth and Charles was one way of keeping Philip II both happy and a potential ally against French aggression in Scotland. It had, therefore, been recommended by those in the Council such as Arundel who opposed direct English intervention in the affairs of its northern neighbour. This proposed match came to nothing, in part because the opinion of the Council was not unanimously in favour, but mainly because Elizabeth had a favourite candidate of her own. This was the home-grown Robert Dudley (Earl of Leicester from 1564), inconveniently married and then conveniently widowed in the autumn of 1560: but not so conveniently as to scotch all sinister rumours surrounding the death of his ailing wife by a fall. His main problem, however, was that he lacked meaningful support in the Queen's Council, and that Cecil and others saw him as a catastrophic candidate: not only a dangerous rival, but also a man tarnished by the unsavoury rumours of his wife's fate. At what point the Queen reluctantly decided to forgo the marriage with Dudley is not clear. Nevertheless, Dudley retained a place in her affections that made him uniquely influential. And with the failure of his marriage plans came a commitment to an aggressive Protestantism which had vital implications for the conduct of foreign policy in the future.

## 3 | Foreign Affairs: France

### Foreign affairs with France in the first years of the reign 1558–9

In Chapter 1, it was made clear that Elizabeth inherited a realm at war with France. It was also explained that the loss of Calais, the sole English territory in France, had been humiliating for the Marian government. This loss had exposed the dangers of yoking English foreign policy to the needs of Spain.

The same chapter discussed the peace negotiations between England, France and Spain that took place at Cateau-Cambrésis: negotiations in which England's position was not strong. In particular, there was the danger that France might question the legitimacy of Elizabeth's title to the throne. Might not a rival claim be made on the behalf of the Catholic Mary Stuart, Queen of Scotland and wife of Francis, heir to the French throne (see pages 154–5)? As it happened, Henry II of France was much less interested in trying to put his daughter-in-law on the throne of England than he was in securing peace. This did not mean that the French were prepared to return Calais, but it did mean that they were prepared to let the English save face somewhat. Hence, it was agreed that Calais would be held by the French for eight

Philip II of Spain, artist unknown, c.1580. What advantages might there be to Elizabeth in marrying Philip of Spain?

years. After that period, England would either get it back, which was, in practice, highly unlikely, or receive some monetary compensation for its loss, which was only marginally more likely. The probability was that England would receive neither the town nor the compensation.

Such proved to be the case. The signing of the treaty was a relief to the English, but what appeared to be an ominous friendship developing between France and Spain following Cateau-Cambrésis was not. Might this not be the start of the anticipated Catholic conspiracy against Protestantism throughout Europe? If so, the old assumptions about France and Burgundy would be frighteningly irrelevant.

However, such fears were somewhat lessened by the apparent willingness of the King of Spain to seek and retain England's friendship in the time-honoured manner:

- Historians traditionally point out that Philip II saw himself as a candidate for the marriage it was assumed Elizabeth must soon make and that he had no desire to see the Guise dynasty of France use Mary Stuart to control, not only Scotland and France, but England as well.
- On the other hand, recent research by Parker suggests that the King's letters reveal a deep anxiety about the religious direction England appeared to be taking and even a desire to launch an invasion if only his finances would permit. They did not. In any case, Philip found himself facing a decade in which the menace of Turkey loomed larger than the heresy of Elizabeth.

## Intervention in Scotland: the Treaty of Edinburgh

Philip's attitude was fortunate for England because 1559 saw two events of great importance in the development of, and tensions within, the country's foreign policy:

- The first was the rising of the Protestant **Lords of the Congregation** against Mary of Guise, the Catholic regent in Scotland. Here was temptation indeed for England to intervene militarily in Scottish affairs. If English forces were able to contribute towards a successful Protestant rebellion, then the danger of Scotland being used as a base for French attacks on England would recede. If French troops could be prised out, then the Guises would lose one of the most important weapons in their armoury. It was, in fact, very important for England to see the power of the Guises curbed.
- This was because the second event of great significance was the death of Henry II and the succession of the young Francis II to the throne of France. The new French royal couple were soon using the English royal arms along with those of France and Scotland: a particularly clear reminder of the potential dangers posed by Mary Stuart to the security of Elizabeth herself.

**Key dates**

Death of French King Henry II: accession of Francis II and Mary Stuart: 1559

Treaty of Edinburgh: French troops withdrew from Scotland: 1560

**Lords of the Congregation**
A powerful pro-Protestant noble faction influenced by the Calvinist ideas of the Scots theologian John Knox (and by their own self-interest).

*Key term*

These two developments were grist to the mill of those who saw foreign policy as a battleground between Protestantism and Catholicism. But Elizabeth's Council was unlikely to speak with one voice on this, or any other, issue. In particular, the remaining members of Mary I's Council, such as Arundel, Winchester and Petre, were opposed to risky intervention in the affairs of other states in the interests of national and international Protestantism. The main supporter of such intervention was the Queen's Secretary, William Cecil. Cecil wanted military support for the Scots and, exploiting fear of the Guises and Elizabeth's fury over the French claims to her title, he eventually had his way. Details of what turned out to be a most gratifying success story for Elizabeth are provided on pages 155–6. In short, the use of English sea and land power brought the French forces in Scotland to the negotiating table.

By the Treaty of Edinburgh (1560), both French and English troops withdrew from Scotland. Traditional assumptions and equally traditional objectives were, it seemed, vindicated by this success. France had indeed proved to be the greatest threat, and that threat had been successfully, if temporarily, thwarted by resolute intervention in Scotland.

## Elizabeth and the rights of fellow sovereigns

It is important to look carefully at Cecil's approach to Scottish intervention, since it provides insight into a number of Elizabeth's attitudes which themselves had major implications for the conduct of foreign policy. Cecil was well aware of the need to take into account his Queen's understandable obsession with the rights of legitimate sovereigns. Support for the Scots nobles was not to be treated as an opportunity for depriving Mary Stuart of her title as Queen of Scots, however many times she chose to sit under canopies bearing the royal arms of England. Cecil was also careful to play down the fact that the Queen would be aiding those whose Protestantism was considerably more radical and Calvinist than her own. He was aware that Elizabeth was unlikely to conduct foreign policy with the interests of Protestant solidarity at or near the forefront of her mind. Her opinion was that such interests led, all too frequently, to rebellion against legitimate authority. The mantle of Protestant champion sat uneasily on her shoulders.

## Relations with France 1562–4

**Key question**
Why did English aid to the Huguenots prove to be unproductive?

If ever the Queen needed an object lesson in the dangers of religious division, and she did not, she need have looked no further than France. The conflict between the Calvinist **Huguenots** and the Catholics was intensified at the accession of Francis II in 1559. This was because the Catholic Guise faction urged the young King to persecute the Protestants. The resulting unrest, the so-called Tumult of Amboise, worked against the Guises and enabled Catherine de Medici, the mother of the ailing King and an enemy of the Guise faction, to persuade Francis to relax the heresy laws. When Francis died in December 1560, Catherine was in a sufficiently strong position to assume the role of regent to her 10-year-old son, Charles IX. By the autumn of 1561, the Duke of Guise had withdrawn from court and was rapidly building up an alliance to defend Catholic interests. Significantly, he sought and obtained financial and other help from Philip of Spain who saw in the crisis a splendid opportunity both to defend his faith and to exploit divisions within France.

**Key term**

**Huguenots**
French Protestants, followers of John Calvin (who was himself French).

A massacre of Huguenots at Vassy by the Duke of Guise presented Elizabeth with the same incentive: to exploit factional hatreds in France and to defend her faith. With a successful Scottish adventure behind them, there was less hesitation about a military intervention in France. Even the Queen, whose hesitations were becoming a factor to reckon with in any policy, was keen to contemplate such a step. What interested the Queen as much as thwarting the Guises was the chance of recovering Calais. The Huguenots might be persuaded to hand over Calais as the price for successful English assistance.

**Key dates**

Death of Francis II: 1560

Treaty of Hampton Court with the Huguenots: 1562

Le Havre occupied by English troops: 1562

Treaty of Troyes ended English armed hostilities with France: 1564

By the Treaty of Hampton Court (September 1562), Elizabeth promised loans and military aid to the Huguenots. But the English troops, under the command of her favourite Dudley's brother, the Earl of Warwick, were as much victims of the incompatible objectives of the government as they were of the successes of the Catholic forces. Having seized Le Havre as a base, the English were soon destroying Protestant solidarity by trying to exchange Le Havre for Calais. This was hardly likely to impress the Huguenots, and they combined with Catholic forces with the intention of expelling the English from French soil. Le Havre surrendered in June 1563. The Peace of Troyes in 1564 ended armed hostilities with France.

This intervention in France usefully reveals the lack of definite and agreed objectives in English foreign policy at this stage. As for Elizabeth, the episode had strengthened her dislike of assisting rebels against a legitimate monarch and had done nothing to encourage her fellow-feeling for continental Protestantism. Dudley and others continued to press for support for their co-religionists, but, as the years went by, Elizabeth's inability to come to firm decisions blended with her distaste for rebellion. Those who wished for a precise and Protestant foreign policy were baulked by the Queen.

## Relations with France 1564–83

There are two main elements in Elizabeth's policy towards France from 1564. These elements are linked:

- The first stemmed from the deterioration of relations with Spain as the decade drew to an end. This meant that the traditional anti-French assumptions might have to be amended in the interests of securing potential allies against Philip II.
- The second element was the threat from the Guises, whose aggressive Catholicism might lead them into the very alliance with Spain that Cecil so gloomily contemplated.

This does not mean that Elizabeth and her councillors came up with some master-plan to counter a future threat: instead, English foreign policy is best seen as a set of responses to various crises.

The diplomatic crisis and suspension of trade between Spain and England (see page 127) in 1569 prompted Elizabeth to enter into a round of marriage negotiations with Henry, Duke of Anjou, who was the second son of Catherine de Medici, between 1570 and 1571. It was, of course, convenient that Catherine was the bitter enemy of the Guise faction. Elizabeth had no intention of marrying Anjou, but the discussions were nearly as good as a treaty of friendship.

In fact, as Anjou faded from the scene, Catherine's youngest son, Francis, Duke of Alençon, was wheeled on stage to take his place: but it was the Treaty of Blois of 1572 which was the significant result of this friendliness. By the terms of this treaty, France in effect abandoned the claims of Mary Stuart to the throne of England. The two countries established a defensive league which was intended to prevent the possibility of Spanish aggression against either.

**Key dates**

Suspension of trade between Spain and England: 1569

Treaty of Blois: 1572

First stage of the Elizabeth–Alençon marriage negotiations: 1572

**Key question**
What impact did the massacre of St Bartholomew's Day have on English foreign policy?

Key date

St Bartholomew's Day massacre: 1572

## The massacre of St Bartholomew's Day

On 24 August 1572 came an event which put this fragile alliance with France to the most demanding of tests: the massacre of St Bartholomew's Day. The massacre had followed from a bungled attempt by Catherine to remove (that is, murder) the Protestant leader Coligny, who was, in her view, becoming dangerously close to her son Charles IX and thus about to embroil the French in a disastrous religious war with Spain. Coligny was killed, and a Paris mob then murdered at least 3000 Huguenots in the city. Protestant England was understandably horrified. Might not Elizabeth herself be the next victim? What would be the fate of English Protestants if Mary Stuart were to succeed to the throne? Small wonder that the militant Protestants of the Queen's Council exerted every effort to persuade her to send an army to the defence of the Huguenots, her religion and her throne. Elizabeth, however, was largely unimpressed by the clamour. Protestant the Huguenots might be, but they were, in her eyes, also rebels against a legitimate monarch. In any case, had she not witnessed the disasters of her previous campaigns on their behalf? Was it sensible to throw away the tentative and newly established friendship with Catherine de Medici for the sake of such a cause?

What the English government actually did was to negotiate with both sides. Unofficially, help was offered to the Huguenots, and yet talks were renewed with Catherine de Medici on the Alençon marriage. It is unfair to label the English response as confused. In all probability, it was Elizabeth who prevented the country from launching into a gravely hazardous military adventure. It would have been hazardous because England lacked the resources to

A contemporary painting of the St Bartholomew's Day massacre by the Huguenot artist François Dubois, who was reputedly an eyewitness. How might the circulation of engravings of such scenes affect the English government's relations with France?

maintain a campaign against the French crown, and because further interference in France in the defence of Protestantism would cement the links between Spain and the Guises. It might even result in the conflict being turned into a Europe-wide religious war. The English response might not have been heroic, but it made sense.

## The Anjou marriage negotiations

There were other reasons for not losing sight of the Alençon marriage (which should be referred to as the Anjou marriage – the suitor was the same, but his title had changed when his elder brother inherited the French throne in 1574):

**Key question**
What was the relationship between the Anjou match and foreign policy?

- First, that most abiding concern of the English, the fate of the Netherlands, was once more in the balance. The Spanish commander, the Duke of Parma, had been particularly successful against the rebel forces in 1578 (see page 129).
- Second, it looked as if Anjou intended to play a significant part in the Netherlands struggle. Catholic though he was, Anjou was fiercely anti-Spanish. To the increasingly desperate rebels of the Netherlands, Anjou looked a better source of help than the hesitant and often unsympathetic Queen of England. But, for Elizabeth, the danger was that Anjou would simply replace Spanish authority over the Netherlands, which was at least hedged about by frequent Spanish inefficiency and permanent Spanish communications problems, with French authority.

One way to neutralise Anjou would be to outbid him by offering firm commitment in the shape of money and troops to the rebellious provinces. This policy was, of course, much favoured by the more zealous Protestants of Elizabeth's Council.

But the Queen's habitual dislike of rebels was unchanged: she preferred to play the marriage card yet again. The difference this time was that Elizabeth was genuinely prepared to marry Anjou. This was partly for emotional reasons. At the age of 46, Elizabeth's days of playing the enjoyable and ego-boosting game of courtship were fast drawing to an end. Faced with the prospect of marriage into one of the greatest royal families, she discovered that she wanted marriage, and badly. There were also cogent political reasons for marrying Anjou. As his wife, Elizabeth could hope to control his behaviour in the Netherlands, while at the same time using him as a threat to persuade the Spanish to negotiate a settlement with the Netherlands provinces along the lines of the Pacification of Ghent (see page 128). This would, at the very least, free the provinces of Spanish troops.

## Opposition to the Anjou marriage

Elizabeth faced both political and emotional opposition, not only from members of the Council but also, it would seem, from public opinion. This determined opposition was based in part on the fear that England would thereby be controlled by France in the French interest, and in part on anti-Catholic feeling. It is hard to

**Key date**
Elizabeth funded Anjou to intervene against Spain in the Netherlands: 1581

escape the conclusion that Elizabeth became a victim of her own propaganda. How could the Virgin Queen, 'nursing mother' and Supreme Governor of the English church, so tarnish herself? Elizabeth gave way: there was no marriage and, in August 1581, she settled for providing Anjou with funds for intervention in the Netherlands. To use a Catholic in the defence of the provinces demonstrates very clearly that the Queen's aims and objectives were entirely traditional, even if her means were not. Rather than seek to defend and spread Protestantism, which would have been an entirely new aim for English foreign policy, she sought to maintain the Netherlands' semi-independence in the interests of England's security alone. Unfortunately for her, Anjou's expedition was a disaster. By 1583, he was back in France and, the next year, dead.

The Anjou episode provides a number of helpful insights into the nature of Elizabethan foreign policy. It serves as a reminder of the centrality of the Netherlands to English concerns. It demonstrates the potential role of marriage in foreign affairs. It also demonstrates the fact that Elizabeth was willing and able to reject the advice of those who demanded a military intervention in the Netherlands for religious reasons. But this does not mean that Elizabeth was able to ignore concerted and virtually unanimous demands, which, in theory, infringed her prerogative over foreign affairs. For the second time, she allowed herself to be persuaded out of a marriage.

## Relations with France 1584–1603

**Key question**
Why had English support been offered to Henry IV?

The death of Anjou was important for Elizabeth's wider interests. Anjou's brother Henry III was childless, and there was a real prospect of the Huguenot, Henry of Navarre, succeeding to the throne of France. But this, the Guise faction could not stomach. From Elizabeth's point of view danger lay in the alliance between the French **Catholic League**, dominated by the Guises, and Philip II. If the League and Philip succeeded in crushing Navarre and the Huguenots once and for all, the Guise might make the channel ports of France available to Spain for an invasion of England. By September 1589, Philip had decided to give the League support in the form of Spanish troops. The Duke of Parma was ordered to move Spanish forces in the Netherlands to the French frontier.

**Key term**

**Catholic League**
Founded in 1576 by Duke Henry of Guise with the aim of destroying Protestantism in France and preventing the Protestant Henry of Navarre from succeeding to the French throne.

### Henry IV of France

Both the Duke of Guise and Henry III had been assassinated by mid-1589, but, even though Henry of Navarre was crowned as Henry IV, the situation was still perilous from the English perspective. The alliance between the League and Philip II was simply strengthened by this setback, and Elizabeth was faced with urgent demands for assistance from Henry IV. She had little choice but to commit herself to sending both money and troops in the autumn of 1589. But by 1590, Spanish troops were in Brittany. If Spain overran neighbouring Normandy, then Spanish-

**Key dates**

Accession of Henry IV of France: 1589

English troops sent to Normandy: 1589

controlled Brittany could link up with the Spanish army in Flanders. This is why Elizabeth constantly complained of Henry IV's lack of interest in dealing with the problem of Normandy.

Henry himself was under no illusions: Elizabeth was, as always, protecting English interests and not those of international Protestantism. Nor did Elizabeth call off her support when Henry IV converted to Catholicism in 1593. In fact, Henry's conversion was politically helpful from the English point of view. Conversion gave Henry the opportunity to unite France. His decision not only pleased the Catholic majority, but also made the Catholic League irrelevant. He also offered **toleration** to Huguenots. France might therefore become once again an effective counterbalance to Spain. English troops were withdrawn from France by 1595, leaving Henry to unite the country by the traditional method of focusing attention on a common and foreign enemy. Only when Henry's national war with Spain started to go badly were English troops sent back (in 1596). As part of her attempt to shore up Henry IV, Elizabeth concluded a triple alliance with the Dutch and France in 1596 and, as part of the alliance, was obliged to recognise the United Provinces as a sovereign state. It was typical of Elizabeth's obsession with the rights of legitimate rulers that she should have been so reluctant for so long to give official sanction to the rights of rebels.

In 1598, Henry IV made a separate peace with Spain, which simply accepted the territorial position laid out at Cateau-Cambrésis so many years and so many lives before. The need for English troops in France was at an end.

## Relations with France: a conclusion

The most important change in foreign policy was to the old assumption that France was the 'natural' enemy. Spain became identified as the greater threat to English interests, in the shape of the Netherlands, and to the security and safety of England itself. The attempt to curb Spanish dominance over the Netherlands might have been a new objective, but the old fear of French control of the self-same provinces was difficult to shake off.

Indeed, the formation of new objectives in English foreign policy was not easy because the aims and objectives of Elizabeth and her councillors were not always identical. There were those who wished to make Elizabeth the saviour of international Protestantism. This new aim, Elizabeth successfully resisted; partly due to her realistic appraisal of English weakness, and partly due to her inability or unwillingness to depart from the assumption she never shed: that the encouragement of rebellion was the unacceptable face of foreign policy. Given the Queen's indecisiveness, it is hardly surprising that she was unable to commit herself to radically new aims and objectives except when those were imposed on her by circumstance.

The broad aims of the government were achieved in the sense that the country had not been invaded or grossly manipulated by France. The objective of preventing the Guise faction from using

**Key dates**

Henry IV converted to Catholicism: 1593

Elizabeth concluded triple alliance with Dutch and French against Spain: 1596

**Key term**

**Toleration**
In the context of religion, the willingness of the state to grant the right to worship freely.

**Key question**
To what extent had English policy towards France changed over the period 1558–98?

the French monarchy, the French Catholic League and/or alliance with Spain to subvert Elizabeth was indeed achieved. English policy was not responsible for this. English military intervention was less than successful, and the eventual neutralising of the Guises owed more to French internal and external politics and the assassin's knife than it did to English interference.

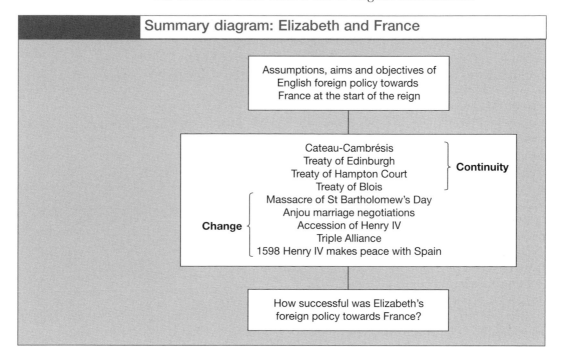

**Summary diagram: Elizabeth and France**

Assumptions, aims and objectives of English foreign policy towards France at the start of the reign

Cateau-Cambrésis
Treaty of Edinburgh
Treaty of Hampton Court
Treaty of Blois
} **Continuity**

**Change** {
Massacre of St Bartholomew's Day
Anjou marriage negotiations
Accession of Henry IV
Triple Alliance
1598 Henry IV makes peace with Spain

How successful was Elizabeth's foreign policy towards France?

# 4 | Foreign Affairs: Spain

## Relations with Spain 1560–74

**Key question**
What factors increased tension between England and Spain up to 1573?

Relations between England and Spain in the early 1560s were less than cordial. Given the religious differences this is hardly surprising. But joint suspicion of the Guises was sufficient to keep the two powers reasonably friendly. This explains why Philip II was keen at this time to dissuade the Pope from excommunicating Elizabeth as a heretic. Better a Protestant Tudor Queen of England than a Catholic Stuart Queen when the latter was a tool of the Guises.

### The importance of the Spanish Netherlands

The Netherlands, which was part of Philip II's Burgundian inheritance, was a potential flashpoint in relations between Spain and England. Important for the English wool trade, the Netherlands had ports which were potential springboards for invasion of England. In 1566 Philip II faced a major rebellion in the Netherlands. Significantly, the immediate cause was resentment at the Spanish King's attempt to run the Netherlands as a colony of Spain. Spanish officials, it seems, were undermining the traditional importance of the great nobles at the Council of State, which was the policy-making body in the

**Key date**
Major rebellion against Spain in the Netherlands: 1566

provinces. If this attempted centralisation seemed sinister to the nobility and the town authorities, it also seemed sinister to England, especially when Philip sent a Spanish army under the Duke of Alva to suppress the rebellion (1567). Spanish troops, Netherlands' ports, and a military commander with an impressive reputation and a remit to destroy heresy: here was a prospect to worry the calmest of Elizabeth's councillors.

Elizabeth did not follow a consistent policy towards the Netherlands in the following decades of turmoil. There are certainly many instances where England's policy seemed to be nothing more than a reaction to circumstance. However, one must take account of the basic assumptions that underpinned Elizabeth's responses. It was important that Spanish authority was not backed by an army of occupation, which would effectively destroy the traditional semi-independence of the Netherlands. Nevertheless, the English had to recognise the fact that, although they might seek to influence events in the Netherlands, they were in no position to direct them. This, Elizabeth was realistic enough to acknowledge. Not all her councillors were so clear-headed.

By 1568, the rebels in the provinces had suffered major setbacks. Two of their leaders, Horn and Egmont, had been executed. Others, including the powerful William of Orange, had been defeated in battle by Alva. Elizabeth was not prepared to commit English forces to the rebel cause, partly due to her sustained distaste for rebellion, and partly because England lacked the military muscle to face a commander such as Alva in open battle. Elizabeth had learned from the disasters of 1563–4 in France (see pages 119–20) that sending a small expeditionary force in theory to help a just rebellion, but in practice to further her own interests, was unlikely to end in success. So, a policy of harassment seemed wise. It was potentially damaging to Spain, it might be possible to dissociate the English government from it if necessary, and it might even yield a profit.

Certainly there were members of Elizabeth's Council who saw a splendid opportunity to strike a blow at Spanish finances when, in November 1568, storm-battered Spanish ships were chased by privateers and sought shelter in the ports of Devon and Cornwall. These ships had 400,000 florins (gold coins) on board as payment for Alva's army. This episode ended with the Queen deciding to take advantage of the money herself. It was, in fact, the property of Genoese financiers. So why should Elizabeth not take over the loan instead of the Spanish King?

That Elizabeth prevented the money going to Alva is indisputable, but her precise motives are less clear. Some historians have argued that the seizure was dangerous, pointless and piratical; others, that it made sense to create whatever difficulties she could for Alva. The episode should be seen as a piece of opportunism that was risky, but justified. Evidence suggests that Cecil identified the advantage to England and to the Protestant cause in general in seizing the treasure, but that the Queen's decision was made only after she had initially agreed to speed the ships on their way to Alva. She was not, therefore,

**Key date**

England seized Philip II's Genoese bullion: 1568

gleefully and instantaneously seizing the first opportunity she could to stir up trouble for Spain. She did not want major conflict with Philip II, and the episode should not be taken as evidence for any such intention. She no doubt wished to make things as difficult for Alva as possible, but seizures of shipping were not uncommon, and the Queen did not expect major repercussions from her action.

Elizabeth had not, however, anticipated the over-reaction of De Spes, Philip's excitable new ambassador. De Spes urged Alva in the strongest terms to seize English ships and property in the Netherlands, even before Elizabeth's decision to take over the loan had been announced. Alva did so with misgivings, and of course the English retaliated by seizing Spanish property in England.

**Key dates**

Pius V excommunicated Elizabeth I: 1570

Treaty of Nymegen: trade resumed between Spain and England: 1573

The excommunication of Elizabeth by Pope Pius V in 1570 is discussed fully in Chapter 4 (see pages 95–7). It is enough to note here that Philip was not consulted by Pius and doubted both the timing of the excommunication and its political wisdom. Nonetheless, he was increasingly ready to encourage plots against Elizabeth, instructing Alva to prepare to send 10,000 troops to England at the time of the Ridolfi plot of 1571 (see page 160). In her turn, Elizabeth encouraged English privateers to co-operate with Netherlands privateers, the so-called 'Sea Beggars', in raiding Spanish shipping. This was also the period in which England and France explored possible marriage alliances and concluded the Treaty of Blois (see page 120). But it must not be assumed that England and Spain were now looking for war.

By 1573, representatives of Alva and Elizabeth had concluded a treaty (the Convention of Nymegen) for the resumption of trade between Spain and England. The English government also withdrew support from raids on Spanish shipping in the Indies. The explanation for this new accord is simple enough. Spain had been militarily more than successful in the Netherlands, France was submerged in turmoil following the St Bartholomew's Day massacre and there was little to be gained by supporting the remaining rebels in the provinces. Once again, Elizabeth adapted her foreign policy to circumstances. And circumstances dictated that apparent neutrality was the best policy to follow. It at least avoided open confrontation with Spain. This is why the Queen was prepared to resist pressure from Walsingham and Leicester who wanted to help the increasingly desperate William of Orange.

## England's relations with Spain 1575–8
### The Netherlands

**Key question**
What evidence is there that, by 1585, English policy towards the Netherlands was in disarray?

By 1575, a subtle change in English foreign policy may be identified. Instead of remaining strictly neutral and detached, Elizabeth began to offer herself as a mediator between William of Orange and the Spanish. This desire to mediate was, of course, purely selfish. Elizabeth suggested a compromise: that the restoration of the 'liberties' of the provinces would be granted in return for the rebels' acceptance of continuing Habsburg rule. This would both make England feel more secure and pamper to

Elizabeth's dislike of rebellion in any form. This new approach was the response to a change in the political and military situation, since it seemed for a time that a new Spanish offensive would either smash the rebels or force them to seek military assistance from the French. Either of these possibilities was deeply worrying from the English point of view.

In fact, the situation changed again in 1576 when the unpaid Spanish army mutinied, sacked the city of Antwerp and brought out the whole of the Netherlands in revolt against Spain. The Estates-General of the Netherlands duly met and called for the removal of Spanish troops and the restoration of the provinces' 'liberties'. The terms of this demand, known as the Pacification of Ghent, were exactly what Elizabeth would have wished. It is a sign of her approval that she immediately offered the Estates a loan of £100,000 if Spain refused to accept the terms.

Spain, in fact, was in no position to refuse. The new Governor-General of the Netherlands, Don John, accepted the terms when he signed the **Perpetual Edict** early in 1577, and the Spanish army withdrew from the provinces. But the edict was unlikely to live up to its name. Spanish weakness was temporary, but suspicion among the Estates, divided by religion as well as by faction, was more or less permanent.

By mid-1577, Spanish armies were back in the Netherlands, and there was a disturbing new element in the conflict. This was the danger of French intervention under the Duke of Anjou (see pages 122–3). Elizabeth's anxiety is well revealed in her offer, not only of an immediate loan to the Estates of £100,000, but also of English troops if the French did become involved. An envoy was sent to Philip to try to persuade him to keep to the terms of the Pacification, but, given the divisions within the Estates and their defeat by Spanish forces at the battle of Gembloux in 1578, such persuasion was unlikely to be effective: and so it proved. Even so, Elizabeth did not send an army to the Netherlands. Hesitation, fear of the consequences of a war with Spain, contradictory advice from her councillors: all these took their toll. It was safer to pay for the services of a **mercenary**, John Casimir of the Palatinate, than to commit England to a conflict of uncertain outcome. In the event, Casimir was worse than useless. His troops were mainly German Protestants who passed their time in attacking and desecrating Dutch Catholic churches. This simply fanned the flames of Calvinist and Catholic distrust among the Estates.

By the end of 1578 Elizabeth's foreign policy was in disarray. The objective had been the traditional one: preventing a major continental power from gaining such complete control of the Netherlands that the country might be used as a base for an invasion of England. But nothing Elizabeth had done had contributed towards a successful resolution of the problem in line with English interests. Instead, she had managed to alienate Spain without earning the trust of the Netherlands. The unhappy prospect of a complete Spanish victory loomed. Spanish power was on the increase. In 1580, Philip II had invaded Portugal:

**Key dates**

Sack of Antwerp: 1576

Pacification of Ghent: 1576

Perpetual Edict: Spanish army temporarily withdrew from the Netherlands: 1577

Parma's victory at the battle of Gembloux: 1578

**Key terms**

**Perpetual Edict**
A declaration, signed by Don John as Governor-General of the Netherlands, that Spanish troops would permanently withdraw from the Netherlands. It was not honoured.

**Mercenary**
A professional soldier who fought for whoever paid him.

within a year, he was King of Portugal and the commander of another splendid fleet. Meanwhile, the new Governor-General, the Duke of Parma, was proving as adept at exploiting the division among the Estates as he was at defeating them in battle. Holland, one of the richest of the provinces, was holding out, but for how long?

If Philip had the means to launch an invasion of England, it seemed as if he also had the will. In 1579 and 1580, he gave some aid to unsuccessful expeditions to Ireland, which went with papal blessing (see page 149). Since there was little to be gained by further protestations of neutrality or offers to mediate over the Netherlands, Elizabeth felt obliged to support a French intervention at the hands of Anjou (see page 123): the lesser of two evils, perhaps. Walsingham reported that the Queen was even prepared to accept the prospect of the replacement of Spanish authority over the Netherlands by that France. However, the French rejected offers of sovereignty put forward by the Dutch. At last it seemed as if England was going to have to shoulder the burden and uncertainty of full-scale help for the provinces. Yet Elizabeth hesitated still. There were letters prepared that would have sent expeditionary forces to relieve Antwerp, a city in desperate plight, but such was Elizabeth's indecision that she could not bring herself to sign them. It was Philip's action in seizing English shipping in Spanish ports that finally brought Elizabeth to conclude a treaty with the Dutch. Philip may not have intended the ships to be part of an invasion fleet, but it looked like that to the English. Under the provisions of the Treaty of Nonsuch (1585), Elizabeth would send to the Netherlands 5000 troops and 1000 cavalry under an English commander. She was given control of the Netherlands towns of Brill and Flushing as security for the expenditure, but rejected the offer of sovereignty over the provinces. In her view, of course, sovereignty was God-given: subjects had no right to offer it. In addition to the terms of Nonsuch, a fleet under Sir Francis Drake was sent to raid the Spanish shipping of the Caribbean and to release the English ships held by Philip. But it would be a mistake to assume that Elizabeth was now heartily committed to a war with Spain. Even at this stage, she was in contact with Parma in the hope of some compromise.

**Key date** | Treaty of Nonsuch: Elizabeth sent troops under Leicester to the Netherlands: 1585

### The expedition to the Netherlands

The chronic indecisiveness of the Queen was such that neither Drake nor Leicester, commander of the force destined for the Netherlands, could be certain that their orders might not be revoked at the last moment. Leicester's task would, in any case, have daunted an experienced military administrator and soldier: Leicester was neither. His correspondence with Burghley and Walsingham reveals a man uncertain of his role, constantly short of money and unable to answer the increasing Dutch suspicion of the Queen's intentions. He was well aware of his own limitations as a military commander, and spent much time trying to persuade the Queen to allow the veteran soldier Sir William

Pelham to join him. But Pelham owed the Queen money, and she was reluctant to let him go until he had paid up. Poor Leicester was also faced with the furious anger of the Queen when he accepted the title of Governor-General. His letters show as much anxiety over the Queen's attitude towards him as they do over the increasingly disastrous military situation. Leicester found himself trying to cope with numbers of towns which were simply defecting to Parma, attracted by the latter's skilful bribery: his 'golden bullets', as contemporaries termed them. In July 1586, Leicester wrote the following letter to the Privy Council:

> If your lordships will know the cause of so sudden defection of these towns, I must pray you to consider withall … I find it is not corruption from the prince [of Parma], for he hath little to give; not desire of the Spanish government, for even the papists abhor it; not mislike of being under her majesty, or her officers … but, indeed, the cause cannot be imagined to be any other than a deep impression in the wiser sort, that her majesty careth not heartily for them. … For my own part, what a man without money, countenance, or any other sufficient means, in case so broken and tottering every way, may do, I promise to endeavour to do, to the best of my power.

Leicester was keen to blame everyone but himself. But his own lack of judgement, as much as the Queen's frequent bursts of meanness, contributed to the breakdown of goodwill between the Dutch and the English. A good example is his disastrous appointment of Sir William Stanley to command the newly captured town of Deventer in 1587. But Stanley was a Catholic, and had fought for the Duke of Alva as a mercenary. The Dutch protested to no avail, and Stanley repaid Leicester's trust by handing the town over to the Spanish.

## The Netherlands: a summary
A review of the situation in late 1587 reveals unrelieved failure:

**Key question**
To what extent was Elizabeth personally to blame for the threat of Spanish invasion by 1587?

- Leicester had returned for the second and last time to England.
- The Queen had spent considerable sums of money, but had never showed any awareness of the need to spend more when the occasion demanded it.
- Elizabeth had chosen the wrong person to represent her in the Netherlands, and had failed to support him properly when he got there.
- The Queen's on-off negotiations with Parma had yielded no results, and the Spanish were making military preparations for the invasion of England. It may even be that the English involvement in the Netherlands played a substantial part in the Spanish decision to invade England: the invasion, in short, was to be part of the Netherlands campaign. Philip's instructions to his military commanders reveal that he had no intention of annexing England to the Spanish empire. His terms for peace

after victory were to be an English withdrawal from the Netherlands and toleration for English Catholics.

Thanks, therefore, in large measure to the Queen's actions, the country faced the prospect of an invasion. Was it not the most fundamental aim of foreign policy to avoid just such an occurrence? Of course, to assess the scale of the Queen's miscalculations requires an appreciation of the likelihood of a successful Spanish invasion.

## 1588: The Armada and after

**Key question**
Why did the Armada fail?

**Key date**

Defeat of the Armada: 1588

It is ironic that what saved the Netherlands from Parma was, in part at least, a diverting of attention towards the projected invasion of England, together with increasing Spanish involvement in the troubled affairs of France (see pages 123–4). Parma was ordered to hold back on any further Netherlands campaigns in readiness to link up with the Armada, the huge Spanish fleet that was to protect the Duke's crossing from Flanders to Kent. Parma's men were to cross in flat-bottomed boats. There were roughly 17,000 troops in the Flanders invasion force, to be supplemented by about 6000 from the Armada once a footing had been won on English soil.

The Armada did not, of course, succeed. But to what extent was this the fault of the plan itself? Its success depended on the Armada clearing all Dutch and English naval opposition, on excellent communications between Parma and the Armada's commander, Medina Sidonia, on preparedness on the part of both dukes, on good weather and on precise timing (high tide was needed to embark the troops). The absence of any one of these factors could lead to failure. The invasion of England was, therefore, always a massive gamble, with disaster being more likely than success.

The so-called Armada Portrait, c.1588, by the English painter George Gower. What messages about Elizabeth are conveyed by this portrait?

By July 1588, the Armada had entered the English Channel. It faced a formidable opponent in the English fleet. Thanks in large part to the reforms of John Hawkins, treasurer to the navy, the fleet was manoeuvrable and well armed. This had been proved by the success of Francis Drake's Cadiz mission in 1587 which had damaged many Spanish ships in harbour and delayed the Armada for a year. In particular, the English had 153 long-range guns against the Armada's 21. This advantage would not allow the English to blow the Armada out of the water, but it did prevent the Spanish from using their favourite tactic of boarding the opponent's ships. The Armada found it impossible to clear the English from the Channel. Indeed, the English fleet, under Admiral Howard and Francis Drake, was largely undamaged when the Armada anchored off Calais on 27 July.

Under these circumstances, Parma was unwilling to attempt a crossing. The problem was not simply the continued presence of the English. The Dutch were similarly undefeated at sea, and would relish the chance to attack the Duke's slow-moving barges. Medina Sidonia hoped that Parma would take advantage of what uncertain protection the Armada could offer and risk the crossing. But he was unsure of Parma's exact whereabouts and state of readiness, and Parma was in no hurry to enlighten him. In the midst of this uncertainty, the English sent fire-ships against the anchored Armada. Medina Sidonia, operating on the reasonable assumption that these were the familiar floating bombs, ordered the Armada to set sail immediately. Some ships cut their anchors, an action that proved disastrous when the Armada had to face bad weather in the weeks to come.

On 29 July, the Battle of Gravelines took place off the coast of Flanders. The Spanish tried to get close enough to the English fleet to board, and the English peppered the Armada from as far away as possible. The English tactics proved most effective. Only three Spanish ships were disabled, but Medina Sidonia had no choice but to pull his fleet out of the fight. The prevailing wind sent the Armada around the north of Scotland and the west of Ireland. Gales, coupled with the loss of so many anchors, sank half the battered fleet. The contemporary English view – 'the Lord blew and they were scattered' – is at least accurate in giving the weather the credit for the destruction of so much of the invasion fleet. Had the Spanish possessed a deep-water port in the Netherlands where they could have sought shelter and the chance to re-fit, then the superiority of English gunnery would have counted for little.

It is also necessary to consider how Parma would have coped with English troops fighting on their own soil had the Armada successfully carried out its task. Against the 23,000 Habsburg forces would have been the south coast militia of roughly 27,000 infantry and 2500 cavalry, together with the army of 16,500 under the command of Leicester at Tilbury. There would also have been a total of 16,000 troops as a bodyguard for Elizabeth herself. This does not take into account other militia in the north.

However, this superiority in numbers may be misleading. Elizabeth lacked the resources to put a professional, Habsburg-style army into the field. It is true that there had been attempts in the 1570s to improve the organisation of military training in England, but these steps had affected no more than one-tenth of the militia. Money for training and mustering forces mainly came from gentlemen whose patriotism was tempered by the desire to avoid paying tax. Burghley, for example, had an income of several thousand pounds, but he made sure that his income was assessed at a mere £133 6s. The militia was, therefore, underfunded and ill-prepared to face an experienced army led by one of the acknowledged masters of the art of warfare. It is as well, therefore, that the English were not put to the test. On the other hand, Parma was by no means confident. In March 1588, he had written to Philip:

> Even if the Armada supplies us with the 6000 Spaniards as agreed – and they are the sinews of the undertaking – I shall still have too few troops. … If I set foot on shore, it will be necessary for us to fight battle after battle. I shall, of course, lose men by wounds and sickness. I must leave the port and town garrisons strongly defended, to keep open my lines of communication: and in a very short time my force will thus be so much reduced as to be quite inadequate to cope with the great multitude of enemies.

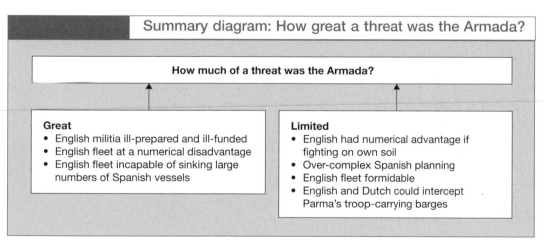

**Summary diagram: How great a threat was the Armada?**

**How much of a threat was the Armada?**

**Great**
- English militia ill-prepared and ill-funded
- English fleet at a numerical disadvantage
- English fleet incapable of sinking large numbers of Spanish vessels

**Limited**
- English had numerical advantage if fighting on own soil
- Over-complex Spanish planning
- English fleet formidable
- English and Dutch could intercept Parma's troop-carrying barges

## The strength of English sea power

The failure of the Armada should not lead to an overestimate of the naval strength of England. Elizabeth's use of the navy as a weapon of war was limited by the fact that she could not afford to maintain a professional force. The problem was that most expeditions were, at least in part, privately financed. This meant that commanders were interested primarily in plunder and tended to disregard orders when these conflicted with the possibility of obtaining rich pickings elsewhere. For example, in 1589 Drake and Norris were in charge of a considerable invasion force aimed at provoking a revolt against Philip II as King of

Portugal. When the Portuguese in Lisbon failed to rebel, the planned attack on the Armada was conveniently forgotten: the fact that the venture was partly funded by merchants was not. The English fleet set sail for the Azores and the joys of plunder. However, unfavourable winds prevented the fleet from reaching its destination. On return to Plymouth, the casualty list was over 11,000. This was a heavy price to pay for a complete failure.

Similarly, when Hawkins devised a plan to stop the flow of Spanish treasure from its overseas colonies back to mainland Spain, this so-called 'silver blockade' had to rely on the uncoordinated attacks of privateers rather than on concerted action by an English fleet. This piracy might be occasionally profitable, and some of the money found its way into Elizabeth's treasury, but it was too haphazard to be fully effective.

In addition, these raids did not prevent the building of two more Armadas in the 1590s. In 1597, the English fleet was so ill-prepared that the Spanish, *en route* to Ireland, had a clear run through the Channel. Storms came to the rescue of England on both occasions.

## 5 | Conclusion: Elizabeth, France and Spain

By the time of Philip II's death in 1598, Spain had been badly mauled in the Netherlands conflict. The Dutch had exploited the mutinous condition of unpaid Spanish troops and had brought off impressive victories which safeguarded the northern provinces (now known as the United Provinces) against the increasingly bankrupt Spanish. As for the French, Henry IV had concluded the triple alliance with the United Provinces and England in 1596 (see page 124). By 1598, France and Spain were at peace, but in a state of mutual hatred that was music to English ears. The conflict between England and Spain continued until 1604, when James I, Elizabeth's successor, brought it to an end.

Elizabeth would seem to have achieved most of her foreign policy aims and objectives. She had avoided an invasion by a foreign power, be it Habsburg Spain or France of the Guises. England had not been yoked to another country in such a way as to lose its independence of action. Unlike Spain, the crown did not, despite its debts, go bankrupt. But economic depression caused by the cessation of Anglo-Spanish trade combined with war taxation to create real resentment in England: resentment which is revealed in the increasingly quarrelsome and disenchanted attitude of Parliament over the issue of monopolies in the final years of Elizabeth's reign (see page 178). On the other hand, it is true that the war with Spain offered men of capital the opportunity of great reward through privateering. Profits and expertise acquired through raids on Spanish colonies and shipping laid the foundations for such enterprises as the East India Company (1600) and others founded in the reign of James I, such as the Virginia Company (1606) and the Newfoundland Company (1610). In this sense, it is possible to argue that Elizabeth's policies did meet the aim of maintaining

**Key date**

Death of Philip II: 1598

English economic interests, at least in the long term, and for the few.

There were major changes in the Queen's objectives as the reign progressed. The assumption that France was the natural enemy changed when Spain offered the greatest threat to the Netherlands. Increasing enmity with Spain and increasing co-operation with the French reflected this change. But the constant objective was to ensure that the Netherlands had sufficient independence for English commerce and security to be maintained. This objective was largely achieved. Although the southern Netherlands remained under Spanish control, the northern provinces did not. It is, however, difficult to assess how far the Queen's actions contributed to this satisfactory result. Philip II felt that English involvement was sufficiently disruptive to justify the expense and danger of the Armada. The Dutch themselves were less convinced of the value of Elizabeth's hesitant and unenthusiastic assistance. In military terms, English help was of dubious value, and for this the Queen was in large part responsible. Leicester was the wrong choice as military commander, and the Queen's treatment of him was unlikely to overcome his defects. Nor were her rather desperate attempts to negotiate with Parma on the eve of all-out war with Spain likely to endear her to the Dutch.

It has to be said that England was fortunate to escape the worst conceivable consequences of its war with Spain: namely, Spanish troops on English soil. It is difficult to avoid the conclusion that the successes of Elizabethan foreign policy owed much to luck and circumstances beyond the Queen's control. Convenient assassination, mistaken decisions by adversaries, helpful weather and Spanish bankruptcy were Elizabeth's allies. They were the kind of allies she liked: they made no financial demands.

Some historians have argued that Elizabeth had aims above and beyond those occasioned purely by narrow self-interest: aims which represented a break with the traditional policies of predecessors. Simon Adams' view is that Elizabeth was motivated by the desire to see Protestant subjects granted freedom of conscience by their Catholic rulers. This, he has suggested, is the explanation behind her complicated relationship with the Dutch and her curiously hesitant manner of assisting them. There is some truth in this, but it is unlikely that Elizabeth wished to secure such freedom solely or primarily as a matter of principle. She avoided employing a policy of religious persecution only when it was to her political advantage, and political advantage, rather than an attachment to the principle of toleration, lies behind her wish to see Philip II grant religious liberty to the Calvinists of the Netherlands. Such toleration would be an obstacle to that complete Spanish control of the provinces which Elizabeth's foreign policy constantly strove to prevent.

Elizabeth had, of course, little sympathy for the views of those councillors who tried to add a new aim to English foreign policy: the defence and furtherance of international Protestantism. The Queen's lack of enthusiasm was probably fortunate, since the country lacked the resources to maintain the position of Protestant champion on the scale envisaged by the zealots. That lack of enthusiasm may have reflected her dislike of aiding and abetting rebels, but it did not entirely prevent her from supporting them in an emergency. After all, she did provide military assistance in the Netherlands, Scotland and France for those fighting against legitimate monarchs. That she did so is a testimony to the extent to which English foreign policy had to respond to events outside its control. Elizabeth found herself following short-term objectives which were frequently dangerous and as frequently distasteful to the Queen herself.

Finally, it is possible to identify tentatively one crucial development in foreign policy which separated Elizabeth's reign from the past: Elizabethan foreign policy did not operate to serve the monarch's personal or dynastic glory. War suited the extravagant posturings of Henry VIII. It did not suit the Virgin Queen.

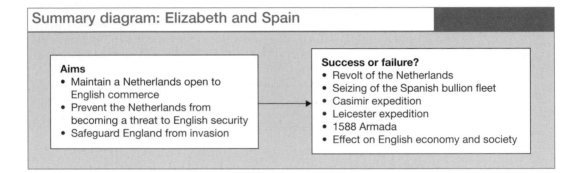

Summary diagram: Elizabeth and Spain

**Aims**
- Maintain a Netherlands open to English commerce
- Prevent the Netherlands from becoming a threat to English security
- Safeguard England from invasion

**Success or failure?**
- Revolt of the Netherlands
- Seizing of the Spanish bullion fleet
- Casimir expedition
- Leicester expedition
- 1588 Armada
- Effect on English economy and society

## Study Guide: AS Questions
### In the style of OCR B
Answer **both** parts of your chosen question.

**(a)** Why did Elizabeth support the Dutch in their rebellion against Spanish rule? (25 marks)

**(b)** Was English support for the Dutch rebels the main reason that Philip sent the Spanish Armada? (25 marks)

---

### Exam tips

*The page references are intended to take you straight to the material that will help you to answer the questions.*

**(a)** This question requires an understanding of the Anglo-Burgundian alliance, of England's dependence on the Antwerp wool and cloth market, of religious elements of the Spanish–Dutch conflict as well as the involvement of France in the Netherlands and England's concern about this. The question implies that you should analyse the reasons for England's support of the rebels and reach a judgement about the role of the factors. There is an element of paradox in Elizabeth's policy, since she was very reluctant to support rebels against the rightful ruler, in this case Philip II.

You might, for example, argue that as Philip's policies became increasingly aggressive towards England, with aid to Ireland and involvement in plots with Mary, Queen of Scots, Elizabeth felt she had no choice but to intervene on behalf of the Dutch rebels. You might explain her change of heart in supporting rebels with reference to the Calvinist theory of the just war against an evil ruler.

You might, for example, argue that Spain's increasing strength after the annexation of Portugal, and the importance of the Netherlands to English trade, as demonstrated by the hardship experienced after the sack of Antwerp, encouraged Elizabeth to take a more active role.

What you should do:

- Identify a range of factors leading to escalating support for the Dutch rebels.
- Organise the factors into different kinds of cause and establish how they link with each other.
- Think about the role played by each factor or cause.
- Try to get into the minds of the Privy Councillors who were encouraging Elizabeth to be involved: which factors were most important to them? Use this to help you argue their relative importance.

What you should avoid:

- Explaining why Elizabeth was reluctant to help the rebels in the Netherlands.
- A narrative account that includes the reasons without explaining why they caused the English to help the Dutch.

**(b)** The focus of this question is Philip II's motivation in sending the Armada of 1588. This is a complex issue, with Philip's motives deduced from a range of evidence including the number of priests aboard the fleet suggesting religious aims and the timing of the Armada, after the execution of Mary, Queen of Scots. The key event with regard to support for the Dutch rebels is the Treaty of Nonsuch, signed in 1585, and some understanding of the difficulties faced by Philip in the Netherlands would be useful. You should analyse the role played by each factor, bearing in mind the evidence of earlier Spanish expeditions to Ireland (Chapter 6, pages 148–9) and reach a judgement about the relative importance.

You might, for example, argue that while the Treaty of Nonsuch provided the immediate motive, Philip had been involved in activities to undermine Elizabeth's rule for some time and England had been provoking him in a number of ways for some years: piracy, seizure of treasure ships and more informal interference in the Netherlands included. Establishing that the Treaty marked the culmination of a series of actions on the part of the English might lead to the conclusion that while the Treaty provided the trigger, Spanish action against England was very likely to occur at some point.

Alternatively you might argue that it was the execution of Mary, Queen of Scots that laid the way open for Philip to attack England by removing the French-backed Catholic heir to the English throne, thus allowing the possibility of Spanish Catholic dominance in England.

What you should do:

- Use the evidence about Elizabeth's actions to identify a range of motives for Philip's reaction, including his religious zeal and his desire to defend his territories and other possessions.
- Plan explanations for each of these factors, going beyond the immediate causes to explain, for example, why Philip was so keen to defend his territories.
- Analyse the relationship between the causes and reach a judgement in relation to the question.

What you should avoid:

- Becoming diverted into a discussion about what Philip intended for England if he succeeded in invading and defeating the English.
- Explaining why the Armada failed.

# Study Guide: A2 Question

## In the style of AQA

'Elizabeth I's foreign policy was confused and haphazard.'
Assess the validity of this view. (45 marks)

### Exam tips

This is a big question that asks you to examine the whole of Elizabeth's foreign policy and see whether you can detect any consistent aims, either throughout the reign, or at different times within it. In order to do this successfully, you will also need to consider Elizabeth's policy with regard to Scotland and Ireland, which is discussed in the next chapter as well.

Try to avoid a purely chronological approach, although you will almost certainly want to highlight key 'turning points'. You may wish to start with an overview of foreign policy to indicate why it might appear 'confused and haphazard'. You could then examine key areas more closely and show where there are underlying threads of continuity.

From the material supplied in this chapter, some constant themes that you might consider are:

- the importance of the Netherlands to England
- the need to preserve and extend trade
- the need for security and possible aggrandisement
- traditional anti-French attitudes
- the need to preserve and spread Protestantism
- the importance of legitimacy and avoiding support for rebels
- the need to seize opportunities because of Britain's 'second-rate' power status.

You may decide that none, some, or all of these objectives were constant throughout the reign, or present in varying degrees at different times. By providing a range of examples of foreign policy which fits the different objectives, you should be able to question the assumption that Elizabeth's foreign policy was entirely 'confused and haphazard' and reach a substantiated conclusion.

# 6 Meeting the Challenge of Foreign Affairs: Elizabeth, Ireland and Scotland

POINTS TO CONSIDER

The particular challenges posed to the Elizabethan government by Ireland and Scotland were:

- Proximity. Scotland was a separate kingdom which enjoyed a fraught relationship with England, its larger and much more powerful neighbour. The Scots had reason to be fearful for their independence, and so the traditional alliance with France was at one and the same time self-defence for Scotland and a potential threat for England – especially if French troops ended up on Scottish soil. Ireland was allegedly subject to the English crown, but English authority was contested to say the least. The country was often fertile ground for rival claimants to the English throne.
- Religion. Elizabeth's status as perhaps the most prominent Protestant ruler in Europe meant that her Catholic enemies might seek to exploit England's problematic relations with Ireland and Scotland to destabilise her regime.

This chapter therefore integrates a discussion of Ireland and Scotland with the wider concerns of Elizabethan foreign policy which were identified and analysed in Chapter 5.

## Key dates

| | |
|---|---|
| 1541 | Henry VIII declared King of Ireland by Act of Parliament |
| 1559 | Rebellion of the Lords of the Congregation |
| 1560 | English army sent to Scotland |
| | Treaty of Edinburgh: French troops withdrew from Scotland |
| 1561 | Mary Stuart returned to Scotland from France |
| | Sussex campaigned against Shane O'Neill in Ireland |
| 1565 | Mary Stuart married Darnley |
| 1566 | Murder of Riccio |
| | Birth of James, son of Mary Stuart |
| 1567 | Murder of Darnley |
| | Mary Stuart married Bothwell |

| | |
|---|---|
| | Mary Stuart was forced to renounce throne in favour of infant James |
| | Shane O'Neill killed |
| 1568 | Mary Stuart fled to England |
| 1569 | Norfolk marriage plot |
| 1571 | Ridolfi plot discovered |
| 1573 | Failure of Smith's Ulster plantation |
| 1579 | Fitzmaurice and Sander landed in Smerwick, triggering uprisings in Ireland |
| 1586 | Babington plot discovered |
| 1587 | Execution of Mary Stuart |
| 1593 | Hugh O'Neill, Earl of Tyrone, elected to title of 'The O'Neill' |
| 1596–7 | Spanish armadas to Ireland scattered by storms |
| 1598 | Battle of Yellow Ford: Hugh O'Neill defeated English forces |
| | Munster plantation destroyed |
| 1599 | Essex appointed Lord Lieutenant in Ireland; left later that year |
| 1600 | Mountjoy Lord Deputy in Ireland |
| 1601 | Spanish army landed at Kinsale. Mountjoy defeated Hugh O'Neill |
| 1603 | Days after the death of Elizabeth I, O'Neill submitted to Mountjoy |

# 1 | Irish Society and England in the Sixteenth Century

## Ireland in the sixteenth century: land and people

> The custom of these savages is to live as the brute beasts among the mountains. … They carry on a perpetual war with the English, who here keep garrison for the Queen. … The chief inclination of these people is to be robbers. … These people call themselves Christians. Mass is said among them, and regulated according to the orders of the Church of Rome. The great majority of their churches, monasteries, and hermitages, have been demolished by the hands of the English. … In short, in this kingdom there is neither justice nor right, and everyone does what he pleases.

So said Captain Cuellar, a survivor from the Spanish Armada shipwrecked in 1588 on the coasts of Ireland. He clearly felt that the Irish he encountered were beyond the pale of civilisation. Of course, the frightened, uncomprehending and mistreated Cuellar was in no position to make an objective assessment of the Irish as he sought desperately through the marshes and forests of the most remote and poorest parts of Ireland for refuge and a passage back to Spain. But Englishmen new to Ireland frequently shared Cuellar's opinion. As they looked out on **Gaelic** Ireland, the Ireland relatively free of English influence, they also felt

**Key term**

**Gaelic**
Ancient Celtic language, culture and customs.

confused and threatened by a society they did not understand. And, like Cuellar, they concluded that the Gaelic Irish were uncivilised. The vantage point of these Englishmen was the Irish territory belonging to the kings of England: the area around Dublin known as the Pale. Indeed, the phrase **'beyond the pale'**, as used earlier in this paragraph, carries with it the meaning of an area outside the bounds of civilisation.

Ireland was disturbingly different from England. The Pale itself had many of the hallmarks of English society – superficially. The monarch's authority was represented in the Pale by a Lord Lieutenant or Lord Deputy. There were law courts in Dublin practising English law, and an Irish Parliament. The gentry of the Pale prided themselves on their 'Englishness' and sent sons to be educated at the **Inns of Court** in London. Outside the Pale were the 'Old English' **feudal** lords. Descendants of the Norman conquerors of Ireland, they were virtually kings in their own lands. Their allegiance to the English crown was tempered by this near-autocratic power. They used their private armies to pursue private feuds. These nobles therefore occupied a middle-ground between the Pale and Gaelic Ireland. Some of them were more 'hibernicised', in other words close to Gaelic society, than others. Rivalries between great Anglo-Irish earls would often be fed by the closeness of their links with one or other of the cultures.

Figure 6.1 shows just how much of Ireland was under the control of Gaelic chieftains. These chieftains generally refused to accept the authority of the kings of England. Gaelic, and not English, law was in force in their territories. Of the many differences between the two legal systems, the most significant related to the inheritance of land and title. The English system was that of **primogeniture**. On the death of an English earl, for example, the eldest son, or daughter if there were no male children, inherited all landed property. In the Gaelic system, the chieftain did not own the land he controlled: he was not a landlord in the English sense. The territory, apart from some allotted to the chieftain by virtue of his title, belonged to the **freemen** as a whole. It was periodically redistributed among them. Nor did the chieftain pass his title down to his eldest son by right. A successor, known as the **Tanist**, was elected by the freemen, who could choose whom they wished from the members of the ruling family. The election would generally take place before the death of the chieftain to ensure an orderly succession. In fact the system frequently stimulated, rather than curbed, violence.

Gaelic Ireland was remarkably localised even by the standards of contemporary England. Chieftains travelled with an armed retinue as much for protection as for display even within their own territories. Towns were few and far between: the economy depended largely on barter, and wealth was measured in livestock. The movement of cattle to and from pastureland in winter and summer was inevitably accompanied by the movement of people. This gave English newcomers the feeling that the Gaelic Irish were **nomads**, and unspeakably primitive and inferior to boot.

**Key terms**

**'Beyond the pale'**
Outside 'civilised' society. The Pale was a fence dividing the English-controlled area around Dublin from Gaelic Ireland.

**Inns of Court**
The London Inns of Court provided, not only a professional training in the law, but also an education and social contacts appropriate to the well-connected gentry.

**Feudal**
A system of authority based on ownership of land.

**Primogeniture**
A system whereby the first-born inherited all the property of the parent.

**Freemen**
Those not bound as property to a lord or chieftain.

**Tanist**
A Gaelic chieftain and landholder elected by freemen.

**Nomads**
People without a fixed settlement.

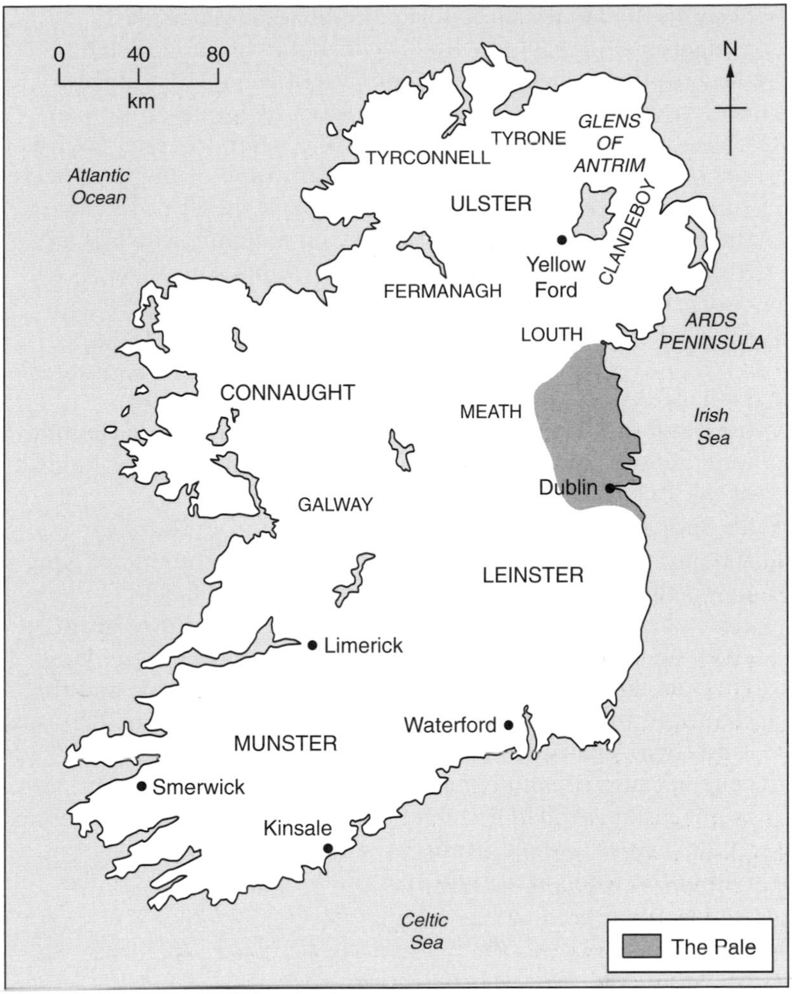

**Figure 6.1**: Ireland in the sixteenth century.

Small wonder, then, that where English customs and Gaelic customs met, confusion (at the very least) would ensue. Mutual incomprehension does not easily engender peaceable relations.

## Ireland and the monarchs of England

Until the reign of Henry VIII, English kings generally relied on a deputy, one of the great Anglo-Irish earls, to maintain the interests of the crown in Ireland. The advantage of this system was that a man such as the Earl of Kildare had power and influence which transcended the divisions between English society and Gaelic society. But, by the 1530s, this reliance on a great feudal lord had been brought into question in two respects:

- First, the Anglo-Irish earls were all too reminiscent of the overmighty subjects whose power had been demonstrated with disastrous consequences in the **Wars of the Roses**. To invest an Anglo-Irish earl with near-absolute authority was outmoded.

**Key term**

**Wars of the Roses**
The struggle between the families of York and Lancaster for the kingship of England which culminated in the rule of the Tudors (1485).

- Second, the Henrician Reformation made it particularly dangerous. After all, the break with Rome brought Ireland to the European stage. Foreign enemies of Henry VIII and his Protestant successors could use Ireland, its loyalty to Roman Catholicism and its Gaelic dissent as a potent weapon against England: either as a springboard for invasion of England or as a means of tying down English troops and thereby sabotaging the economy of the country. To rely on a deputy who was an Anglo-Irish Catholic lord with Gaelic connections was dangerous.

Henry VIII responded to the potential threat in two ways:

- First, direct rule from London replaced delegation to overmighty Anglo-Irish subjects. Lord Lieutenants or Deputies were chosen, not from the Anglo-Irish earls or the Old English of the Pale, but from London courtiers.
- Second, the King chose to change his title from 'Lord of Ireland' to 'King of Ireland'. The adoption of the title of King paved the way towards an attempt to **anglicise** Gaelic chieftains. By the system known as '**surrender and re-grant**', a chieftain handed over the territory he controlled to the king. He then received it back with the title of English earl and the chance to pass on the land and title by primogeniture. This was unlikely to 'civilise' Ireland in the short term and would, of course, cause resentment among the freemen. What right, they might justly ask, had the chieftain to surrender land belonging to the clan as a whole? And, if the new earl subsequently fell foul of the King, what right had the King to confiscate that land?

## 2 | Elizabeth and Ireland: Problems and Possible Solutions

### The situation in Ireland at the start of Elizabeth's reign

The problems in Ireland facing the Queen at the start of her reign were:

- Given the clash of English and Gaelic cultures, Ireland lacked any central authority.
- The traditional system of allowing overmighty subjects to govern in the monarch's name had been found wanting.
- The post-Reformation English monarchy had to beware lest Ireland became a pawn in a Europe-wide conflict. For Elizabeth, there were certain uncomfortable parallels with Spain and the Netherlands (see pages 125–6).
- The attempts made by Henry VIII to extend the crown's influence over Gaelic Ireland had been largely unsuccessful.
- Ireland was expensive, since it was becoming increasingly obvious that a standing army under the control of London would be necessary to maintain English interests.

**Key date**
Henry VIII declared King of Ireland by Act of Parliament: 1541

**Key terms**

**Anglicise**
To impose English law, systems of authority, customs and manners on another people.

**Surrender and re-grant**
Where a Gaelic chieftain would hand over the land he controlled (but did not own) to the crown. He would then receive it back with the title of an English earl. Such land could then be passed on to his descendants.

**Key question**
What challenges did Ireland pose to Elizabeth?

- The imposition of a deputy from England was likely to cause resentment among the 'Old English'.
- Policy towards Ireland had to take account of the fact that many English, and particularly the Puritans, detested the Irish, who were regarded as beast-like papists.

It would be tempting to assume that no monarch of England could possibly 'solve' the problems posed by Ireland. But England had considerable advantages when dealing with its sister island. Most importantly, it had a significantly larger population and vastly greater resources. This meant that an English monarch could, in the last resort, raise an army in England which no Gaelic chieftain or Anglo-Irish lord could hope to meet in formal battle with any chance of success. Even if a **guerrilla campaign** were to be fought against such an army, little could be done to prevent the English from destroying the crops and livestock which meant both life and wealth to Gaelic society.

It could be argued that Elizabeth had three possible courses of action in handling challenges posed by Ireland:

- First, she might ignore the rest of Ireland – that is, most of Gaelic Ireland – beyond the Pale and the southern counties. But both the internal and the international situation made this extremely inadvisable. The endemic violence and ambitions of chieftains in Ireland meant that the areas under English influence would be constantly under threat. More importantly, as we have seen, the religious and political crises of Europe meant that Ireland could never be a mere matter of domestic policy for England.
- Second, Elizabeth could attempt to colonise areas where English influence was limited or non-existent. This might prove attractive to Old English or the land-hungry English of the mainland. This would also pander to English views of the Gaelic Irish as barbarians and justify colonisation as a gift of civilisation. But the Gaels were, of course, unlikely to see colonies in this light. Colonies would, therefore, need to be defended by a system of fortresses or garrison towns to be secure against Gaelic attack.
- The third option was a full-scale military conquest. This would not be easy given the Gaelic preference for guerrilla warfare, and would need to be followed up with a system of fortresses and/or colonisation. The second and third options, in order to be successful, would require long-term planning and very substantial investment.

**Key term**
**Guerrilla campaign**
Fighting a war by stealth rather than through formal battles.

## Shane O'Neill

**Key question**
What do the career and fate of Shane O'Neill reveal about the difficulties facing the Elizabethan government in Ireland?

The career of Shane O'Neill provides the historian with an excellent opportunity to study the way in which Elizabeth tackled the problems posed by Ireland. Under the 'surrender and re-grant' policy, Shane's father, Con O'Neill, had abandoned his Gaelic title of 'The O'Neill', had promised to adopt the English language and habits, had surrendered 'his' lands and had been granted them back with the title of Earl of Tyrone. The O'Neill base was in Ulster, an area remote from English influence. But Shane had been chosen as his father's Tanist in defiance of the English law of primogeniture, which made the eldest son, Matthew, heir to his father's title and earldom. In the event, Shane instigated the murder of Matthew and Con was forced out of Tyrone.

By 1561, Shane had been proclaimed a rebel by the Earl of Sussex, the Lord Deputy, but the former's military strength, increased by his use of Scottish mercenaries and his unprecedented step of arming peasants, meant that Sussex could do little until reinforcements arrived from England. However, once they arrived, Shane could not risk a formal battle. He could not prevent the Lord Deputy from marching through Shane's territories and slaughtering enormous numbers of livestock. This exhibition of power caused Shane to negotiate an audience with the Queen, who was treated to a display of Gaelic court manners that astounded the English courtiers and emphasised very clearly the gulf between the two cultures. But O'Neill's howling and pleading in the traditional manner was not the sign of a defeated man.

What, then, could Elizabeth do with him? To defeat him militarily would involve massive expenditure: and, even then, success could not be guaranteed. In any case, it has been made abundantly clear in previous chapters that massive expenditure and Elizabeth were uneasy bedfellows. She therefore tried the risky stratagem of curbing Shane by giving him an important role as a servant of the English crown. He was encouraged to remove Scottish settlements in Ulster, always a thorn in the side of the English given the strained relations between Scotland and England. But it is hard to see how using Shane in this way was likely to tame him. There was little that Elizabeth could realistically offer him that he would value. Sussex recognised this, and tried to solve the problem by bringing Shane to battle after the latter's return to Ireland.

Indecisive skirmishing duly followed, and the Lord Deputy had little alternative but to make a treaty with O'Neill. Extraordinarily enough, the treaty accepted him as 'The O'Neill' in the Gaelic fashion. That this was a humiliation for the government is evident from a failed attempt to murder Shane with a poisoned cask of wine. No-one was under any illusions as to the danger posed by Shane. He had attempted to negotiate for French military assistance by offering the crown of Ireland to Charles IX, had also negotiated with Mary, Queen of Scots and, for good measure, had sought to pose as a defender of the faith against Protestant heresy.

In the end, the greater armed strength of England proved indirectly to be Shane's downfall. In 1566, Sussex's successor, Sir Henry Sidney, pursued the standard tactic of marching through O'Neill's land causing as much devastation and capturing as many fortresses as possible. To recoup some of his losses, Shane attacked the O'Donnells of Tyrconnell, but his forces were badly mauled at the battle of Farsetmore (1567). It is a mark of his

**Key dates**

Sussex campaigned against Shane O'Neill in Ireland: 1561

Shane O'Neill killed: 1567

Hugh O'Neill, Earl of Tyrone, elected to title of 'The O'Neill': 1593 desperation that he appealed for help to the MacDonnells, bitter enemies some two years before. A meeting with them degenerated into a squalid brawl and Shane's miserable death. His head – thoughtfully pickled for the journey – was sent to Dublin.

No doubt Elizabeth's government was more than pleased to hear of Shane's fate, with or without his pickled remains. But they had less reason to feel self-satisfied as it was ill-luck, poor judgement and his own excesses that had brought Shane to his sordid end. Nevertheless, the downfall of Shane O'Neill had two major consequences for Elizabeth's Irish policy. First, it gave her the chance to reassert royal claims to Ulster as a whole. In 1569, an Act of Attainder (legalising the confiscation of the lands of rebels) abolished the title of 'The O'Neill'. Second, Shane's death gave the government the chance of an Ulster **plantation**: the first attempt so to do in Elizabeth's reign.

**Key terms**

**Plantation**
Colonisation by settling in numbers.

**Colonisation**
One country seizing foreign territory by dispossessing original owners and occupants.

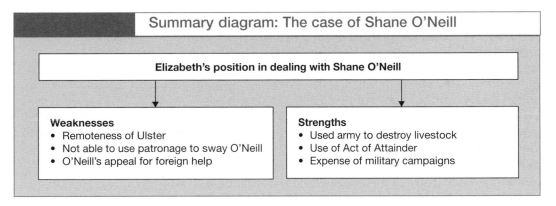

**Summary diagram: The case of Shane O'Neill**

**Elizabeth's position in dealing with Shane O'Neill**

**Weaknesses**
- Remoteness of Ulster
- Not able to use patronage to sway O'Neill
- O'Neill's appeal for foreign help

**Strengths**
- Used army to destroy livestock
- Use of Act of Attainder
- Expense of military campaigns

**Key question**
Why did the plantation policy fail?

**Key date**
Failure of Smith's Ulster plantation: 1573

## Control by colonisation: the failure of the Ulster plantation 1573

**Colonisation** should be seen as a mechanism for conquering Gaelic Ireland. However, the attempts to colonise Ulster in the 1570s were expensive failures and demonstrate the lack of detailed planning in the government's strategy. In Elizabeth's eyes, one advantage of the proposed colonisation was that it was to be undertaken by private individuals, albeit with some financial support from the crown. But it is clear that these attempts were simply not thought through. Elizabeth gave official sanction to a plan by Sir Thomas Smith, a member of her Privy Council, to establish a colony in the Ards peninsula. She granted Smith lands which belonged to the O'Neills of Clandeboy.

To ignore the rights of Sir Brian McPhelim O'Neill was foolhardy, and the settlers, under the direction of Smith's illegitimate son, lacked the military muscle to survive in the face of attacks from Sir Brian. After the murder of his son in 1573, Smith had to hand the enterprise over to Walter Devereux, Earl of Essex. Essex had greater financial resources, some of which came from the Queen, but relied like Smith on the efforts of land-hungry English adventurers who needed rapid success to maintain their enthusiasm. The Queen likewise demanded swift results without providing Essex with the support he needed for an overwhelming military victory. Elizabeth even demanded that Essex abandon the enterprise if he failed to make it pay its own way: a curious attitude to what was, after all, a major military campaign.

Essex left a trail of massacres and damage behind him, but, in an area where there were few towns and against an enemy who refused to fight set-piece battles, Essex came to the conclusion that only fortress garrisons could subdue Ulster. In this, the Queen agreed, but failed to provide the funds needed fully to implement the scheme.

By 1576, Essex had exhausted himself to little effect. The Queen granted him the title of Earl Marshal of Ireland, but it was no consolation for his crippling losses and failures. Sickness and depression brought him to his deathbed in Dublin. For this, Elizabeth must accept much of the blame.

## Control by colonisation: the plantation of Munster from 1568

Munster was a more attractive proposition for English adventurers and settlers than Ulster. It was richer, more fertile and considerably more accessible. Indeed, it had received earlier attention from land-hungry English than had Ulster. Men such as Sir Peter Carew (pronounced Carey) from Devon were not concerned with the rights of Gaels or Old English if they could get their hands on land. In 1568, Carew launched a series of aggressive claims against certain gentry in the Pale itself, as well as in Munster, based on the alleged holdings of one of his Norman ancestors. Carew had the support of the English Lord Deputy and the Privy Council. The encouragement of this naked aggression could only increase tension between the English government, the 'New English' colonists and the Old English.

In 1569, rebellion broke out as a direct result of the resentment caused by English policy. The motives of Sir Edmund Butler, a member of the generally pro-English House of Ormond, were clearly to destroy the small English plantations: Carew's in particular. What is significant is that Butler collaborated with Gaelic chieftains: a testimony to the depth of his resentment, caused largely by the remarkable insensitivity of Elizabethan policy. The rebellion was stamped out, as was a revolt under James Fitzmaurice Fitzgerald (referred to hereafter as Fitzmaurice), but the latter sought not only to establish common cause with Gaelic Ireland, but also to convert rebellion into a crusade against the heretical Queen of England. Fitzmaurice had received some limited and covert aid from Philip II of Spain. The combination of anti-English feeling and Catholicism was a potent brew, strengthened as it was by the papal excommunication of Elizabeth in 1570 (see pages 95–7). However, it is easy to overestimate the support aroused by the call of religion. Perhaps it was a useful justification for rebellion, but, if so, was probably a less important factor than the hatred of English adventurers.

Key dates

Fitzmaurice and Sander landed in Smerwick, triggering uprisings in Ireland: 1579

Spanish armadas to Ireland scattered by storms: 1596–7

Battle of Yellow Ford: Hugh O'Neill defeated English forces: 1598

Munster plantation destroyed: 1598

Essex appointed Lord Lieutenant in Ireland; left later that year: 1599

Mountjoy Lord Deputy in Ireland: 1600

Spanish army landed at Kinsale. Mountjoy defeated Hugh O'Neill: 1601

Days after the death of Elizabeth I, O'Neill submitted to Mountjoy: 1603

**Key question**
What does the rebellion in Tyrone reveal about the nature of the late-Elizabethan court?

## The Fitzmaurice invasion

By the end of the decade Fitzmaurice had returned with a small, papal-sponsored force (see page 129). His landing at Smerwick in July 1579 triggered uprisings in Ulster, Leinster and throughout Munster, and brought the dithering Earl of Desmond into rebellion. Philip II sent troops to help with the revolt. The new Lord Deputy, Lord Grey, reacted with relentless repression and some savagery. He read a Catholic conspiracy into every act of defiance and resentment: Anglo-Irish and Gael alike were sent to the gallows, whatever their actual motives for opposing the government. His ruthlessness in destroying livestock and harvest brought famine and death throughout Munster. Even the Pale suffered.

The eventual defeat of the rebellions paved the way for a more thorough and systematic colonisation between 1579 and 1583, based in large part on the confiscated lands of the Desmonds. It is important to note that the loyal Old English were offered few or no opportunities to take advantage of the available land. Instead, lands were touted for sale in England, where the land-hungry younger sons of the Carew type were encouraged to fulfil their ambitions to be great landowners in the rich lands of Munster. Many did so, but the plantations in Munster were largely destroyed in uprisings in 1598. Once again, the government sought to keep its own expenses down by pandering to greed. Adventurers had been encouraged to over-reach themselves. Many had acquired so much land that they were unable to exploit it. Neither Elizabeth nor her advisers had learned much from the mistakes of the Ulster plantations.

## The rebellion of Hugh O'Neill, Earl of Tyrone

After the death of Shane O'Neill (see page 147), the government had adopted a cautious approach in Ulster. The old 'surrender and re-grant' policy resurfaced, and attempts were made to play one chieftain off against the other to prevent the rise of another dominant lord on the model of Shane. Hugh O'Neill, a grandson of Con O'Neill, was educated as a royal ward and attached to the household of the Earl of Leicester. He was, in time, granted the title of Earl of Tyrone. But Hugh was in a position fraught with difficulty. He was an obvious candidate for the Gaelic title of 'The O'Neill'; an attractive prospect to him. He also liked being an Anglo-Irish noble. However, as time went on, it became clear to him that he lacked influence where it most mattered in Elizabethan England: at court and on the Privy Council. His friends Leicester and Walsingham were dead, and he had no-one who could speak for him at the centre of power. He saw Ireland increasingly at the mercy of relatively minor English officials and adventurers: the title of Earl of Tyrone would not alone enable him to fulfil his ambition of ruling Ulster without interference. His attempt to gain a commission from the Queen to govern Ulster was unsuccessful, and he responded by turning to Gaelic Ireland, where traditional antagonism to English encroachments proved to be a useful weapon.

In 1593, he was elected to the title of 'The O'Neill', but followed a less traditional path by building up a far more powerful and extensively trained fighting force than his predecessors had possessed. By 1595, Tyrone was in open rebellion and looking for help from Spain. Philip II was not one to throw away money on lost causes, but Tyrone's effective and modernised army interested him, especially when it became clear that Elizabeth's forces were finding it a formidable opponent. In 1597, an Armada was dispatched for Ireland, only to be scattered by the winds. Undaunted, Tyrone inflicted a remarkable defeat on a 4000-strong English army at Yellow Ford in 1598. Indeed, it could be argued that the successes of Tyrone revealed the folly of Elizabeth's past meanness. All her parsimonious free-enterprise schemes, all the inadequate but still substantial monies provided for the campaigns of Lord Deputies, all the attempts to 'civilise' the Gaelic Irish, all in jeopardy and all potentially wasted. It was at this point that the Munster plantation was virtually swept away. Tyrone was, in effect, at the head of a confederation of Gaels and some Old English who had in common their antagonism to Elizabeth's policies. Indeed, if Tyrone were to succeed in linking up with a Spanish invasion force, then the English might well be forced back into the Pale and the surrounding southern counties.

The defeat at Yellow Ford so infuriated the Queen that she finally decided to devote sufficient resources to a full-scale military conquest of Ireland. But it was nearly too late. In 1599, the Queen's favourite, Robert Devereux, Earl of Essex, was sent to Ireland with an army of 16,000 infantry and 1300 cavalry. Essex was not a good choice. He achieved nothing. Ireland was not a happy hunting ground for those who relied on the affection of the Queen for their position. Essex made a truce with Tyrone and scampered back to London (see Chapter 8).

The perilous position for the English in Ireland was redeemed only by the appointment of the dour Charles Blount, Lord Mountjoy, as military commander. Landing in 1600, he managed to motivate the dispirited English forces and succeeded in pushing Tyrone back towards Ulster, only to be faced with a formidable Spanish invasion of 3400 crack troops at Kinsale. It was, indeed, a close-run thing. Tyrone made an error in risking a full-scale battle outside Kinsale, and was heavily defeated by Mountjoy. By January 1602, the Kinsale garrison had surrendered, Munster was well on the way to being pacified and Tyrone was back in Ulster. Hugh O'Neill finally submitted six days after Elizabeth died, but only on generous terms. He was recognised as the Chief Lord of Ulster under the crown: the very position he had sought and fought to achieve. Elizabeth's successor, James I, was therefore obliged to pursue the old-fashioned and discredited policy of allowing overmighty subjects to rule Ulster ostensibly in his name.

## The Irish Reformation
In 1560, an Act of Uniformity declared Elizabeth to be Supreme Governor of the Church of Ireland, very much on the model of

the English Act of 1559 (see page 44). It showed some awareness of the need to bear in mind Irish conditions by permitting priests ignorant of English the use of a Latin version of the prescribed prayer book. However, any assessment of the impact of the Elizabethan religious settlement on Ireland must recognise its essential failure. The Elizabethan brand of Protestantism was seen by the Irish as nothing more than the religious version of English political encroachments and was treated accordingly. Effective Protestant preachers could not be attracted to Ireland: livings were poor, and the language barrier was virtually insurmountable. There was no pool of Protestant clergy available to take the place of religious conservatives. The only meaningful attempt to improve clerical education came with the founding of Trinity College, Dublin in 1592.

## Elizabeth and Ireland: conclusion

A reminder of the basic criteria marking a successful Irish policy is now in order:

- The first is that the government should prevent Ireland from being used by a foreign power as a base for an invasion of England. In this, Elizabeth was successful, although of course she was unable to prevent Spain from landing small invasion forces in Ireland itself.
- Second, Ireland should be controlled in a manner which suited English interests. Ideally, Gaelic Ireland should be increasingly anglicised. In this, Elizabeth's policy was largely a failure. Mountjoy's campaigns may have subdued the country, but it was not pacified in the long term. The net result of this and other policies in the 45 years of Elizabethan rule was that antagonism between England and the Gaelic population was intensified. Even worse, the influx of 'New English' administrators and colonists, operating with government complicity in defiance of the interests of the Old English, effectively alienated many of the traditional loyalists from the country of their origin. Elizabeth had sown the seeds of an Irish nationalism which transcended Gaelic and Anglo-Irish divisions. This meant that any 'solution' in Ireland was likely to be based on military conquest and occupation. Private enterprise colonisation was cheap, but no real alternative. And the longer the Queen delayed in committing adequate funds to military campaigns, the more dangerous the climate became. Tyrone's successes had put in jeopardy almost all English authority outside the Pale and surrounding counties. Mountjoy's victory was impressive precisely because defeat was all too possible.
- The imposition of the Elizabethan Protestant religious settlement on Ireland is the third element in any successful policy. After all, religion was a vital weapon in the political control of the country. But here, Elizabeth's failure was complete.

- Fourth, Elizabeth should have curbed the ability of the Irish nobles to defy the authority of the crown. Any success here was compromised by the defiance of Tyrone.

Finally, what was the cost of Elizabethan rule to Ireland itself? By the time of Elizabeth's death, large areas of the country, particularly Ulster, had been devastated. Crops were burned, trade was disrupted, and towns were in ruins. Famine was widespread, and parts of the rich land of Munster were uninhabited. The prospect of the assimilation of such an Ireland within an English nation-state was remote indeed.

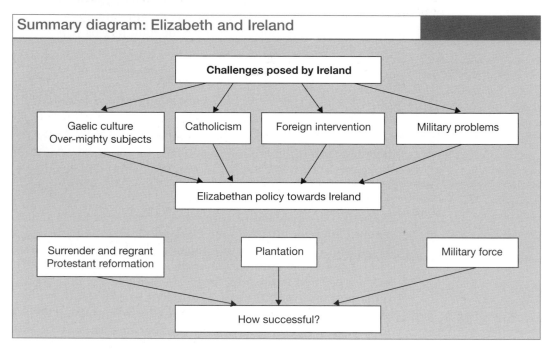

Summary diagram: Elizabeth and Ireland

## 3 | Elizabeth and Scotland

### Introduction

Elizabeth's relations with Scotland almost entirely revolved around the figure of Mary Stuart, Queen of Scots. An account of the career of Mary reads like a particularly unlikely plot from a spectacularly extravagant and romantic historical novelist. Here we had a young Queen of Scotland: a woman, it seems, of beauty, intelligence and charm. She married the young heir to the throne of France, and became Queen of France on his accession as Francis II. But Francis died young, and the widow returned to her native Scottish shores. She already had a claim to the throne of England, and married Lord Darnley, an English nobleman, who had a claim of his own. But the marriage was unhappy. The jealous Darnley snatched from his Queen's presence a favourite of hers, an Italian secretary named David Riccio, and murdered him in cold blood. However, Darnley was himself murdered. His house was blown up, and his strangled body found in the garden.

Key dates

Mary Stuart married Darnley: 1565

Murder of Darnley: 1567

Mary Stuart married Bothwell: 1567

This near-contemporary drawing shows the scene of Darnley's murder. Darnley, in bed, is saying, 'Judge and avenge my cause, O lord.' To what purpose might a drawing such as this have been put at the time?

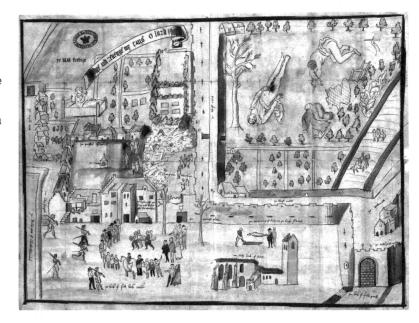

Suspicion fell on the Scottish nobleman, James Bothwell. Mary married none other than Bothwell, and was imprisoned by horrified opponents. She subsequently escaped to England, where, after years of imprisonment, she was executed by the English Queen.

Although this sequence of events seems desperately improbable (and likely to impress a publisher with an eye for sensational fiction), the basic factual outline is accurate. Most significant is Elizabeth's action. To execute a fellow monarch hardly seems in keeping with her general obsession with the rights of legitimate authority. The implication is, of course, that Mary represented a particularly dangerous threat to Elizabeth herself. The following two sections explain the nature of this threat, which lay partly in the uncertainties and tensions of traditional Anglo-Scottish relations and partly in the unique position of Mary herself.

## The Scottish background

It was one of the central assumptions of English foreign policy in the sixteenth century that the kingdom of Scotland represented a threat to England. In large part, this was because of the closeness of Scotland's relations with France. From the French perspective, England was the traditional enemy. It therefore made sense for the French to exploit the antagonism between Scotland and England to damage the latter as much as possible. Chapter 5 contains a detailed discussion of this issue (see page 116). From the Scottish perspective, England was a real danger. With a far greater population and vastly greater resources, the southern kingdom was an adversary Scotland could not afford to face alone.

The earlier Tudors had sought to draw Scotland ever closer to the English orbit. The attempts made by Henry VIII and Somerset to marry Edward to the infant Mary, Queen of Scots were discussed in Chapter 1 (see page 8). The Scots had invoked French help, which appeared in the form of 10,000 troops in June of the same year. Mary Stuart was taken to France for education and then marriage to the Dauphin, Francis. This was bad enough from the English point of view, since the marriage underpinned the Scottish–French alliance. But the full danger was apparent on Elizabeth's accession, since Mary Stuart had a strong claim to the English throne herself. This was based largely on the alleged illegitimacy of Elizabeth, and is discussed in detail below. The French might exploit Mary's claim in a number of ways. The powerful Guise family saw it as an opportunity to destabilise the heretical Protestant regime of Elizabeth.

However, it would be a mistake to assume that all Scots were happy to fall in with the world-view of the Guises. To some, their Queen's foreign marriage seemed to reduce the country to the very state of dependency they had striven to avoid. In fact, to the increasing number of Protestant nobles, dependence on the Catholic France of the Guises seemed a worse fate than a closer relationship with Protestant England. The Scottish outlook was not, therefore, entirely without hope from the English point of view.

## Mary Stuart and the English succession

The genealogical table in Chapter 1 on page 18 shows that, by hereditary descent, Mary Stuart was Elizabeth's rightful heir. On the other hand, the last will and testament of Henry VIII had bypassed her line (and therefore the Catholic heirs). But it was open to doubt whether the King had the right to alter traditional rules of inheritance. Admittedly, that right had been granted to the King by Parliament, but Parliament's right so to do was at least open to question.

To consider Mary as the rightful queen in place of Elizabeth was another matter. There was no dispute that Elizabeth was the daughter of Henry VIII, but was she his rightful heir? After all, if one were to argue that her mother Anne Boleyn's marriage to the King was illegal, on the grounds that the King's previous marriage to Catherine of Aragon was never lawfully dissolved, then Elizabeth's title to the throne might be brought into question. In theory, English Catholics might take this line. In practice, however, very few English Catholics disputed Elizabeth's title. Bitter enemies like the Guises had, needless to say, no such qualms. Mary's use of the royal arms of England was a sign of the antagonism that the Guises felt towards the English Queen.

Mary's claim to succeed Elizabeth, however, caused Elizabeth's councillors much additional anxiety. From the viewpoint of many Protestants in and outside the Privy Council, Mary's Catholicism rendered her unacceptable as Elizabeth's successor. This made it imperative in their eyes that Elizabeth should marry quickly to provide a Protestant heir. As Elizabeth grew older and hopes of her marriage began to fade, Mary's importance increased. The danger was that Elizabeth might lose the allegiance of those who kept their eyes fixed firmly on the future. Finally, there was the nightmare suffered by those convinced of the existence of an international Catholic conspiracy. Might not supporters of Mary wish to secure her succession by the simple expedient of murdering Elizabeth? As we shall see, fears for Elizabeth's safety grew as relations with Catholic Spain worsened.

Mary Stuart, then, was a convenient focus and weapon for all those who opposed the reign of Elizabeth I on religious grounds. In the following sections we trace the various challenges this posed to the government of Elizabeth and identify the policy of that government towards the Scottish Queen. In so doing, it should be possible to answer questions vital to any analysis of the nature and success of English policy, namely:

- To what extent was the Queen responsible for Scottish policy?
- How far was policy clearly thought out? Did it merely respond to events, or was there evidence of long-term planning?
- What were the principles whereby relations with Mary were conducted? What changes, if any, were made to such principles?

## Rebellion in Scotland 1559

**Key dates**

Rebellion of the Lords of the Congregation: 1559

English army sent to Scotland: 1560

Treaty of Edinburgh: French troops withdrew from Scotland: 1560

In the spring of 1559, Protestant nobles, calling themselves Lords of the Congregation, rose in rebellion against the French Catholic regent of Scotland, Mary of Guise (mother of Mary Stuart). Their motives were partly religious, but also reflected their resentment at what they saw as a loss of Scottish sovereignty stemming from the links with France. This rebellion could be seen, of course, as a great opportunity for England. Support for the rebels, carefully emphasising a common Protestantism, might lead to a new relationship with Scotland which would go some way towards lessening the threat apparently posed by the Guises. In June 1559, Henry II of France died. The young French King and Queen, Francis II and Mary Stuart, were encouraged by the Guise faction to use the coat of arms of the monarchs of England. Councillors such as William Cecil saw this as a clear confirmation of the existence of a Catholic plan to press the claims of Mary to the throne of England, while at the same time securing control of Scotland. They therefore urged immediate military intervention in Scotland.

## The Treaty of Edinburgh 1560

**Key question**
How far was William Cecil responsible for the success represented by the Treaty of Edinburgh?

What Cecil had to reckon with was Elizabeth's attitude towards the Scottish rebels. Elizabeth, as ever, showed little enthusiasm for international Protestant solidarity and had no intention of hiding her dislike of the religious mentor of the Lords of the Congregation, John Knox. Knox's pamphlet of 1558, *The First Blast of the Trumpet against the Monstrous Regimen of Women*, had been targeted at Mary of Guise and Mary I of England, but its savage criticism of women in positions of government had deeply offended Elizabeth. And, of course, to aid and abet rebels was wrong, and the fact that it was politically advantageous to do so did not, in Elizabeth's view, make it right. Elizabeth's attitude towards rebellion meant, on the one hand, that she was frequently unable to take advantage of situations as they arose, as a true pragmatist would have done, and, on the other, that she was dismissive of policies which genuinely sought to further the long-term interests of the nation itself. Fortunately for those interests, William Cecil was aware of the Queen's unwillingness to support the Lords of the Congregation.

However, he managed to play on her anger at the French royal couple's claim to her title to propel her into providing some grudging assistance for the rebels:

- Starting with the secret supply of arms and money to the Scots, Elizabeth was then persuaded to send a fleet to the Firth of Forth to prevent any French attempt to relieve their main garrison in the town of Leith.
- Cecil also managed to get an English army sent to Scotland to assist with the siege of Leith in March 1560.
- The French agreed to negotiate in June, and the resulting Treaty of Edinburgh was something of a triumph for the English. The withdrawal of all English and French troops from Scotland was agreed, and the French commissioners promised that Mary Stuart would not use the royal arms of England. Mary herself refused to ratify the treaty, but this did not hinder the withdrawal of French troops.

It is important to note that credit must be given to William Cecil for the successful action resulting in the Treaty of Edinburgh. Elizabeth's part was performed with reluctance and a kind of brutal indecisiveness which drove her councillors to distraction. The Queen nearly managed to strangle the Edinburgh treaty at birth by sending last-minute instructions to Cecil in which he was told to refuse to sign unless the French agreed to hand over Calais. Fortunately, she was too late. The treaty had already been signed.

## The return of Mary Stuart

Francis II died in December 1560. Mary Stuart's position in French politics collapsed along with that of the Guises as Catherine de Medici asserted her control (see page 119). Mary therefore returned to Scotland, where her presence raised many awkward questions for England. First and foremost was marriage. English councillors were all too aware that in Mary Stuart they had on their doorstep a young widow with a rich dowry. Since Mary was the unrecognised, but legitimate, heir to Elizabeth, this made the Queen of Scots' next marriage of vital interest to the security of England. Meanwhile, Elizabeth's apparent lack of interest in marrying was a source of enormous frustration to those Protestants for whom the prospect of a Catholic heir was too much to bear. Whatever were her reasons, it must be accepted that Elizabeth's failure to marry placed her personal feelings above the interests of her kingdom. After all, her elder sister and brother had died young, and, in 1562, she in her turn nearly succumbed to an attack of smallpox.

**Key question**
How did the Darnley marriage affect English policy towards Scotland?

Mary Stuart returned to Scotland from France: 1561

Key date

Back in her kingdom, Mary Stuart at first showed an astute grasp of political realities. On arrival, she had issued a proclamation forbidding any alteration to the state of religion as she found it. This meant an acceptance of the Protestant ascendancy. Similarly, while she did insist on her right to practise her own faith, she was prepared to attend Protestant baptisms and weddings when it was politically expedient to do so. Her apparently statesmanlike behaviour and her genuine charm had secured the loyalty of important men who had no liking for her religion. One such example was William Maitland of Lethington. Secretary of State under Mary of Guise, Maitland also held the post under Mary and showed himself to be an excellent advocate for her case to be officially recognised as Elizabeth's heir.

Mary's qualities could only be viewed with disquiet by her English Protestant opponents. Clearly, if Elizabeth could not be propelled into marriage, then it was essential to her interests that Mary be persuaded to marry a candidate acceptable to England. Ideally, this would be an English Protestant nobleman. The Scots thought, until enlightened, that Elizabeth had in mind Henry Darnley, son of the Countess of Lennox. But Darnley was anything but Elizabeth's candidate, since he had Catholic sympathies and, through his mother, something of a claim of his own to the English throne (see the genealogical table on page 18). Elizabeth, extraordinarily enough, proposed her favourite, Dudley, as Mary's suitor. The Scots assumed that this idea was a mere ploy to delay any marriage, and so was not to be treated seriously. This is very possible. But it is just conceivable that Elizabeth felt a Dudley marriage to be a sound move. She may have been sufficiently arrogant to believe that she could preside over a curious three-way relationship and groom her favourite's children to take over her throne.

In fact, Mary had little intention of accepting Elizabeth's promptings. She had hoped for a match with the son of the King of Spain, but was disappointed. She therefore turned to Darnley, and benefited from a miscalculation on the part of Elizabeth and Cecil. As an English subject, Darnley needed permission from Elizabeth to visit Scotland. The government raised no objection when Darnley made his request, but, while he was in Scotland, Mary married Darnley in July 1565. The Protestant ascendancy in Scotland was shaken. Both Maitland and the Earl of Moray, the half-brother of Mary Stuart, found their positions under threat and their advice suddenly unwelcome. Moray, after an abortive rebellion, fled to England.

How dangerous was the English miscalculation? First, the Darnley marriage had been a grave blow to the ascendancy of the Protestant Scottish nobles with whom the Privy Council had established a sound working relationship. The Treaty of Edinburgh looked like so much waste paper. English Catholics would be encouraged by the prospect of co-religionists succeeding in time to the English throne. Admittedly, there was little immediate threat to Elizabeth. Whatever Mary Stuart might boast in unguarded moments, the Scots were too disunited and poor to constitute a military danger. But this was little real consolation to men such as Cecil whose antipathy to Mary Stuart and her religion led them to see the Darnley marriage as part of the alleged international Catholic plot against Europe's foremost Protestant power. There was, however, nothing much they could do about it. The Queen would not sanction an attempt to depose Mary Stuart. It is therefore hard to avoid the conclusion that the early successes of English foreign policy in Scotland counted for little. Force of circumstance, some miscalculation and her antipathy towards marriage had left Elizabeth looking extremely vulnerable in the longer term. As the years went by, how was the Virgin Queen to keep the loyalty of nobles who could see that the future lay with the children of the Stuart and Lennox line? For, by January 1566, Mary was expecting a child.

## Mary Stuart and the murder of Darnley

Mary Stuart's strong position in her relationship with Elizabeth was demolished by the unhappiness of her marriage to Darnley and the extraordinary and torrid series of events that resulted from it. In March 1566, Darnley and some of his friends dragged Mary's Italian secretary, David Riccio, from her presence and murdered him. Darnley's motive was jealousy and his action an **indictment**, not only of himself, but also of the Queen's indiscreet conduct. There were no dramatic repercussions immediately. Perhaps profiting from the antagonism between Darnley and Mary, Moray returned to Scotland and was reconciled with his half-sister. Meanwhile, Mary's envoy, Sir James Melville, travelled to England in the hope that Elizabeth might be persuaded into a formal acceptance of Mary and her newborn son, James, as her successors. This he was unable to achieve, but it seems clear that a number of very influential nobles were keen to reveal themselves privately to be in favour of his suit. These included Norfolk, the most powerful nobleman in the country, and, oddly enough, Leicester himself. The latter's motives may well have been an understandable desire to safeguard himself once his status as favourite was no longer any protection.

Then, in February 1567, came the murder of Darnley. Mary's complicity was apparently all too clear when she married the Earl of Bothwell, the very man suspected of being responsible for her husband's death. Mary's exact state of mind at this time can only be guessed at. The fact that she was prepared to marry Bothwell according to Protestant rites is significant: for whatever reason, emotion had overpowered her shrewd political sense. The ensuing turmoil gave an opportunity for Moray to lead a Protestant faction which seized the Queen, forced her to abdicate and crowned her child as James VI.

Elizabeth was, unsurprisingly, aghast at the deposition, and sent an envoy to demand the release and restoration of the former Queen of Scots. Indeed, Elizabeth was in a state bordering on frenzy. It does not seem to have occurred to her that an unhoped-for opportunity existed to rebuild a pro-English regime in Scotland. What mattered to her was not political **expediency**, but

**Key question**
Why did Elizabeth not seek to gain advantage from the abdication of Mary in 1568?

**Key terms**

**Indictment**
Accusation of guilt.

**Expediency**
Convenience.

**Key dates**

Murder of Ricco: 1566

Birth of James, son of Mary Stuart: 1566

Mary Stuart was forced to renounce throne in favour of infant James: 1567

Mary Stuart fled to England: 1568

the political principle nearest to her heart: the inalienable rights of the legitimate ruler. Even when Mary fled to England in the summer of 1568, Elizabeth persisted in considering how she could restore her. However, her councillors persuaded her to postpone any action, suggesting that Mary might be subject to some kind of judicial investigation into her role in the death of Darnley. This would at least give the government some breathing space in which to decide what to do with her.

## Mary in England

**Key question**
Why was Mary's presence in England so problematic for the English government?

Mary in England posed particular problems: even in her place of custody in remote Staffordshire. Her behaviour in Scotland had not affected her claim to the succession to the throne of England, and her actual presence in England might well loosen the allegiance of Catholics to Elizabeth. It was also conceivable that she would be the centre of plots to assassinate Elizabeth. After all, assassination on religious grounds was not uncommon in contemporary Europe. In addition, even Mary's implacable opponent Cecil was aware that she had considerable political skill and personal magnetism. These qualities and the passing of time would efface the charges that had been laid against her by Moray in front of the Privy Council. Certainly Mary could not be allowed the freedom, at the English court or elsewhere, to build up a faction to support her claims.

It seemed, however, that Mary did not need personal liberty to attract support. By the spring of 1569, it would appear that some people of great influence were prepared to recognise Mary's position as Elizabeth's heir, providing she were safely married to a suitable Englishman. The Duke of Norfolk, the premier nobleman of England, was the most obvious candidate. However, he was not unsympathetic to Catholicism. It is a sign of the dangers posed by Elizabeth's continued avoidance of marriage that a group in support of the Norfolk marriage included Leicester. Were the marriage to take place, then the way might then be open for the restoration of Mary to her Scottish throne.

It was only a question of time before Elizabeth heard of the scheme. Leicester tearfully confessed and retired to the comparative safety of his sick-bed. Norfolk was summoned to court and informed in no uncertain terms that he was to give up any such plans. However, the situation was more volatile than Elizabeth realised. Norfolk was faced with Mary's demands that he should release her by force if necessary. At the same time he was under pressure from certain northern earls to mobilise his supporters to free Mary, go through with the marriage and place pressure on Elizabeth to recognise Mary as her successor. It is clear that some sort of rising in the north had been planned. The northern earls Northumberland and Westmorland were Catholic themselves and had estates in the counties of the north least affected by Protestantism. But once Norfolk, after some agonised consultation with his own followers, had submitted to Elizabeth and was lodged in the Tower of London, Northumberland and Westmorland found themselves out on a limb. They were themselves summoned to the royal presence, but were too compromised by their discussion of the succession and contacts with the Pope and Spain to risk their fates at court. They were therefore pushed into open rebellion.

## The Revolt of the Northern Earls and the Ridolfi plot

The course and failure of the rebellion are discussed on pages 93–5. The Duke of Norfolk had survived despite his links with the rebels, but had learned little from his narrow escape. He would not give up the prospect of marriage with Mary: a testimony to the influence of her presence on Catholic sympathisers. Mary, quite naturally, was more than ready to pursue any channel which would free her from her irksome captivity. She became embroiled in the schemings of one Roberto di Ridolfi, an Italian merchant with connections in many European courts. Ridolfi had a plan for seeking military assistance for Mary from the Spanish commander in the Netherlands, the Duke of Alva. Norfolk was persuaded by Ridolfi to agree to a request for such assistance. Were that to be forthcoming, Norfolk was to raise his own followers. The plot was discovered, and Norfolk's role exposed. At his trial in January 1572, his defence largely consisted of the argument that he was a duke, and therefore that his word counted for far more than anyone else's. This was not well received. Norfolk was duly executed in June 1572.

Mary Stuart was herself in some danger. Cecil, now Lord Burghley, was instrumental in leading the Privy Council to put pressure on the Queen to have Mary executed. The Parliament of 1572 was probably called due to unremitting pressure from the Privy Councillors, who hoped that acts would be passed to attaint the Queen of Scots and to exclude her from the succession. Elizabeth fought these proposals with her customary skill. She refused to have anything to do with the **Attainder** Act, and diverted Parliament's attention to the **Exclusion Act**, which she then shelved.

The massacre of the French Protestants on St Bartholomew's Day (August 1572) simply confirmed the views of those who, like Burghley, assumed the existence of a murderous Catholic conspiracy: a conspiracy represented in England, of course, by Mary Stuart. Elizabeth remained, as ever, unmoved by the renewed pleas to put Mary to death. It may be that she had now discarded any real intention of restoring Mary to her Scottish throne, but the gulf between Elizabeth's attitude to Mary and that of her Privy Council was nevertheless distressingly wide. This meant that genuine discussion and calm planning on this issue became impossible. The councillors therefore had to find other ways to influence the Queen: and the best method was to frighten her with details of immediate and personal threats to herself and her throne.

**Key dates**

Norfolk marriage plot: 1569

Ridolfi plot discovered: 1571

**Key terms**

**Attainder**
An Act of Attainder was a method of securing conviction of an alleged traitor without trial (and seizing his or her lands for the crown).

**Exclusion Act**
When passed by Parliament and agreed by the monarch, this would, in law at least, prevent a claimant from succeeding to the throne.

**Key question**
What factors led to the death of Mary, Queen of Scots?

## The downfall of Mary Stuart

The political climate of the 1580s provided just the opportunity the Privy Council needed to persuade Elizabeth to take action over Mary:

- In 1580, a papal pronouncement stated that anyone who assassinated Elizabeth with the 'pious intention of doing God service not only does not sin, but gains merit'.
- In 1584, the murder of William of Orange provided apparent evidence that all Protestant monarchs were in danger from Catholic terrorism.
- The same year saw the exposure of the Throckmorton plot in England, in which the Duke of Guise was to lead an invasion aimed at releasing Mary Stuart and deposing Elizabeth. Burghley and Walsingham were sufficiently alarmed to draw up the Bond of Association (October 1584), by which signatories pledged to defend Elizabeth by force and, in effect, to murder anyone implicated in plots against the monarch. The bond was never invoked as such, but the highly charged atmosphere, in which fear of Jesuit missionaries coincided with fear of Spanish invasion, had its effect on Elizabeth herself. She was frightened, and a frightened Elizabeth was an insecure safeguard for Mary Stuart.

Concern over the threat of Spain led Elizabeth and her councillors to act together in seeking a defensive league with James VI against Spain. James, after all, had little to gain from a Spanish invasion of England. Only his mother stood between him and the succession to the throne of England after Elizabeth's death. He did, however, stand to gain a useful pension if he accepted such a league. In 1585, the league was formalised and James received an annual pension of about £4000. Informally, this meant that he was accepting his mother's continued imprisonment. The policy of keeping James reasonably happy with the pension and subsidies was sensible, although few councillors trusted him. What was even more attractive to the young King than money was a letter written by Elizabeth which promised that nothing should be done to harm his title to the English crown.

For Mary, a Spanish invasion was her last hope of freedom and, just possibly, of the prize that had never been close enough for her to grasp: the throne of England. In May 1586, she formally disinherited her son in favour of the King of Spain in the hope that this would stimulate Spanish efforts on her behalf. In this way, the seeds for her eventual execution were sown, as she could not resist dabbling in further plots against Elizabeth.

In 1586, Anthony Babington, a fervent Catholic and supporter of Jesuit missions, was in contact by letter with Mary. His offer was straightforward enough: to release Mary and subsequently murder Elizabeth. Mary appears to have dictated a letter in reply which endorsed the plan, with the suggestion that Elizabeth should be murdered before, rather than after, Mary's release. But matters of timing were all irrelevant, because the whole

**Key date**
Babington plot discovered: 1586

correspondence was being read with much satisfaction by Walsingham himself. Babington was arrested, and readily confessed his part in the whole scheme.

But what was to happen to Mary herself? A committee of nobles, Privy Councillors and justices meeting at Mary's new place of custody, Fotheringay Castle, found her guilty of plotting to assassinate Elizabeth. Elizabeth refused to have the sentence published, and the Privy Council persuaded her to summon Parliament in the hope that she could be forced by sheer weight of opinion to sign a death warrant. Parliament duly petitioned for Mary's execution. Even so, the Queen would not commit herself. Her chronic indecision was fed by her simple revulsion at condemning to death a fellow monarch and a fear of the likely reactions of neighbouring states, particularly, of course, the King of Scotland. It is a mark of Elizabeth's desperation that she should, against advice, sound out Mary's Puritan gaoler, Sir Amyas Paulet, on the possibility of his disposing of Mary without implicating the Queen. Not unreasonably, Paulet refused. His letter to the Queen took the high moral ground. His life was, he said, in Elizabeth's hands:

> … but God forbid that I should make so foul a shipwreck of my conscience or leave so great a blot to my poor posterity to shed blood without law or warrant.

The warrant, indeed, was all ready for signature: but how was the Queen to be persuaded to sign it? Once again, the Privy Council tried to force Elizabeth to act by playing on her fears for her own safety. She was fed fictitious stories about Spanish landings in Wales and Mary's escape. Pen and ink were sent for, and she signed the warrant, but instructed her second secretary, Davison, not to have it sealed and dispatched. Davison, however, sealed it and dashed off to consult his fellow councillors. The decision was taken to dispatch the warrant and not to tell the Queen until the execution was over. Mary was beheaded on 8 February 1587, and the Queen turned, with all appearance of genuine fury, on Davison. He found himself heavily fined and a prisoner in the Tower of London. Burghley was denied access to the Queen for a month.

Execution of Mary Stuart: 1587

Key date

In the meantime, Elizabeth wrote letters to James VI in which she proclaimed her innocence. James was only too pleased to receive such protestations. They enabled him to avoid a military conflict with a country whose crown he was now closer to gaining than ever before.

## Mary, Queen of Scots: a summary

It could be argued that, following Mary's execution, the central aims of English policy towards Scotland had been achieved. Mary's death was the ultimate way to neutralise her influence. The Scottish King was reasonably friendly towards a kingdom he fully expected to inherit, and the possibility of the French or Spanish using Scotland as a weapon against England was non-existent.

Key question
How effectively did the English government handle the challenge of Mary Stuart's presence in England?

A contemporary Dutch sketch of the execution of Mary, Queen of Scots. Why was the execution not held in public?

On the other hand, it is hard to escape the conclusion that good fortune played a significant role in an eminently satisfactory outcome. Indeed, if attention is turned to the actions of the English government, we see frequent turmoil, miscalculation and delay: all fuelled by Elizabeth's parsimony, prejudice and indecisiveness and by disagreements with councillors on priorities. Even so, Elizabeth's reluctance to act against a fellow sovereign prevented the development of a politically dangerous martyr's cult around Mary which conceivably would have compromised the loyalty many Catholics felt towards Elizabeth herself.

It is impossible to assess the extent to which Elizabeth was in actual danger of assassination because of Mary's presence and willingness to engage in plots. But it is fair to say that the danger would have been less if Mary were not so near at hand and so convenient a rallying-point and incentive for Catholic extremists. Of course, had Elizabeth married and borne children, then the danger of Mary Stuart would have been largely neutralised. Only a few Catholic die-hards would have remembered a one-time Scottish queen residing in comfortable prisons in the English Midlands. Those prepared to murder Elizabeth might have baulked at the thought of murdering a royal family.

Speculation apart, how effectively was Mary Stuart handled as Elizabeth's prisoner? Certainly, the Privy Council responded efficiently to the need to keep her secure. There was little or no prospect of even her most enthusiastic and imaginative rescuers freeing her. The surveillance system established by Walsingham produced the evidence needed to convict her.

As for Elizabeth herself, her refusal to be pressured by her Privy Council and Parliament into executing Mary, particularly after the Ridolfi plot, made sound political sense. The effect of an execution at that time on the fraught relations with Spain and France could hardly have been positive. On the other hand, Elizabeth's refusal probably owed more to her beliefs in the inviolability of the monarch's position than to political acumen. In the event, the manner of Mary's execution gave James VI the opportunity to avoid a military confrontation with England, but again, this owed more to the fortunate combination of Elizabeth's dithering and a convenient scapegoat than it did to political expertise.

## The final years: relations with James VI

Elizabeth's failure to marry has been seen as a symptom of her lack of interest in the fate of her country after her death. This monumental egotism also informed her relationship with her most likely successor, the King of Scotland. James was never officially promised the succession, and it is unlikely that Elizabeth named him on her deathbed. James succeeded because he was the only realistic candidate, and was supported at the centre of English government by men such as Burghley's son, Robert Cecil. When Elizabeth died on 24 March 1603, they were in the position to issue a proclamation announcing James's accession. It was a curious end to the Tudors' relationship with Scotland. Henry VIII had wanted to assimilate Scotland into England: his second daughter had shown no such interest. The line of the Tudor monarchs died out as the King of Scotland took the English throne.

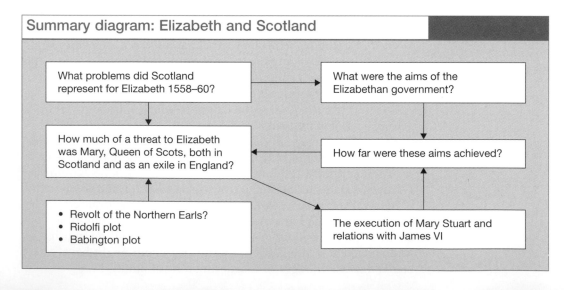

Summary diagram: Elizabeth and Scotland

What problems did Scotland represent for Elizabeth 1558–60?

What were the aims of the Elizabethan government?

How much of a threat to Elizabeth was Mary, Queen of Scots, both in Scotland and as an exile in England?

How far were these aims achieved?

- Revolt of the Northern Earls?
- Ridolfi plot
- Babington plot

The execution of Mary Stuart and relations with James VI

## Study Guide: AS Questions

### In the style of OCR A

How successfully did Elizabeth deal with the problems presented by Mary, Queen of Scots?                                        (50 marks)

---

*Exam tips*

Mary, Queen of Scots gave Elizabeth many problems. The main ones were:

- Constitutional: Mary was a rival claimant to the English throne and a target for conspiracies and plotters.
- Political: when Mary sought protection in England, Elizabeth's Privy Council and Parliament were divided about how best to deal with her.
- Religious: Mary's devout Roman Catholicism gave hope to English Catholics and created anxiety among Protestants.
- Foreign: England's relations with Spain, France, Scotland and the Papacy were all adversely affected by Mary's presence in England.

'How successfully' requires an assessment of whether or not Elizabeth tackled these problems effectively. Were her methods appropriate and more sensible than those who criticised them? A judgement needs to be reached on which problems were overcome, which took longer to resolve and which (if any) proved insoluble. The highest marks are likely to be awarded to essays that give a comparison of the problems and the effectiveness of the solutions.

## In the style of OCR B

Answer **both** parts of your chosen question.

(a) How far was Mary, Queen of Scots' claim to the English throne the most significant problem she created for Elizabeth? (25 marks)

(b) Why was Mary, Queen of Scots executed in 1587? (25 marks)

---

*Exam tips*

(a) The question implies there were a number of reasons why Mary posed a problem and that you should consider their relative importance. Remember that Mary was not the official heir, but the French backed her claim to England. The 'Auld Alliance' between France and Scotland had been threatening to Elizabeth since she succeeded to the throne. You will also need to consider developments in Scotland under Mary as well as the threat she posed when in England. Make sure you include a balance of different kinds of factors in your answer.

You might argue that Mary's claim to the throne was what led to the various plots in her name and that their number as well as the range of foreign involvement meant that they were very serious. However, you might evaluate this argument by explaining that none of the plots came near to success and that they were known about by the English government.

You might, for example, argue that after Mary's marriage to Darnley it was clear that England had little influence in Scotland and the danger posed by a Franco-Scottish alliance was very great. You might evaluate this argument by pointing out that this problem was relatively short-lived, as Darnley's murder led to Mary's deposition and the seizure of power by the Protestant faction. This could be compared with the long-term problem posed by Mary's presence in England from 1568.

What you should do:

- Be clear about what 'problem' means in this context.
- Make sure that you give sufficient consideration to the problem raised in the question.
- Identify a range of other problems and weigh up their relative importance.

What you should avoid:

- A narrative of the life of Mary, Queen of Scots.
- A digression into the issue of the succession, Mary's claim and the issue of Elizabeth's marriage.

(b) There are two ways of looking at this question: you could ask why Mary was executed at all, or you could ask why the execution took place in 1587 (and not earlier). There is no expected approach, but your answer might be different according to where your emphasis lies. Remember that there are various issues to consider, including the role of the Privy Council and Parliament as well as the danger that Mary posed to

Elizabeth. A comparative analysis might be useful in evaluating your conclusion: you could ask why Mary was not executed earlier.

You might, for example, argue that the repeated plots involving Mary undermined Elizabeth's determination not to execute Mary, while the Bond of Association meant that after the Babington plot it was more difficult to avoid trying Mary for treason.

You might, for example, argue that in the early years of Mary's residence in England she posed less threat, but in the more dangerous international situation of the 1580s it was increasingly difficult to keep Mary from plotting with England's enemies and since the Scots did not want her back there was little alternative but to execute her.

What you should do:

- Plan your answer to make sure that you are clear exactly what you intend to explain.
- Identify a range of causes and decide how they link together: is there a chain or a web of causes that you could analyse?
- Decide what you will argue about the relative importance of the different causes before you start so that your argument runs throughout the essay.

What you should avoid:

- A detailed description of the course of the plots involving Mary.
- A narrative account of the means by which the Council persuaded Elizabeth to sign Mary's death warrant and Elizabeth's reaction at hearing of Mary's death.

## Study Guide: A2 Question

### In the style of AQA

'The execution of Mary, Queen of Scots in 1587 was a gross miscalculation.' Assess the validity of this view.　　　　(45 marks)

---

*Exam tips*

This question requires an examination of the consequences of the execution of Mary, Queen of Scots and also a consideration of whether the advantages of the execution outweighed the disadvantages. Justification for the execution can be considered with reference to:

- Anglo-Scottish relations
- Elizabethan religious policy
- the Rebellion of the Northern Earls and Elizabeth's excommunication
- concerns about Spain and security
- the Ridolfi plot
- the Throckmorton plot
- the Babington plot.

It can certainly be argued that the longer Mary lived, the more plagued Elizabeth's religious settlement would be and the more insecure the Queen herself on the throne. However, the consequences of the execution (for which you may need to refer back to earlier chapters) include:

- helping to forge an alliance between the French Catholic League and Philip II of Spain
- the Spanish Armada
- the undermining of the moderate Elizabethan religious settlement.

Finally, you may wish to question whether the advantages outweighed the disadvantages, with reference to:

- easing the succession
- the breakdown of relations with Spain as something already well underway
- greater internal security.

# 7

# Meeting the Challenge of Government 1558–88

**POINTS TO CONSIDER**

This chapter will focus on the first three decades of Elizabethan government and will discuss the following issues:

- The role of nobility, court, Privy Council and ministers
- The role of Parliament
- The financial policies of the crown: sources of crown income, overseas trade, the problem of inflation

Chapter 8 discusses the final 15 years of the reign, where challenges to good governance intensified just at the time when the government appeared to be growing old and stale.

**Key dates**

| | |
|---|---|
| 1558 | Government heavily in debt |
| 1560–1 | Recoinage completed |
| 1563 | Statute of Artificers removed a national wage limit |
| 1568 | Peers summoned to discuss the case of Mary Stuart |
| 1571 | Sir William Cecil ennobled as Lord Burghley |
| 1572 | Trial of Norfolk before his peers |
| | Burghley made Lord Treasurer |
| 1585 | System of Lords Lieutenant responsible for county administration made permanent |
| 1586 | Parliament petitioned for the execution of Mary Stuart |
| 1587 | Sir Christopher Hatton made Lord Chancellor |

## 1 | The Role of Nobility, Court, Privy Council and Ministers

### The relations between crown and nobility under the early Tudors

Historians used to hold that great feudal magnates, by virtue of their heredity and landed wealth, powers of patronage and ability to raise forces of armed men, represented an 'overmighty nobility', ready and willing wherever possible to subvert the power of the monarch. These disobliging nobles were supposedly subjected to the cool and calculating attentions of Henry VII. The first of the Tudors so entwined them in a legal and financial web that they were transformed from near-independent princes surrounded by subservient local gentry into men whose status was dependent, less on the extent of their lands, and more on their roles at court as defined by the King. Similarly, the traditional loyalty of the gentry towards the regional magnate was subverted by their frequent employment as agents of the crown.

Christine Carpenter has more recently stressed the dangers run by Henry VII in what she saw as a needless and fundamentally un-English attempt to dominate, rather than enlist the traditional co-operation of the nobility.

Arguably, Henry VIII had far more fellow-feeling for the nobility, but was nevertheless able and willing where necessary to crush even so powerful a noble house as the Howards: at the end of Henry's reign, the Duke of Norfolk was brought to the Tower and his son, the Earl of Surrey, to the block.

## Elizabeth's attitude towards the nobility

In this as in so much else Elizabeth followed her father. Fellow feeling for her 'Good cousins', as she was wont to address her highest nobility in letters, led her to empathise with their sense of dignity. On one level, she remonstrated with Sir Philip Sidney for daring to dispute with an earl on a tennis court; on another, and mindful of his disgrace and rank, she hesitated over the execution of Norfolk and twice cancelled the execution order.

Members of the ancient nobility were her natural counsellors and were consulted as of right when a momentous occasion demanded: the trial of Norfolk in 1572 took place before virtually a full complement of earls; and even Northumberland and Westmorland, although not members of the inner circle of advisers that was the Privy Council, were summoned in 1568 (the year before their rebellion) to discuss the case of Mary, Queen of Scots.

Elizabeth's respect for noble **lineage** did not make her politically naïve or unreasonably trusting. After all, as we have seen, religion was a new and dangerous guest at the feasting of queen and nobility; religion might whisper treason in the ears of those who felt excluded from a Protestant regime and were bitter at receiving only crumbs from the table.

The Revolt of the Northern Earls (see pages 93–5) should therefore be seen as a potent mix of religion and personal grievance on the part of Northumberland and Westmorland. The Queen and Cecil had ensured that the government of the northern marches was not entrusted to them. The Council of the North itself was headed by the Earl of Sussex, and Northumberland had been pointedly excluded from it. It could be argued, as Haigh does, that Elizabeth's policy of excluding, rather than gratifying, such men as Northumberland and Westmorland was itself dangerous. MacCaffrey, on the other hand, sees the two as 'political dinosaurs' who blundered into a doomed rebellion.

**Key question**
What was the relationship between the royal court and the nobility?

**Key dates**

Peers summoned to discuss the case of Mary Stuart: 1568

Trial of Norfolk before his peers: 1572

**Key term**

**Lineage**
Belonging to a well-established noble family.

The Northumberland and Westmorland episode should be seen as atypical of a regime which generally saw the ancient nobility as a vital part of itself. Cecil himself might have lacked the prestige bestowed by lineage, but, as **Master of Wards**, he sought to defend the coming noble generation and see them educated to take their rightful place at the heart of the commonwealth. And, on a personal level, the Queen enjoyed flattery, and wanted it from those whose words mattered to her: in short, her nobility.

## Politicising the court

Since Elizabeth had arguably sacrificed married love and marriage itself for the exercise of power, it was the court that was to provide her with the most enjoyable arena in which to display it. This is why, in Haigh's terms, she politicised her court and made politics courtly: alternatively, one might argue that she personalised politics in the traditional manner of the monarch, but was particularly good at it. The two-way nature of Elizabeth's court is reflected in the way in which courtiers were made political figures and political heavyweights were obliged to become courtiers, since it was in the network of personal relationships revolving around the Queen that power lay: hence the oft-quoted comment of Sir Christopher Hatton, who combined the polished skills of the courtier with a shrewd grasp of the political realities as Lord Chancellor: 'The Queen did fish for men's souls, and had so sweet a bait that no-one could escape her network.'

One key bait was royal patronage:

- Henry VII had arguably succeeded in making place at court the mark of status, and a share in royal patronage, together with influence over its distribution, was the means by which Tudor nobility confirmed their rank and retained the support of the gentry in their localities.
- There were offices in the two component parts of the Court proper: namely, Chamber and Household, whose members would include principal secretaries of state, clerks of the council, the signet and privy seal, grooms of the chamber, yeomen of the guard, keeper of the privy purse and (by way of contrast) the Queen's mole-catcher.
- Also available were wardships, military posts, ambassadorships, **clerical preferment**, licences to import and export; and the established or on-the-rise courtier could expect many a petition for such patronage and many accompanying offers of loyalty. Such loyalty was, indeed, often worth having, given that a noble would wish to see his own candidates elected to Parliament and his own voice dominating his own shires.
- Very, very occasionally, it might be possible for the greatest courtiers to wield some crown patronage on their own (as did Burghley through his role as Master of Wards).

**Key question**
Why was presence at court so important for the nobility?

**Key date**

Sir Christopher Hatton made Lord Chancellor: 1587

**Key terms**

**Master of Wards**
Responsible, through the Court of Wards and Liveries, for the guardianship of the crown's wards.

**Clerical preferment**
Promotion for members of the clergy.

## The intimacy of court life

There is little doubt that the Queen had succeeded in making herself the fount of power and that, almost always, she defined the nature of the relationship between herself and her male courtiers. Patronage, and therefore political influence, was part-and-parcel of a bewildering network of relationships which were at times intimate, relaxed, playful and feminine and at other times, and even simultaneously, formal, ritualistic and saturated with the authority of a monarch. The intimacy extended itself to nicknames bestowed on chief courtiers: Leicester was 'Eyes', Hatton was 'Lids', and Burghley was 'Sir Spirit'. But the intimacy was on Elizabeth's terms and could be withdrawn in an instant. Sir Walter Raleigh (nicknamed 'Water' and, as captain of the guard, a man with frequent access to the Queen) found himself in the Tower of London once Elizabeth heard of his secret marriage to one of her Maids of Honour, Elizabeth Throckmorton, who was expecting his child.

## Patriarchy and the Queen's court

The Raleigh incident demonstrates the highly charged atmosphere of the Queen's court. Its standards, expressed through imagery of the Virgin Queen, were partly the workings of Elizabeth's psyche and partly the attempts made by male courtiers to come to terms with what was, in a **patriarchal** society, enormously difficult to swallow: rule by a woman. It was more palatable if Elizabeth could be presented as unique and not a trendsetter for future female rulers. Elizabeth was presented variously as Deborah, the Protectrix of the Protestant Church of England, and as **Gloriana**, the triumphant monarch of an age of peace and plenty: courtiers were prolific with classical and courtly love allusion to the untouchable, but worthy-to-be-touched mistress. Towards the end of her reign, and with an uncertain future beckoning, the allusions became somewhat more hysterical and even appropriated Catholic imagery of the Virgin Mary. In Helen Hackett's words:

> In later years, increasingly hyperbolic and fantastic representations of Elizabeth, including assertions of her immortality, and use of overtly Marian typology, coexisted with expressions of disillusionment and criticism.

## Patronage and Essex

We should note Hackett's comments about disillusionment. As the Queen grew older it seems that her political circle narrowed (see Chapter 8). Arguably, as her reign stumbled into caricature, Elizabeth lost none of her taste for the flattering words of attractive men, but was less ready to take the trouble to control the combination of positive personal relationship and political status which had marked the rise of, say, Leicester and Hatton. Instead, she was prepared to accept the adulation of Leicester's stepson, the Earl of Essex, and to smile at some of his hot-headed behaviour, but she did not permit him to dominate or manipulate

**Key terms**

**Patriarchal**
Male-dominated.

**Gloriana**
The title given to the Faerie Queene in Edmund Spenser's poem of the same name; Gloriana represented Elizabeth.

her patronage. She frequently refused his requests, and such refusals were a humiliation, as his own followers shared in his failures. The Essex rising was the result (see page 192).

## The functioning of the Elizabethan Privy Council

The Privy Council itself was the product of a deliberate reduction in the size of late medieval King's Council, since it had been felt that a more streamlined body would be more efficient and less prone to factional infighting.

The functions of the Privy Council mirrored those of the King's Council:

- to advise the monarch
- to adjudicate in disputes which affected the good order of the realm
- to administer the government of the kingdom in all its forms.

The Privy Council therefore dealt with military matters, enforced religious conformity, applied social and economic policies and directed local government (such as it was).

As the King's Council became the Privy Council and numbers of councillors got smaller, then it inevitably lost a sense of being a

**Key question**
What evidence is there that a narrowing of the Privy Council led to political instability?

A contemporary drawing of the Queen with Burghley and Walsingham. How might this drawing be used to illustrate the workings of the Elizabethan Privy Council?

sounding-board for the opinions of the political élite as a whole. This is why, as we have seen, a wider circle of nobles and/or Parliament might be consulted in time of crisis. The transformation of the King's Council began under the Yorkist kings and accelerated under Henry VII and Henry VIII, but it is S.J. Gunn's view that it was in Elizabeth's reign, and under the influence of William Cecil, that the Privy Council became the 'heart of the Tudor regime'.

It has been argued, notably by Christopher Haigh, that the narrowing of the political élite was particularly evident in the Elizabethan Privy Council and that, by gradually excluding traditional magnates, Elizabeth's Privy Council stimulated political instability.

Of course, such magnates would not expect to be part of the hub of the Privy Council dealing with daily administration, since it demanded regular weekly attendance: typically, its members would be the Lord Treasurer, Lord Chamberlain, Lord Admiral, Comptroller of the Household, the Secretary and the Treasurer, together with whoever had the Queen's deep personal regard: Leicester, and then Essex. Magnate members could be called on to attend when a particularly important issue surfaced, and so could feel that their position was recognised and advice valued.

However, as the reign progressed, or, to put it another way, as the Queen grew older, the composition of the Privy Council did indeed change: and, crucially, the great provincial magnates were replaced by those in whom Elizabeth placed a particular trust: relations, intimates, familiar faces. It therefore became a narrow and certainly less representative body. Haigh tellingly cites numbers of magnates:

- in 1570, there were 19 privy councillors, with six magnates
- by 1586, there were still 19 members, but only two traditional magnates
- by 1597, there were no traditional magnates in a Privy Council that had shrunk to 11 members.

However, it is easy to overstate the actual impact of these very real changes. Were the Queen to become the puppet of a tiny, Privy Council-based faction, then the narrowing of the administrative élite would be dangerous indeed. It is true that her reign was characterised by an inner ring of key councillors: in the 1560s, Leicester and Cecil, supplemented at various times by Parry, Bacon, Winchester and Pembroke; in the 1570s to the 1580s Leicester and Cecil (ennobled as Lord Burghley in 1571), Walsingham, Hatton and Sussex (who died in 1583). But there is no evidence to suggest that even the most adept councillor of the inner circle felt confident that he could manipulate the Queen. Elizabeth, in fact, preferred to discuss matters of state with the inner circle on a one-to-one basis, and was quite capable of playing off one against the other in the interests of her freedom of manoeuvre. And so, the narrowing of the Privy Council did not lead to a sapping of the Queen's will or ability to rule.

**Key date**

Sir William Cecil ennobled as Lord Burghley: 1571

**Key question**
To what extent did factionalism damage the Privy Council itself as a vital agent of government?

# Factionalism in the Privy Council

John Guy sees the real disagreements and divisions within the Privy Council as symptomatic of personal rivalries rather than rampant factionalism based on ideological or religious hatreds. This is certainly true from the 1570s onwards where, as Simon Adams puts it, both council and court 'displayed a political homogeneity [togetherness] previously unknown'. The fall of Norfolk in 1572 had removed the last traces of ideological, pro-Catholic opposition in the Privy Council. So, we can perhaps argue that the Elizabethan Privy Council from the 1570s agreed on the fundamentals of policy:

- the need for the Queen to marry
- the need to settle the succession
- the need to uphold and defend Protestantism.

There remained, of course, flashpoints where those personal rivalries coalesced with differences on how policies were to be put into effect. Examples included:

- the dispute over the choice of suitor (Leicester's own suit, or the Anjou marriage)
- Leicester's underhand support of Mary, Queen of Scots' claim to the succession
- the Leicester/Walsingham pressure for an anti-Spanish military intervention in the Netherlands.

But the Queen could and did knock heads together, rage and storm, flatter and cajole, and dismiss from court. In this manner, she prevented personal rivalries from becoming politically destabilising or the breeding-ground for faction. It is perhaps only in the final years of the reign (see Chapter 8) when an ageing Queen allowed an increasing dominance of Council and Court by Sir Robert Cecil that faction reared up in the spectacular and doomed form of the attempted coup by Essex.

In the end, one needs to integrate the debate over factionalism in the Privy Council and court into our picture of the nature of the Queen's rule. We have noted the effective way in which she upheld her own authority. After all, the Queen's foreign policy revealed a monarch who was the past mistress of procrastination (which is, after all, hesitation converted into a political art-form). Her procrastination was a weapon against a Council which at times used every means at its disposal to force the Queen into policies whose wisdom she doubted, whose expense she deplored and whose religious world-view she suspected.

This interpretation therefore posits neither a Privy Council that was riven by faction nor one which successfully dominated the Queen. Even so, there are instances where the Queen was unable to fend off the weight of Council pressure. For instance, Privy Council opposition to the Alençon match was probably the deciding factor in its ultimate rejection (see pages 122–3). But these are exceptions that proved the nature of Elizabeth's rule: her undoubted charisma, her glamour, her tactics and her anger all gave her an advantage which could be overcome, but only rarely and by dint of great effort. Leicester and Hatton resorted to persuading the ladies of the Chamber to shed salt tears in the Queen's presence over the Alençon match. But such manipulation carried its dangers, as the Queen was not easy to deceive. Walsingham's slipper in the face (see page 199) was occasioned by the Queen's discovery that he had deliberately kept her uninformed of the strength and threat of the Spanish fleet to encourage her to pour money into Leicester's Netherlands campaign.

## 2 | The Role of Parliament

The role played by Parliament in the extraordinary religious and constitutional changes in the reigns of the earlier Tudors should immediately be recognised. By Elizabeth's reign it was the monarch's necessary partner in the law-making process: the sovereign legislature was therefore King (or Queen) in Parliament, and the statute law so passed was supreme. But if Parliament was a partner in the process, it was very much a junior one.

### The 'Whig' interpretation of the role of Parliament

So-called 'Whig' historians (see page 4) have argued that the Elizabethan House of Commons was not content with a junior role in any shape or form. The 'Whig' argument has the following features:

**Key question**
What is the 'Whig' interpretation of the Elizabethan Parliament?

- MPs came to insist on rights of free speech in Parliament.
- In particular, MPs refused to allow the Queen to dictate religious policy as part of her prerogative and role as Supreme Governor of the Church of England.
- The House of Commons began to dominate its partner in Parliament, the House of Lords.
- In this way, MPs sowed the seeds which germinated in the struggle between King and Parliament for sovereignty in the English Civil War (1646–52).

### An evaluation of the 'Whig' interpretation of the role of Parliament

First, in the 45 years of Elizabeth's reign, Parliament was summoned only 13 times and in 26 of those years there were no sessions at all. Parliament was, as ever, summoned and dissolved at the will of the monarch, whose motive was generally financial: Parliament was expected to make a grant of taxation following an explanation from a government speaker of why, regretfully, it was necessary in the interests of the commonwealth to make such an appeal. Given that sessions lasted a few months at the most, and were taken up with business which was largely dictated by the Queen and Privy Council, it is difficult to envisage the House of Commons demanding rights of free speech on all matters.

**Key question**
What are the fundamental weaknesses of the 'Whig' interpretation of the role of Parliament?

In fact, and unlike her Tudor predecessors, Elizabeth actually intervened twice (in 1571 and 1593) to prevent discussion of foreign affairs on the grounds that, in order to respect the crown's prerogative, Parliament could not discuss any matters of state (including issues of marriage and succession) without her express permission. MPs were to content themselves with freedom of speech on matters of '**commonweal**', i.e. the social and economic good of the community, and on the many private bills placed before Parliament. There were those who actively resented this and, indeed, any limitation on the right to speak, but they were, in Michael Graves' words, 'standard-bearers without an army'. The Wentworth brothers, Peter and Paul, went so far as to demand the right to speak freely on any subject whatsoever, whether it was business before Parliament or not. Peter's outbursts resulted in his imprisonment on two occasions: once, by Parliament itself after he criticised the Queen, and once on the Queen's instructions for his stubborn insistence on the liberties of the Commons. Peter Wentworth was, in short, a nuisance, and his **fulminations** simply disrupted parliamentary business: few MPs wept for him.

Second, the monarch's power extended to the right to **veto** bills. We noted (see page 67) that the Queen vetoed a Communion Bill in the 1571 Parliament that sought to impose harsher penalties on Catholics, even though the bill had the support of the Privy Council and represented the heart-felt views of the Protestant political élites.

Third, Neale and others grossly underestimated the power of the House of Lords which was, after all, the most socially prestigious of the Houses. In particular, Burghley could and did use his seat in the Lords, and client MPs in the Commons, to orchestrate parliamentary business. In 1572, for example, he was behind a Lords' request to the Commons to expedite more quickly official bills rather than pursue its members' private bills.

## The Privy Council and Parliament

However, in rejecting wholesale the 'Whig' interpretation of a strident, often oppositional House of Commons and reminding ourselves of the extent to which the Queen held all the cards, we are in danger of offering an un-nuanced and misleading picture. In particular, we should integrate our discussion of Parliament into our picture of the activities of the Privy Councillors, who were often keen to manipulate whatever could be manipulated in their efforts to persuade the Queen to make decisions. In short, as Parliament was recognised as a legitimate means of representing the views of the political élites to the Queen, then it might be used as an additional means of putting pressure on her. Clearly, support in the form of parliamentary petition or bill was worth having. Haigh demonstrates that the 1572 Parliament was called, not to grant taxation, but because the Privy Council pushed the Queen into sounding out her political élites on the issue of Mary, Queen of Scots; and the Council then propelled bills through Parliament which petitioned (unsuccessfully) for a charge of treason against Mary and her exclusion from the English throne.

Indeed, if the Council could and did use Parliament as part of their campaign to persuade the Queen, they were generally as unsuccessful as they were at court. The closest the tactic came to success was in the joint petition of Parliament in 1586 asking for the execution of Mary: and, even then, Elizabeth would make no answer.

The Queen's tactics exploited, as ever, her strengths. When she felt it necessary, she delivered speeches to Parliament herself which were a judicious mix of flattery, grave warnings on infringing the monarch's prerogative to decide on policy, vague promises of reform and a strong flavouring of her personal dignity: they also displayed her political astuteness.

## Parliament and the monopolies crisis, 1597 and 1601

Indeed, the strength of the Queen's position and her political skill is best revealed in the bitter clashes over monopolies between MPs and the government in the parliaments of 1597 and 1601.

The last decade of Elizabeth's reign was marked by the proliferation of monopolies (see page 23) granted to courtiers. This form of patronage appealed to the Queen because it cost her nothing, but granting monopolies over basic commodities such as salt lined courtiers' pockets at the expense of the whole country, since prices rocketed alarmingly. Privy Councillors benefited too much from monopolies to respond with any sympathy to MPs' grievances, and Robert Cecil's bad-tempered handling of Parliament exacerbated the situation to the extent that subsidies demanded by the government were unlikely to be approved by the Commons. At this point, the Queen stepped in. The Speaker was instructed to convey her promise to repeal or suspend some monopolies, and her concession defused the situation at once.

Although the stridency of the Commons' complaints has been used by historians to adduce an oppositional stance on the part of Parliament, the monopolies issue is best seen as an exemplification of the adage 'the exception proves the rule'. It represents an atypical example of the severing of links between the Privy Council and Parliament over a specific issue whose resolution nevertheless testifies to the fundamental stability of the Queen's relationship with Parliament.

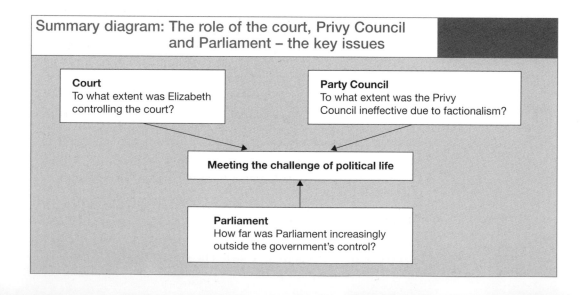

Summary diagram: The role of the court, Privy Council and Parliament – the key issues

**Court**
To what extent was Elizabeth controlling the court?

**Party Council**
To what extent was the Privy Council ineffective due to factionalism?

**Meeting the challenge of political life**

**Parliament**
How far was Parliament increasingly outside the government's control?

# 3 | The Financial Policies of the Crown

Key question
How effective were
the crown's financial
policies?

Key dates

Government heavily in
debt: 1558

Burghley made Lord
Treasurer: 1572

In keeping with its approaches to high politics, Elizabethan
government persevered in using traditional methods in tackling
finance. The aims were to balance the books: an indebted crown
was an endangered crown, and bankruptcy (by no means an
impossibility) would imply political as well as fiscal (economic)
powerlessness.

Making economies:

- Court salaries were pegged back.
- Expenditure on the royal household was curbed by limiting the
  more extravagant menus.
- Surplus royal palaces were sold.
- Gifts of crown land, property or money were generally
  restricted to favourites such as Leicester.
- Winchester continued with his Marian policies of using
  surveyors to maximise the revenue from crown lands, extended
  the surveyor system to support Mary's revision of the book of
  rates to improve customs revenue and raised rents from crown
  tenants in line with inflation. Winchester died in 1572, and
  when Burghley succeeded him as Lord Treasurer he preferred
  to 'farm out' the collection of duties to individuals who would
  pocket any profit they made after paying the government a
  fixed rent.

In times of peace, such policies were relatively successful: the
Marian debt of £227,000 was wiped out. Short-term borrowing
(from the City of London in particular) and Forced Loans (where
the lender was required, rather than asked, to lend to the crown),
together with the subsidies regularly voted by Parliament and
which were sometimes channelled into **ordinary**, rather than
**extraordinary, expenditure**, were sufficient to provide cash-in-
hand.

Key term

**Ordinary and
extraordinary
expenditure**
Parliament would
expect to provide
tax only for
extraordinary
government
expenditure, such
as defence or war,
and not for
everyday running of
government.

Admittedly, the government did nothing to address the
underlying and fundamental problem: that the crown income was
simply inadequate and needed a form of parliamentary taxation
that would contribute towards its ordinary needs. Such ideas were
not unheard of: in 1555, the Marian government had sought
(unsuccessfully) a parliamentary subsidy without making any claim
that it was for extraordinary purposes. But the nettle was a very
difficult one to grasp, since those who might lead in imposing a
tax burden on the wealthy were the wealthy themselves. Burghley
certainly had no intention of leading by example: the Lord
Treasurer made sure that his income was vastly underassessed,
and his attitude was symptomatic of the aristocracy as a whole
(see page 133). The result was that the subsidies voted by
Parliament proved very difficult to collect in full.

The burden of local taxation increased very substantially under
Elizabeth. The following burdens fell largely on parish and county:

- poor relief
- maintenance of roads

- paying the costs of the local militia: an important reorganisation of 1573 but an ever-increasing burden in times of war and threat of war
- the upkeep of fortifications.

## Relations between locality and crown

Despite the local tax burden, relations between locality and crown were, on the whole, positive. This was because nobility and gentry recognised the prestige conferred by links with court, such as:

- the system of lord lieutenants and deputy lieutenants for counties (made permanent in 1585), which brought together courtiers and lesser peers or gentry
- the respect afforded to the status of the justice of the peace (JP).

Such links encouraged local nobility and gentry to identify with the needs of the country.

**Key date**

System of Lords Lieutenant responsible for county administration made permanent: 1585

## Overseas trade

As part of the government's attempt to maintain a favourable balance of payments, attempts were made to encourage overseas trade through voyages of exploration. It was certainly dangerous, given Spanish possession of the Netherlands, to rely on the cloth market at Antwerp to sell England's most important export commodity. In similar vein, new markets for cloth were opened up (after disruptions of trade through Antwerp in 1563) with the northern Netherlands and Germany. The Hanseatic League was compelled to accept an agreement in 1560 which virtually ended restrictions on English trade in the Baltic and the Eastland Company (1579) subsequently regulated trade in that region, which was primarily with Poland. Merchants were similarly incorporated in the Turkey Company of 1581 and the Barbary Company encouraged trade with the Levant and Morocco.

**Key question**

How effective were the government's attempts to improve overseas trade?

Trade with Latin America, given the monopoly claimed by Spain and Portugal, took the form of Sir Francis Drake's attacks on Panama (1572–3) and the Peruvian coast (1578–9). There were unsuccessful attempts to colonise parts of North America, such as Virginia in 1585–7.

Evaluating the overall success or otherwise of these overseas ventures is anything but easy, given the absence of reliable data. On the negative side:

- Cecil concluded in both 1560 and 1580 that England bought more than it sold.
- Traditional markets remained far more important than the new ones.
- The Italians, Dutch and Germans had far more sophisticated banking and credit systems than England. It was, indeed, 1571 before it was legal in England to take money at interest; a restriction which was honoured by tradition, but condemned by necessity.
- The Privy Council's chosen method of encouraging overseas trade was hardly redolent of thrusting, entrepreneurial zeal,

since its idea of a new trading company was a regulated monopoly not dissimilar to the old-fashioned trade guilds of towns.

More positively:

- Merchants were often able to sidestep the restrictive practices of the trading companies.
- Merchants were able to trade on a large scale without a sophisticated credit and banking system (bonds, notes and bills of exchange promising repayment at a future date offered a workable alternative).
- The stimulus to English shipbuilding was a very real one: Palliser calculates that, for example, between 1571 and 1576 at least 51 ocean-going ships were built.
- In keeping with its desire to restrict imports and encourage exports, the Privy Council welcomed Flemish cloth-workers fleeing from Alva's persecutions in the 1560s. Settling mainly in East Anglia, Kent and Essex, their skills in what was called the New Drapery, producing lighter, more varied cloth, opened a valuable Mediterranean market to English cloth.
- Similarly, printing workers from Germany and glass workers from France, Flanders and Italy helped to contribute to a significant expansion in those industries.

However, it is important to recognise that such enterprises could be successful only if there existed demand for the products, and it is clear that growing demand came largely from the domestic market. This was partly fuelled by significant population increase, based on a rising birth-rate and increased life-expectancy, and partly on an increasing income for gentry landowners, town élites and yeoman tenant farmers, who were in a position to benefit from price rises which were themselves partly the result of increasing demand.

## The problem of inflation

**Key question**
How successfully did the crown tackle the economic and social challenges posed by inflation?

The issue of inflation troubled Tudor commentators such as Sir Thomas Smith, especially given the potential social problems if wages did not rise at the same rate as prices. By and large, inflation was marked from the 1520s, accelerated in the 1540s and 1550s, slackened somewhat in the 1560s and 1570s and accelerated again in the final decade of Elizabeth's reign (and beyond). There are a number of possible causes of such inflation:

- Population increased by just over 40 per cent between 1541 and 1600, and it could be argued that prices rose as a result of soaring demand, which agriculture in particular struggled to meet.
- Debasement of the coinage (see pages 3 and 8) under Henry VIII and Somerset was used to finance extravagant military adventures, but, given the reduction of precious metal in coinage, was likely to stimulate inflation as money inevitably lost value.

- Contemporaries were also inclined to blame the turning over of arable land to pasture through enclosure, which was likely to cause food prices to soar, particularly in times of shortage after poor harvests.

None of these possible causes can be rejected, but it is important to recognise that inflation was a Europe-wide phenomenon, and that therefore the specifically English issues, such as debasement and enclosure, cannot fully account for it. It is certainly possible that increased flow of gold and silver into Europe courtesy of the Spanish South American empire may be a significant factor, especially as piracy brought much coin into England itself.

In the early years of Elizabeth's reign, Cecil, together with scholar, MP and diplomat Sir Thomas Smith, advised that the debased coinage be called in and replaced with new coin. This was successfully achieved in 1560–1, but both men were to be disappointed in the expectation that it would cure or even curb inflation: indeed, inflation itself increasingly reduced the value of the new coinage. Its impact, therefore, needs to be assessed in other ways. Sterling work (no pun intended) had already been done by Northumberland and Mary in restoring the gold coinage: it was the silver coins that received Elizabeth's attention. Perhaps the most important result of the recoinage was in terms of the Queen's internal and international prestige, since it presented an image of stability and confidence. Palliser revealingly points to the epitaph on Elizabeth's tomb, which celebrates the restoring of 'purity' to coinage as one of her greatest achievements.

The government's approach to the gap between wages, prices and unemployment was similarly traditional. In 1563, the Statute of Artificers removed a statutory, uniform wage ceiling and instead allowed JPs to fix wages with due regard to local conditions. However, it also became an offence to pay or demand more then the local rate. This is hardly far-sighted or innovatory legislation, and reflected the government's response to pressure from merchants and landowners. The Statute duly attempted to discourage labour mobility (particularly the movement of landless labourers to towns) by imposing compulsory seven-year apprenticeships and forbidding workers to change their employment without a certificate giving permission. John Guy judges that the short-term impact may have encouraged wage rises, but, post-1585, real wages fell again. And, in any case, the attempted restrictions on labour mobility were anything but enforceable.

The social effects of inflation have been much debated by historians. It is probable that those who gained from inflation were the agricultural producers, the larger and middling landowners and perhaps tenant farmers, who could benefit from higher prices and, in the case of landowners, from racking up rents. Conversely, those who suffered most were landless labourers. It is also possible that a rising merchant class gained from the gap between prices and wages. However, generalisations of this sort are fraught with difficulty. Local studies, such as

**Key dates**

Recoinage completed: 1560–1

Statute of Artificers removed a national wage limit: 1563

Finch's work on five Northamptonshire gentry families, suggest that luck, personality, financial prudence and favourable marriage settlements may explain success in the inflationary climate rather better than class-based models of economic behaviour.

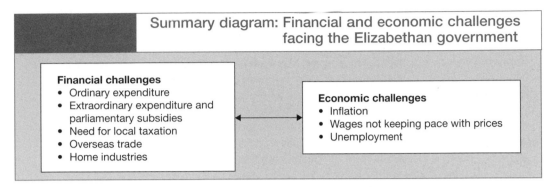

Summary diagram: Financial and economic challenges facing the Elizabethan government

**Financial challenges**
- Ordinary expenditure
- Extraordinary expenditure and parliamentary subsidies
- Need for local taxation
- Overseas trade
- Home industries

**Economic challenges**
- Inflation
- Wages not keeping pace with prices
- Unemployment

# 4 | Conclusion: Meeting the Challenge of Government

The first decades of Elizabethan government were characterised by a style of government that was traditional and prudent in its finance and traditional in its social and economic policies. It sought to uphold the traditional prestige of its nobility, to maintain the class and economic structure of the country and to utilise Parliament in the traditional manner as a source of extraordinary revenue. But the greatest potential challenge to such methods was the inescapable fact that the heart of government was a queen and not a king. Traditional methods rested on traditional power relationships, with the will of the monarch as the motive force, consulting with but ultimately directing the political nation. The assumption was that a king was necessary: but Elizabeth demonstrated that such was not the case. In so doing, she did not so much redefine monarchy as caricature it. Personal monarchy was, in her terms, monarchy by personality. Courtiers were held within a web of intimate relationships woven by the queen, and were rarely able to entrap her within webs of their own making.

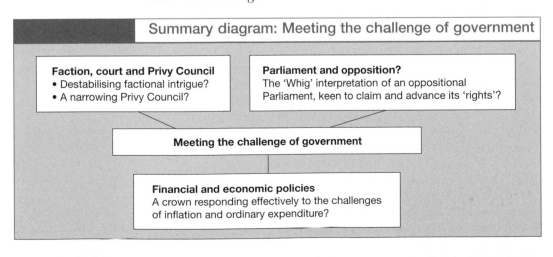

Summary diagram: Meeting the challenge of government

**Faction, court and Privy Council**
- Destabilising factional intrigue?
- A narrowing Privy Council?

**Parliament and opposition?**
The 'Whig' interpretation of an oppositional Parliament, keen to claim and advance its 'rights'?

**Meeting the challenge of government**

**Financial and economic policies**
A crown responding effectively to the challenges of inflation and ordinary expenditure?

## Study Guide: AS Questions

### In the style of OCR A

Assess the importance of the Privy Council in Elizabethan government. (50 marks)

---

### Exam tips

This question requires candidates to know the role performed by the Privy Council and to evaluate its importance alongside other organs of government. Its main functions were to advise the Queen, to administer the realm and to implement decisions taken by the Queen and council. Since its leading councillors headed departments of state, and were responsible for the royal finances, courts of law and national security, it is not surprising that they exercised considerable influence. By the 1580s many of them were Lords Lieutenant of their county and the lynchpin between the localities and central government. However, the council was neither a united nor an unchanging body. Although there was much continuity among some key office-holders, factional rivalry may have lessened its importance. You should understand that the Queen held ultimate authority and give examples of when she stood firm in the face of the more outspoken members. You should also compare the role of the Privy Council with that of Parliament and point out that some Privy Councillors sat in the House of Lords or had clients in the Commons who sought to pressurise the Queen into making favourable decisions. An assessment requires you to reach a judgement and to avoid excessive descriptions of the Privy Council's work and its councillors.

## In the style of OCR B
Answer **both** parts of your chosen question.

**(a)** Why did nobles want to be present at court?          (25 marks)
**(b)** Why was control of Parliament important for Elizabeth's government?                                        (25 marks)

---

### Exam tips
*The page references are intended to take you straight to the material that will help you to answer the questions.*

**(a)** On the surface this question simply asks about the motives of the nobility. However there is far more to be explained. The role of the court in government and the benefits of being at the centre of power and decision-making, and patronage must also be explained. Hence there are many interlinking facets to this question. In evaluating the explanation it might be useful to assess the impact of exclusion from court, for example in the case of the Northern Earls (Chapter 4, pages 92–3) and the Earl of Essex (Chapter 8, page 191).

You might, for example, argue that because of the informal social hierarchy, status was achieved through both noble birth and government or court office but that a combination of the two was regarded as necessary. In the inflationary climate few nobles could afford to eschew royal patronage. You might consider the attitudes and values behind the struggle for political favour in the context of Tudor government in general or Elizabeth's court in particular.

You might evaluate your explanation by comparing the position of nobles such as Robert Dudley, Earl of Leicester, and William Cecil, Lord Burghley, with that of Northumberland and Westmorland in 1569 and Essex in the later 1590s.

What you should do:

- Plan your answer by first separating out the complex attitudes and values that underpinned court life in the sixteenth century.
- Identify individual reasons for the motives of nobles in general and of sub-groups of the courtiers.
- Analyse how the different factors interacted, using specific examples to support your argument.
- Evaluate your explanation, for example by comparing the experience of those who gained and retained the Queen's favour with those who did not.

What you should avoid:

- Describing the court careers of individual nobles.
- Explaining the course of noble-led rebellions.
- Explaining the benefits of political patronage for the Queen.

**(b)** The question assumes that Parliament had some importance for Tudor government and you should be clear about all the workings of Parliament: elections including who was eligible to vote and stand for Parliament, the most common issues for debate and the main concerns of the MPs, the two-house system, the passage of bills and the management of Parliament. This question concerns the last of these, but without an understanding of the whole topic you may misunderstand the government's motives.

You might, for example, argue that the most important function of Parliament from the government's point of view was to grant extraordinary taxation, so management of money bills was the primary aim. You might use examples of conciliation over issues such as the Queen's marriage and the succession question to confirm this view.

You might argue, for example, that Parliament was the chosen arena for Puritan challenges to the church settlement and that, given the Queen's antipathy towards changing the settlement, careful management was needed. You might link this to the idea that there was concerted opposition to certain crown policies among MPs.

You might, for example, take the instances when the Privy Council wished to force a decision from Elizabeth over certain issues such as Mary, Queen of Scots or the succession and set this against their needs in other, more typical sessions of Parliament in order to evaluate the intentional factors you have identified.

What you should do:

- Identify the general reasons for calling Parliament and make sure you can explain why management was necessary to carry out its functions.
- Identify typical and individual examples where the government aimed to manage Parliament.
- Plan a line of argument that shows how the different reasons link together.
- Remember to analyse and evaluate your explanation, using supporting evidence.

What you should avoid:

- Describing how the government controlled Parliament.
- Explaining individual incidences of control without showing how they illustrate the argument.
- Describing the historical debate over the House of Commons and the extent to which it challenged monarchical authority in Elizabeth's reign.

# Study Guide: A2 Question

## In the style of AQA

'Queen Elizabeth I regarded Parliament as a waste of time.'
Assess the validity of this view. (45 marks)

---

### Exam tips

This quotation implies that Parliament had very little importance in the Elizabethan era and that the Queen could easily disregard it and, indeed, preferred to do so. You will need to consider evidence that both supports and rejects this view and you will probably also want to refer to the historiography on the subject, and explain, rather than simply describe, the modern rejection of the views of Neale about Parliament's growth during this period.

Evidence in favour of the quotation might include reference to:

- Elizabeth's personal role at the head of government
- the role of Elizabethan ministers
- political patronage
- the Privy Council
- the limited number of Parliaments and action taken against 'awkward' parliamentarians (e.g. arrest of MPs who discussed reform of the Church of England in 1587).

This needs to be balanced against the 'use' to which Parliament was put and the Queen's attempts to win it over. Issues might include reference to:

- the question of the succession
- the dispute over religion
- the dispute over monopolies
- social policy and the Poor Laws (see the next chapter).

You should also make clear that Parliament fulfilled the important role of granting money to the crown and that Privy Councillors (especially William Cecil) took care to arrange parliamentary business and to attend parliamentary sessions. You might also wish to distinguish between the Lords (which contained men who had significant roles in government) and Commons. (You may need to refer to other chapters to find some of the supporting evidence here.)

# 8 Meeting the Challenge: The Final Years 1589–1603

**POINTS TO CONSIDER**

John Guy's seminal *Tudor England* (1988), in discussing the final two decades of Elizabeth's reign, offered as a chapter heading 'The Tudor *Fin de Siècle*'. The French 'end of the century' term is often taken to imply a sense of senile and decadent lethargy, and there is plenty of evidence to suggest that the term may not be misapplied: the Queen, arguably, slipped from politically astute indecisiveness into an enfeebling hesitancy. As she withered physically, so her hold on the court and the wider political life of the country slipped from her grasp.

A negative interpretation of the Queen's final years was favoured by those historians such as Neale who saw the majority of Elizabeth's reign as a golden age. Neale clearly regretted its decline, and it might be argued that his picture exaggerated the contrast: he painted it too golden, but also too tarnished. It is therefore essential that we look at the different features of the end of the reign to evaluate the Neale 'decay' interpretation:

- Factions and court (the Essex Rebellion)
- Social and economic distress in the 1590s
- The succession

**Key dates**

| | |
|---|---|
| 1588 | Earl of Leicester died |
| 1595 | Food riots in London |
| 1598 | William Cecil, Lord Burghley, died |
| 1599 | Essex sent to Ireland to crush the Tyrone Rebellion |
| 1601 | Essex Rebellion |
| | Poor Law legislation |
| 1603 | Elizabeth I died |

## 1 | Factions and Court: The Essex Rebellion

Robert Devereux, Earl of Essex, was a man who thought much of his ancient lineage and traces of royal blood. There was no reason why he should not, as the Queen felt the same way. Being the stepson of the Earl of Leicester was no handicap, and it is likely enough that the Queen's aim was to mould Essex for government

**Key question**
Why was the Earl of Essex a potential threat to the Elizabethan regime?

The allegorical portrait, 'Time and Death.' Unknown artist, c.1610. How might the allegorical portrait support the 'decline' interpretation?

Key dates

Earl of Leicester died: 1588

William Cecil, Lord Burghley, died: 1598

in the same way that she had moulded Leicester. This would reflect the positive and negative features of her deep personal regard: a willingness to forgive in him what she would not forgive in others, but also a readiness to lash out in fits of jealous anger when she felt her affection was being taken for granted or exploited: a willingness to be impressed by a certain military style, but also a desire to tame martial extravagances in the interests of sound, sober work in the Privy Council. The real problem was that Essex was a caricature of Leicester: more reckless, more proud, more extravagant, more convinced that he was always right, and self-destructive. Where Leicester, faced by the Queen's fury, retreated to his sickbed, Essex, punished by a well-merited slap in the face, dared to place his hand on his sword.

These astonishing incidents aside, it is ill-advised to accept the full weight of the 'decline' interpretation. It may be that the Queen was less dominant as definer of the personal relationships which underpinned the court, but she nevertheless did not allow herself to be manipulated by her courtiers. There are a number of compelling examples which demonstrate her continuing hold on the court. It was the Queen's decision, for example, to keep the secretaryship vacant following the disgrace of Davison in 1588 (see page 162); she therefore resisted both Essex (who wanted to see Davison restored) and Burghley (who wanted to see his son installed). Only in 1596 did Robert Cecil secure the post, and only then when his father was too crippled to continue to cover the vacancy himself. It was also the Queen's decision to deny Essex the influence over royal patronage that a favourite craved: in short, Essex was unable to advance the prospects of his followers and so was denied that ultimate sign of status and pre-eminence. He had the ill-judgement to stake his credibility on the appointment of Francis Bacon as attorney-general in 1594 and failed to deliver.

## The personality of Essex

The problem for the Queen was that such strategies did not tame Essex, or turn him into a serious politician, but simply fuelled his resentment and made him look to wilder means to secure a position that he was conspicuously failing to earn. Temperamentally, he preferred solutions which depended on assertions of his military prowess, lineage, honour and challenging rivals to duels to solutions requiring political finesse and patience. Occasionally, Elizabeth did respond more favourably to some of his awful sulking. She granted him the title of Earl Marshall so that he retained his **precedence** over the Lord Admiral, the newly created Earl of Nottingham. But he seems to

**Precedence**
Having a higher ranking than others.

Key term

Lord Treasurer William Cecil, Lord Burghley, and his son, Robert Cecil. Unknown artist, c.1596.

have interpreted this as the blueprint for dominating Queen and council. Risk-taking and emotional bullying would secure him his demands.

His mind-set was such that factional rivalry at court was interpreted by him as an attack on his honour and the 'natural law' by which old-established military aristocracy (such as himself) were to triumph over lesser men and **parvenus** (such as Sir Walter Raleigh and the Cecils). In other words, Essex was a man out of his time.

## Essex and the Tyrone Rebellion in Ireland 1599

The Queen gave Essex the opportunity to prove or hang himself by accepting his arguments in favour of a substantial army (led, of course, by himself) to quell the Irish rebellion of the Earl of Tyrone in 1599 (see page 150). He then proceeded to ignore specific instructions, failed to exploit what military advantages he had, negotiated with Tyrone without authority and returned to England having been expressly forbidden so to do. He burst into the Queen's bedchamber with the expectation that his explanation alone would suffice. It did not. He found himself sent to answer before the Council for his actions, banished from court, temporarily placed under house arrest and suspended from the Privy Council and from his role as **Master of the Ordnance**. He was fortunate to survive a charge of treason.

**Key terms**

**Parvenus**
Newcomers.

**Master of the Ordnance**
Responsible for the supply of military equipment to armed forces.

**Key date**

Essex sent to Ireland to crush the Tyrone Rebellion: 1599

Robert Devereux, Earl of Essex, c.1596, after Marcus Gheeraerts the Younger. Compare and contrast the way Essex and the Cecils are portrayed in the two portraits.

## The Essex Rebellion 1601

Essex's position was unenviable, and rendered untenable when the Queen refused to renew his patent on sweet wines. His ability to raise loans had now vanished, and his income from his lands was insufficient to fund his habitual extravagance. As a result, he faced the collapse of his factional support. In one desperate last gamble, he called on his allies, aristocrats of like mind who deplored what they saw as the domination of the Elizabethan government, and particularly the Privy Council, by men other than themselves. With his allies he attempted to stage what can only be called a court *putsch*. Essex's initial plan was, by force of arms, to secure the palace of Whitehall, the Queen's person, the Tower and other strategic London sites in a move which would once and for all destroy the Cecil faction and oblige the Queen to declare James VI as her successor. There were rumours that the Privy Council had caught wind of the plot, and Essex's hand was forced when, on 8 February 1601, four Privy Councillors arrived at Essex House with a message from the Queen offering to consider his complaints. They were therefore in an ideal position to note Essex's preparations at first hand, and so he took them into his custody and marched out at the head of a glittering troop of nobles, gentlemen and their servants with the hope of raising the city to his cause. He was obliged to fall back on Essex House once it became clear that the city's trained bands were encircling him and that heralds were abroad proclaiming his treason. With the Tower artillery trained on his residence, he capitulated (gave himself up). Elizabeth, with a minimum of customary hesitation, signed the warrant for his execution, but was merciful towards those nobles who had joined him in his London escapade.

## Interpreting the Essex Rebellion

To see the Essex Rebellion as a symptom of a collapsing government, narrowly exclusive and antagonistic towards the ancient nobility, is to see Essex's behaviour and complaints as largely justified. This would be unwise. After all, Essex was himself a Privy Councillor; that he was dismissed was the result of his own folly, extravagancies and fundamental lack of political skill. Rivalry with the Cecils was inevitable, but this need not have ruled out compromise and co-operation: it is John Guy's judgement, for instance, that he was able to sustain a working relationship with the Cecils (and Raleigh) in 1596 on the urgings of Francis Bacon. But this all collapsed with his cries of 'dishonour' when faced by the Nottingham and face-slapping affairs. Essex's idea of the political rough-and-tumble involved swords: his fellow Privy Councillors disagreed. Of course, it could be argued that Elizabeth's evident affection for him simply encouraged him in his folly. Perhaps: but he chose to ignore the strong evidence that her favour had its limits.

Wherever the blame lay, the Essex Rebellion brought the country close to civil war. There is certainly some evidence that Essex, in canvassing anti-Cecil support in the localities, might have encouraged a dangerous polarisation of opinion: a form of

Essex Rebellion: 1601 **Key date**

*Putsch*
A take-over of the government. **Key term**

**Key question**
How should the Essex Rebellion be interpreted?

country versus court conflict which anticipated the situation which led to the outbreak of civil war in the seventeenth century. But Essex did not control the Lord Lieutenants of the counties, and any attempt to raise troops without their orders would have been simply impractical.

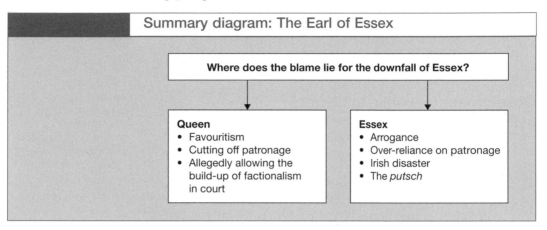

Summary diagram: The Earl of Essex

**Where does the blame lie for the downfall of Essex?**

**Queen**
- Favouritism
- Cutting off patronage
- Allegedly allowing the build-up of factionalism in court

**Essex**
- Arrogance
- Over-reliance on patronage
- Irish disaster
- The *putsch*

**Key question**
Why were the 1590s a particularly grim time for the poor?

Key date

Food riots in London: 1595

## 2 | Social and Economic Distress in the 1590s

### Evidence of social distress and discontent

Catastrophic harvest failures in 1586–7 and particularly c.1594–6 have been cited as leading to mortality rates and poverty on such a scale that the government was simply unable to cope. In particular, the Elizabethan Poor Law was allegedly exposed as utterly inadequate. There is certainly evidence to support such a case. The Privy Council in the 1590s was fearful of a repetition of the Kett-style camps of 1549 (see pages 8–9), which would indeed have marked a breakdown of local authority in the face of distress. No such camps appeared, but there were food riots in London, the south-east and west in 1595 and in Norfolk and East Anglia in 1596–7. The London riots involved considerable numbers of apprentices and produced an overreaction from the Privy Council, as the almost obsessive pursuit of those involved in the so-called Oxfordshire Rising of 1596 would suggest. It seems that a plot was hatched to seize arms from the house of the Lord Lieutenant and march to the aid of the London apprentices. In fact, it came to nothing, but the so-called ringleaders were examined by a committee of the Privy Council and executed, even though no violence had taken place and no one of any social standing whatsoever had been implicated. Clearly, then, this response implies that the Privy Council felt the stability of the country to be in danger. Was the Council correct?

Estimating the numbers of the very poor, best defined as those below subsistence level, at any one time or over a period is fraught with difficulty. From a survey of the historiography, Palliser concludes that 'rural areas could normally support their indigenous poor, sending on their way paupers and vagrants who tried to come in from elsewhere'. But it is likely that, in times of acute distress, the problem was simply exported to the towns as the desperate poor migrated in the search for food and work. And, of course, the problem was exacerbated (made worse) by population growth. This made the problem particularly stark in London. And so, we can argue that the late 1590s represent what was probably the worst time for the poor, given that harvest failures and subsequent rising prices coincided with falling wages, that plague disrupted economic life and that there is some evidence of malnutrition shading into outright starvation in the more remote rural areas.

## Government response to distress

At the start of the sixteenth century few would have considered that poor relief was the responsibility of central government anyway. In the pre-Reformation period, much charity had been dispensed by the religious orders, and private charity was encouraged as a good deed which would be rewarded by God. And it was accepted that, as a mark of social status and a reflection of traditional hospitality, the noble landowner would arrange for alms (charity, usually in the form of food) to be distributed to the poor at his gate. Those too young, old or ill to work might be licensed to beg by their town or rural parish. However, this frequently indiscriminate and unsystematic charity was short-circuited, and some historians would say catastrophically, by the abolition of religious orders in the Reformation, and by the Protestant rejection of the Catholic teaching that salvation might be earned by good deeds. Indeed, as the centralisation of authority around court and council intensified, local nobility looked outward towards London and towards their own class rather than towards the poor in their own parishes. Their new homes proclaimed their status to their peers: a new desire for privacy replaced old-fashioned hospitality towards the local community with entertainment for one's fellow nobles. It was unsurprising, then, that government itself should look for ways to fill in the gaps in relief for the poor: especially as popular discontent was politically dangerous.

> **Key question**
> How did the government respond to social and economic distress?

### Poor relief: the deserving and the undeserving poor

Sixteenth-century governments attempted to distinguish between the deserving and the undeserving poor, but were inclined to assume that the undeserving poor included anyone who was physically fit but without work (on the dubious grounds that there was work available for anyone who wanted it). Anyone considered a **vagrant** (which might include those genuinely moving out of their own parishes in search for work) was faced with corporal punishment (and worse): an act of 1572 specified whipping and ear-boring for the very first offence; a second offence was considered a **felony** and the third was punishable by death. Similarly, as act of 1576 had authorised the building of houses of correction in every county.

Statutes were not necessarily enforced by JPs, and the harsher ones were ignored. Nor was it easy to replace private charity with

> **Key question**
> To what extent were the social and economic policies of the Elizabethan government intended to increase central authority and impose social control on the poor?

> **Vagrant**
> A wandering beggar.
>
> **Felony**
> A serious crime.

Key terms

A contemporary drawing of a vagabond being whipped at the tail of a cart. What does this source suggest about attitudes towards begging?

some sort of compulsory public obligation, since compulsory public obligation meant some form of tax, and increases in tax generally meant parliamentary and local opposition.

Some towns, such as Norwich in 1549 and York in 1550, took the lead in introducing compulsory payments towards poor relief and a 1563 Poor Law Act made a gesture in the direction of statutory compulsion by instructing parishes to keep a list of those who failed to contribute towards a poor rate. Persistent offenders could be prosecuted, but enforcement was haphazard at best. However, the government's mind was concentrated wonderfully by the 1569 Revolt of the Northern Earls (see pages 92–5), as it was assumed that they had picked up support from discontented local poor. In 1572, the Act Directing the Levy of a Compulsory Poor Rate required the payment of a weekly rate for poor relief, to be administered by churchwardens, parish constables and four overseers (appointed by JPs) per parish. Overseers, who were responsible for levying the poor rates and work for the able-bodied poor, were to be recruited from substantial householders of the parish, such as yeomen: although they were unpaid, they were obliged to serve.

**Key date**

Poor Law legislation: 1601

**Key question**
What attitudes towards the poor are indicated by government legislation?

## Poor Law Acts of 1598 and 1601

New legislation followed renewed distress in 1598:

- Apart from confirming the compulsory poor rate, the new act required the setting up of pauper apprenticeships to train boys until 24 and girls to the age of 21.

- Vagrants were to be subject to the usual whipping and then returned to their parishes of origin.
- More houses of correction were to be built so that the able-bodied poor could be put to work (reflecting the persistence of the view that unemployment was the fault of the unemployed). Begging was outlawed.

This act was followed and confirmed by the 1601 Act, which tinkered with the number of overseers (reducing them from four to two) and allowed a pauper girl to leave her apprenticeship if she married before its termination date.

It is tempting to read into Elizabethan Poor Law legislation the interpretation that it represented a far-sighted blueprint for poor relief, as part of a deliberate policy of increasing central government's role in, and control of, the localities. The fact that the 1601 Act remained the basis for the country's Poor Law for 200 years increases that temptation. In support of that interpretation, we might cite some further legislation introduced by the Privy Council which not only directed local authorities to relieve distress, but also sought to control social behaviour. From Henry VIII's reign onwards, occasional printed collections of relevant statutes and circular letters specifying action to be taken, say, to preserve public order were sent to JPs. By the middle of Elizabeth's reign came the first publications of **Books of Orders**. Significantly, these were not collections of statutes, but instructions to JPs on the implementing of the crown's social and economic policies. These were based on the crown's prerogative power to enforce such policies and, as they were not passed by Parliament, some JPs doubted their legality. The Book of Orders for the **dearth** of 1586–7, for example, instructed those with stocks of corn to take them to market. JPs were to ensure that searches for hoarded grain were carried out and that corn was to be sold in small amounts and at prices the poor could afford: similarly, bakers were to produce bread that was equally affordable. There was to be no reselling in the first hour of trading, so that the poor had every opportunity to buy. Similarly, Books of Orders were issued in plague years 1587, 1592 and 1593 and were intended to enforce **quarantine** on infected houses.

The Poor Law and the Books of Orders may be taken as an indication of the acceptance by the government that traditional charity was neither adequate nor, more arguably, appropriate to the needs of the poor in times of crisis, since both represented an attack on traditional alms-giving and, indeed, neighbourliness towards the sick. However, it would be unwise to see them as the first stirrings of a **welfare-state ideology**. In the first place, Paul Slack reminds us that the government called on the church to promote good old-fashioned neighbourliness, and we might add that attempts were made to force those many members of the aristocracy who were increasingly drawn to live amongst their peers in London to return to their country estates and practise traditional hospitality and generosity to the poor there. Also, the Poor Law and Books of Orders were responses to crises, rather

## Key terms

**Books of Orders**
Instructions to Justices of the Peace directing them to take specific action in times of plague or famine.

**Dearth**
When food was expensive.

**Quarantine**
Sealing up of infected houses.

**Welfare-state ideology**
The belief that the state has a responsibility to look after those in need.

Key terms

**Paternalism**
Behaving to those in need in the traditional manner of a father towards his children.

**Indiscriminate charity**
Charity distributed without the testing of need.

than a fully thought-out programme. They represent, perhaps, a reasonably creative mish-mash of pragmatism and principle, tradition and innovation. Into the melting-pot of Privy Council ideas went Tudor **paternalism**, the influence of puritan urban élites and their dislike of **indiscriminate charity**, a regard for the traditional charitable role of the local nobility, a willingness to learn from continental practice and, most potent of all, a fear of public disorder.

What emerged reflected some of these contradictory ingredients. In effect, the distinction between the deserving and undeserving poor was hardened, and came to be seen as a distinction between the respectable poor and those beyond the pale. The Poor Laws provided JPs and others in authority with a social control mechanism, since they were in a position to deny relief to those considered disorderly, such as frequenters of ale-houses. Ipswich Puritans, for instance, refused relief to anyone not attending church. The empowering of the parish officers via the national initiative encouraged the 'middling sort' (who might find themselves parish overseers) to share the world-view of their social superiors, rather than that of the labouring poor.

### The effectiveness of Elizabethan social and economic legislation

Did the Elizabethan social and economic legislation actually work? If one were to judge by the money raised by the poor rates, then the answer must be 'no'. Paul Slack comments: 'The deliberate redistribution of wealth from rich to poor by 1603 was minimal.' It was certainly significantly less than private charitable giving for poor relief, and even that, if J.F. Hadwin's calculations are correct, declined in real terms in the 1590s, when the need was greatest. One can but conclude that the overall effect of the Elizabethan measures was very limited.

The Privy Council had adopted measures because it feared the type of rebellion that characterised Somerset's regime. Those rebellions did not take place: indeed, even food riots were limited in scale and frequency. But this does not mean that their measures explain the lack of disorder. We might conclude that real distress was limited in place and time and that the Privy Council fell victim to paranoia. However, given that popular risings were often led by discontented lesser gentry or the 'middling sort', it may be that the real success of the late Elizabethan government lies in the way it unintentionally encouraged the middling sort to identify with the ruling classes.

## 3 | England, Scotland and the Succession

Key date

Elizabeth I died: 1603

It is unlikely that Elizabeth named her successor. Had she done so, then neither Essex nor Cecil need have engaged in secret contact with James VI of Scotland, who was the most likely candidate. The most plausible explanation of her failure to do so is the unbridled egotism that underpinned her view of monarchy. Her throne was hard won, and she had no intention of seeing her courtiers drift away from her as she aged. Had she named a successor, then their attentions would, in part, have been focused elsewhere as they jockeyed for future positions under the future monarch.

According to David Loades, Essex had been in touch with James as early as 1593 and had, in all probability, done everything possible to present the Cecils as antagonistic towards the Scottish King's hopes. But Essex's death opened the door to a mutual understanding between the Scots King and Robert Cecil via ciphered letters and trusted representatives.

In February 1603, the Queen was clearly seriously ill. Cecil moved into action; the nobility were consulted and Lord Lieutenants briefed on the need to ensure local security in anticipation of James' succession. On 20 March, with the end clearly approaching, Cecil sent James a draft of the intended proclamation of his succession, with which James was only too happy to concur. The Queen, having refused physicians, food and bed, died on a pile of cushions on the floor of her bedchamber on 24 March. A carefully stage-managed proclamation, ceremony and procession took place in London: and bonfires were lit in London to celebrate James' accession. Those bonfires, and the street parties that accompanied them, were a mixture of relief at an orderly succession and the chance to greet a king at last.

# 4 | Summary: The Final Years. The Tarnished Image of Gloriana?

Age does, of course, tend to tarnish. Elizabeth was 70 years old when she died, and no flattery could hold back the ravages of time on her body any more than the increasingly desperate propaganda of England as a land of peace and plenty could conceal the effects of long years of war and dearth. The new King was welcomed, and that was because he was different to Elizabeth: he was new, and he was a king.

Elizabeth had been increasingly indecisive as she grew older, more prone to rages, more forgiving of her favourites. But there is plenty of evidence that neither the Queen nor her government fell into inactivity:

- Essex went too far, and was punished.
- Ireland was pulled back from the brink.
- The Poor Law was no solution to social and economic distress, but neither was it the sign of a government unresponsive or bereft of ideas.
- The Queen's response to the Monopolies crisis (see page 178) demonstrated her continued engagement with political life.
- Sir Robert Cecil did come to dominate the Privy Council, but he knew better than to ignore the great nobles or, indeed, the fact that the Queen ruled.

What neither Elizabeth nor her government did was to tackle underlying problems and issues which a less impressive regime might struggle to contain: but then this was a characteristic of the whole reign, and not just those final years.

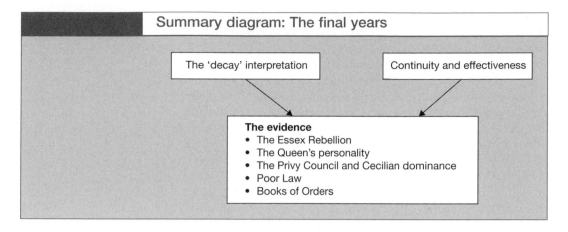

**Summary diagram: The final years**

The 'decay' interpretation

Continuity and effectiveness

**The evidence**
- The Essex Rebellion
- The Queen's personality
- The Privy Council and Cecilian dominance
- Poor Law
- Books of Orders

# 5 | Conclusion

Elizabeth's motto was *Semper Eadem*: 'ever the same' (see page 56). Perhaps, in the last few days of Elizabeth's reign, Sir Robert Cecil might have reflected on it as he warily approached the Queen, who was clearly dying. The story goes that he told her that she must go to bed, and she rounded on him, saying 'Little man, little man! The word "must" is not to be used to princes.' In her rebuke is a theme central to this book: the Queen's sense, and jealous guarding, of the high majesty of her position and title.

Her sharp and dismissive words are clearly the words of a remarkable woman. And one of the most remarkable aspects of her long reign was her ability to break most of the rules. These rules were made by men:

- The first and most important was based on the idea that a throne held by a woman was at best a misfortune. It was, therefore, the rule that a queen be taken under an appropriate male wing through a suitable and swift marriage. But Elizabeth I chose not to marry, and so did not, despite all the considerable pressure her (male) councillors and her (male) Parliament could apply. She might at least be expected to name a successor, but she would not.
- A second rule was that no woman should have authority over the teaching of the church. But the Church of England was, as we have seen, shaped largely by the wishes of the Queen.
- A third rule was that a queen should pay heed to and follow the advice offered by her Privy Council: that select band (of men) who expected to hold the reins of government. And Elizabeth heeded that advice – sometimes, and when it suited her. If it did not suit, then the Privy Council was subjected to a formidable display of evasion, bullying and hesitation. She was also rather good at throwing slippers. Her secretary, Walsingham, caught one full in the face. Occasionally, the Queen might be manipulated to take a course of action of which she disapproved. But her councillors did not succeed in wresting control from her. The decision was hers.

Until the very last years of her reign, Elizabeth I managed to baffle, irritate, drive to distraction but earn the admiration of this male-dominated world. Indeed, her reign fostered a public image which exploited the weaknesses of her position as a woman by converting them into strengths. Unmarried, she was represented as married to her country. Her successes, apparently so different from the supposed failures of other female rulers, were seen by her Protestant subjects as evidence of God's favour. Although he could hardly be expected to concur that Elizabeth had the favour of God, Pope Sixtus V commented on how well she ran her country, despite her sex. 'She is only a woman, only the mistress of half an island, and yet she makes herself feared by Spain, by France, by the Empire, by all!' Indeed, and as twentieth and twenty-first century movie makers and audiences can attest, it is hard to resist what can only be called the glamour of Elizabeth I.

This is not to overstate her achievements. 'Ever the same' might also reflect the fundamentally traditional nature of Elizabethan government. Crown finances were never placed on a firm footing. The long years of Cecilian expertise and administrative skilfulness never produced much more than pragmatic responses to problems as they arose; and those responses owed more to standard Tudor paternalism than they did to blueprints with long-term solutions in mind.

The rise of the courtier at the expense of the great feudal magnate continued, but the monarch remained at the centre of a personal monarchy and consulted great nobles whenever the occasion demanded. There was no real sense, even in those final years where the Privy Council appeared to be falling under Cecilian dominance, that a court versus country divide was developing. Lord Lieutenants continued to represent central government in the localities, and the better-off gentry, serving as JPs, sheriffs or deputy lieutenants, increasingly looked beyond the boundaries of parish and county towards the country as a whole. A potential and particular sense of national identity was engendered by the Henrician break with Rome, but its reality came about as the Elizabethan Church of England laid down meaningful roots from the later 1570s onwards.

In Chapter 1 we argued that the phrase 'Mid-Tudor crisis' was largely inappropriate if one interpreted crisis to mean a collapse, or near collapse, of existing systems of authority. Elizabeth did not have to resolve such a crisis. Neither should one argue for a 'late-Tudor crisis' in the Queen's final years. Of course, the personal monarchy and its underpinning systems of authority collapsed some 40 years after Elizabeth's death. But we cannot read the causes of the English Civil War back into Elizabeth's reign.

## Study Guide: AS Questions

### In the style of OCR A

How far do you agree that social and economic issues were the **most** serious problem facing Elizabeth's government after 1588? (50 marks)

---

### *Exam tips*

Elizabeth's government faced many problems between 1588 and 1603 and you need to plan your answer so that enough attention is given to assessing the social and economic issues before you evaluate and compare them with other problems. It is important that the main social and economic issues are covered first. These are likely to include:

- famine and food riots often linked to enclosures
- rising numbers of unemployed and 'masterless' men
- the urban poor and rural vagabonds
- recurrent plague in several cities
- price inflation caused in part by the war against Spain.

Assess these issues in terms of their frequency, scale and seriousness. Then compare them with other problems such as O'Neill's rebellion in Ireland, the effects of the Spanish war, Parliament's criticism of monopolies, Essex's Rebellion, and the succession. Focus on why these were problematic and how far the government overcame them, before reaching a judgement as to whether social and economic issues were the most serious problem.

---

## In the style of OCR B

(a) Why did the Earl of Essex rebel in 1601?                    (25 marks)

(b) Why was a new Poor Law passed in 1601?                    (25 marks)

---

### Exam tips

*The page references are intended to take you straight to the material that will help you to answer the questions.*

(a) This question is apparently straightforward, asking about the motives of a particular individual. Implicit, however, is the need to explain why others were prepared to join him. Besides this, it is worth reminding yourself that the only other noble rebellion of the reign was in 1569, so what is being explained is a highly unusual event, so it might be worth reviewing the normal means by which nobles vied with each other and satisfied their desire for power (Chapter 7, pages 170–3).

You might, for example, start by explaining the political and financial predicament in which the Earl of Essex found himself by the end of the century (pages 188–93). However, you will also need to explain why rebellion was his preferred option at this point. To do this you will need to consider the dominance of the Cecil faction in government and at court and why this had come about. A comparison with Elizabeth's more adept handling of rivalries at court earlier in the reign would be useful (Chapter 7, pages 170–2).

You might further argue the relative significance of Essex's character against Elizabeth's handling of him, perhaps as a result of her declining powers, in reaching a judgement about which factors were more important.

What you should do:

- Start your plan by working out what Essex's motives and intentions were. You should also consider the motives of others involved in the rebellion as he could not have rebelled without some followers.
- You should then identify the circumstances that caused him to have these motives and intentions and make sure you can explain how they link together.
- Make sure you can also explain why other nobles did not join rebellions, despite provocation, for example the Duke of Norfolk in 1569 (pages 93–4): comparative analysis is a useful method for evaluating an explanation.

What you should avoid:

- Describing the course of Essex's career at court.
- Describing other rebellions, such as the rebellion of the northern earls, without making use of the evidence in your analysis.

**(b)** To answer this question you will need to understand both the situation that created increasing numbers of poor at certain times in the sixteenth century and the precise circumstances of the late 1590s. You will also need to know about earlier Poor Laws and how they were administered in order to explain why the existing legislation was inadequate or unsatisfactory. As suggested in Chapter 8 (pages 194–6), central government seemed to be taking a greater responsibility for social control and you will need to decide how important a motive this was for passing the 1601 Act.

You might, for example, argue that the new law reflected a growing understanding of the reasons for poverty and vagrancy, recognising the need to distinguish between the deserving poor and those who were able-bodied but lazy. You might further argue that the particular hardships of the later 1590s provided the opportunity to revise legislation and incorporate the experience of larger cities into the laws.

You might, for example, argue that fear of unrest or rebellion such as those in Edward's reign (Chapter 1, pages 9–12) was the primary motive of government, rather than paternalistic caring for the less fortunate in society, citing examples of particular punishments to support your ideas.

What you should do:

- Start your plan by identifying a range of intentions for the new laws.
- Next you should look for the particular events or circumstances that lay behind these intentions as well as the attitudes that underpinned thinking about the roles of different groups within the socio-political hierarchy.
- Make sure that you show how these circumstances and ideas helped to form the intentions of the ruling élite.
- Analyse the role played by the different factors and evaluate your explanation, perhaps by comparing earlier legislation with that passed in 1598 and 1601.

What you should avoid:

- Explaining the reasons for increased economic problems without linking this to the laws passed.
- Describing the exact terms of all the Tudor poor laws and the changes in treatment of beggars and deserving poor: instead, use selected examples to support your argument.

## Study Guide: A2 Question

### In the style of AQA

How far would you agree that the final years of Elizabeth I's reign were an unmitigated disaster? (45 marks)

---

### Exam tips

Before beginning this answer you should decide what your view will be. There is plenty of material to support the view that Elizabeth's final years were 'years of decline', but even if this is accepted, you may wish to suggest that they were not an 'unmitigated disaster'. Conversely, you could cite a number of positive elements and argue entirely against the view of the question. The choice is yours, but any judgements need to be well substantiated. Material suggesting 'disaster' could include:

- factions at court
- the influence and actions of the Earl of Essex
- the position in Ireland
- social and economic problems
- religious issues, e.g. separatism (see Chapter 3) and the position of the Catholics
- war with Spain (continued to 1604, see Chapter 5).

Such points should be balanced against a more positive assessment that might consider:

- government stability and the influence of Robert Cecil
- internal peace (including the survival of the religious settlement)
- the absence of direct external threats
- the easy transition to the reign of James I on Elizabeth's death.

---

# Further Reading

Susan Doran, *Monarchy and Matrimony: The Courtships of Elizabeth I* (Routledge, 1996).

Michael Graves, *The Tudor Parliaments: Crown, Lords and Commons, 1485–1603* (Longman, 1985).

John Guy, *Tudor England* (OUP, 1990).

John Guy, *My Heart is My Own: The Life of Mary Queen of Scots* (HarperPerennial, 2004).

Christopher Haigh, *Elizabeth I* (Longman, 1988).

Christopher Haigh, *English Reformations* (Clarendon, 1993).

Jennifer Loach, *Edward VI* (Yale, 1999).

# Glossary

**Absolution**   Releasing from sin.

**Acumen**   Knowledge and experience.

*Adiaphora*   A Greek term, meaning in this context 'things indifferent to salvation'; in other words, religious practices which might not in themselves be welcome, but which were not likely to affect one's destination in the after-life (heaven or hell).

**Anabaptists**   A Protestant Separatist movement from Switzerland and Germany that grew up in the first years of the Lutheran Reformation. Some Anabaptists preached extreme political and religious views, including the abolition of private property.

**Anarchy**   Lawlessness, rejection of authority.

**Anglicise**   To impose English law, systems of authority, customs and manners on another people.

**Anticlerical**   Opposition to the position and authority of the clergy.

**Anticlericalism**   Dislike of clerical claims to authority.

**Apostolic Church**   Made up of the first Christian churches, founded by the earliest followers of Christ.

**Appellants**   Anti-Jesuit missionary priests who appealed to the Pope against the appointment of George Blackwell as Archpriest.

**Archpriest Controversy**   A dispute over the appointment of George Blackwell as an Archpriest with authority over the mission to England.

**Attainder**   An Act of Attainder was a method of securing conviction of an alleged traitor without trial (and seizing his or her lands for the crown).

**Autocratic**   Ruling without consultation or sharing power.

**'Beyond the pale'**   Outside 'civilised' society. The Pale was a fence dividing the English-controlled area around Dublin from Gaelic Ireland.

**Book of Common Prayer**   Laid down the orders of church services, including morning and evening prayer, Communion, marriage, baptism, burial and other rites.

**Books of Orders**   Instructions to Justices of the Peace directing them to take specific action in times of plague or famine.

**Break with Rome**   The rejection of the authority of the Pope over the English church.

**Capitalism**   An economic system based on competition and an unrestricted market.

**Cardinal legate**   A top-ranking papal representative whose decisions could be overruled only by a pope.

**Catholic League**   Founded in 1576 by Duke Henry of Guise with the aim of destroying Protestantism in France and preventing the Protestant Henry of Navarre from succeeding to the French throne.

**Celibacy**   Abstaining from marriage/sexual relations.

**Classical movement**   A series of meetings, mainly or entirely of Protestant clergy, for study and prayer.

**Clemency**   Leniency.

**Clerical preferment**   Promotion for members of the clergy.

**Clericalism**   Belief in the authority of the priesthood over the laity.

**Clerics**   Churchmen.

**Cloister**   Part of the interior of a monastery or, in this sense, the monastery itself.

**Colonisation**   One country seizing foreign territory by dispossessing original owners and occupants.

**Commonweal**   The public good or welfare.

**Communion**   The offering of the bread and wine to the congregation.

**Confession**   The practice of acknowledging sins to a priest in the hope of God's forgiveness.

**Conservative**   One who upholds traditional values and ways.

**Counter-Reformation**   Historians' term referring to the reform movement within the Catholic Church.

**Court of Wards and Liveries** Responsible for administering the crown's feudal revenues.

**Covenant**   An agreement whereby a church member agreed to conform to church discipline.

**Dauphin**   Eldest son and heir of the French King.

**Dearth**   When food was expensive.

**Debasement of the coinage**   Reducing the amount of precious metal in the coinage supplied through the royal mints.

**Diocese**   The church territory, divided mainly into parishes, under the authority of a bishop.

**Discipline**   As in 'godly discipline': the control of social and moral behaviour in accordance with the correct interpretation of the gospel.

**Dispensation**   Permission given to step outside the usual rules.

**Dissolution of the monasteries**   In 1536 all monastic property was seized by the crown; a significant portion was sold on to the nobility.

**Dominicans**   A Catholic religious order devoted to preaching and combating heresy.

**Dukes of Burgundy**   Although the French lands of the Duchy of Burgundy had been annexed by the French crown in the fifteenth century, the title and its Netherlands lands were inherited by the Habsburgs.

**Ecclesiastical**   Of the church.

**Elevation of the Host**   The Host is the wafer of bread consecrated by the priest which Catholics believe to be the body of Christ. The priest raised the Host as a sign of its transformation in essence from bread to body ('transubstantiation').

**Enclosures**   Where land formerly farmed by a whole village as common land was fenced off by landowners and turned over to pasture of animals. Needed fewer agricultural workers.

**Episcopate**   The bishops.

**Erastian**   Giving priority to serving the needs of the state.

**Eucharist**   The bread and wine offered to the congregation in the Communion service.

**Evangelising**   Preaching God's message and the teaching of the Church.

**Ex officio oath** A legally binding promise to respond truthfully to whatever question was asked, but without prior knowledge of the question.

**Exclusion Act** When passed by Parliament and agreed by the monarch, this would, in law at least, prevent a claimant from succeeding to the throne.

**Excommunicated** To be completely isolated from the Christian community and denied access to all the services and rites of the church (including burial).

**Expediency** Convenience.

**Factions** Rival groups of nobles.

**Felony** A serious crime.

**Feudal** A system of authority based on ownership of land.

**Fiscal** Relating to finance.

**Freemen** Those not bound as property to a lord or chieftain.

**Fulminations** Bitter and explosive complaints.

**Gaelic** Ancient Celtic language, culture and customs.

**Gloriana** The title given to the Faerie Queene in Edmund Spenser's poem of the same name; Gloriana represented Elizabeth.

**Guerrilla campaign** Fighting a war by stealth rather than through formal battles.

**Heresy** Holding beliefs in opposition to those taught by the church.

**Heretics** Those who do not accept the teaching of the church.

**Hierarchy** An organisation with authority depending upon rank.

**Historiography** Interpretations of the past embodied in the writings of historians.

**Homilies** Short sermon-like passages that could be read instead of preaching.

**Hugger-mugger** Secretive.

**Huguenots** French Protestants, followers of John Calvin (who was himself French).

**Humanist** Participant in the intellectual movement associated with the revival of the learning of classical Greece and Rome. Humanists looked towards a greater understanding of the Christian scriptures and were dismissive of what they saw as superstitious practices in the church.

**Iconoclasm** The destruction of those religious images which were seen by Protestants as detracting from the worship of God alone.

**Indictment** Accusation of guilt.

**Indiscriminate charity** Charity distributed without the testing of need.

**Inflation** Where money loses its value and prices rise.

**Injunction** A royal proclamation on religious matters.

**Inns of Court** The London Inns of Court provided, not only a professional training in the law, but also an education and social contacts appropriate to the well-connected gentry.

**Jesuits** A missionary religious order founded in 1534 and recognised officially by the Pope in 1540. Jesuits were characterised by a rigorous but emotional piety based on disciplining the will.

**Jure divino** A Latin phrase meaning 'by the law of God'.

**Laity** The church congregation; strictly, any person not in the employ of the church.

**Lay** From laity, meaning those who do not have official posts within the church.

**Letters Patent**   A legal instrument used by the monarch to confer a title or post.

**Lineage**   Belonging to a well-established noble family.

**Lords of the Congregation**   A powerful pro-Protestant noble faction influenced by the Calvinist ideas of the Scots theologian John Knox (and by their own self-interest).

**Marian exiles**   Those Protestants who fled to Protestant centres such as Zurich and Geneva on the accession of the Catholic Mary I in 1553.

**Martyr**   A person willing to suffer for faith's sake.

**Master of the Ordnance**   Responsible for the supply of military equipment to armed forces.

**Master of Wards**   Responsible, through the Court of Wards and Liveries, for the guardianship of the crown's wards.

**Mercenary**   A professional soldier who fought for whoever paid him.

**Minister**   The Protestant equivalent of the Catholic priest. Most Protestants preferred the former to the latter as 'priest' carried with it suggestions of a special status with special powers.

**Minority**   The period before a monarch comes of age and is able to rule alone.

**Missionary priests**   Catholic priests sent to England from the continent to win back souls for the Roman Catholic Church.

**Monopoly**   A licence granted by the crown that gave an individual or a group the sole right to produce or trade in a particular commodity.

**Nomads**   People without a fixed settlement.

**Oratory**   Persuasive speech.

**Ordinal**   The book containing the regulations for becoming a minister or bishop.

**Ordinary and extraordinary expenditure** Parliament would expect to provide tax only for extraordinary government expenditure, such as defence or war, and not for everyday running of government.

**Ornaments**   The clothing required of the clergy.

**Orthodoxy**   The official teaching of the church.

**Papal Bull**   A document containing a pope's explicit instructions which the faithful were to obey.

**Papistical**   A Protestant term, intended to be offensive, meaning 'Catholic-like'.

**Parvenus**   Newcomers.

**Paternalism**   Behaving to those in need in the traditional manner of a father towards his children.

**Paternalist**   Literally, a father figure and one who rules as a traditional father, making decisions with the best interests of the family in mind but without consultation.

**Patriarchal**   Male-dominated.

**Peace of Cateau-Cambrésis**   This treaty marked the end of the long struggle between France and Spain for the control of Italy. England had been Spain's ally against France in the Marian period, Although conflict between France and England was ended by the treaty, France did not relinquish Calais.

**Perpetual Edict**   A declaration, signed by Don John as Governor-General of the Netherlands, that Spanish troops would permanently withdraw from the Netherlands. It was not honoured.

**Piety**   Holding and displaying strong religious beliefs.

**Plantation**   Colonisation by settling in numbers.

**Pluralism**   A priest owning more than one living and therefore being responsible for more than one parish.

*Politique*   Someone motivated by practical politics, often uninterested in religious matters.

**Pragmatic**   Making decisions on the basis of what was practical in a particular set of circumstances, rather than through theory or principle.

**Precedence**   Having a higher ranking than others.

**Predestination**   A Protestant doctrine associated particularly with John Calvin which stressed the power of God and the weakness of humankind. God, being all-powerful and all-knowing, had decided before a person's birth whether their fate would be salvation or damnation.

**Primogeniture**   A system whereby the first-born inherited all the property of the parent.

**Prophesyings**   Meetings of ministers and other interested parties in which ministers honed their preaching skills in front of a critical audience.

**Purgatory**   In Catholic doctrine, a place where the souls of the dead are cleansed by suffering as preparation for heaven.

*Putsch*   A take-over of the government.

**Quarantine**   Sealing up of infected houses.

**Radical**   Proposing or leading to rapid and highly significant change.

**Real Presence**   The teaching ('doctrine') that Christ was truly present in the bread and wine at Communion.

**Recant**   To withdraw former statements of belief.

**Recusancy**   The refusal to attend the services of the Church of England.

**Recusant**   Someone who refused to attend the services of the Church of England.

**Regency Council**   Group of councillors ruling in the name of a monarch.

**Regent**   A person ruling in place of a monarch (usually because the monarch was too young to rule independently or was absent).

**Roman Catholic Mass**   A service in which the officiating priest consecrates bread and wine. In Roman Catholic teaching it is through the agency of the priest that bread and wine become, in essence, Christ's body and blood.

**Royal prerogative**   Decisions which, by right, should be made by the monarch alone.

**Royal Supremacy**   The right of the monarch to govern the Church of England as imposed and enforced by the Act of Supremacy.

**Secular**   Non-spiritual.

**Secular priests**   Catholic priests who are not also members of the Society of Jesus or other religious orders.

**Seigneurial religion**   A religion relying upon the support, and serving the needs, of the upper class.

**Spanish Inquisition**   The Spanish branch of the Holy Office, charged by popes with the uncovering of heresy. Methods might, with the participation of secular authority, include torture.

**Spanish Match**   The marriage between Mary I of England and Philip II of Spain.

**Surrender and re-grant**   Where a Gaelic chieftain would hand over the land he controlled (but did not own) to the crown. He would then receive it back with the title of an English earl. Such land could then be passed on to his descendants.

**Synods** Regional or national decision-making meetings of church representatives.

**Tanist** A Gaelic chieftain and landholder elected by freemen.

**Tithe** A tenth part of the fruits of the land or of labour which by law were to be given to the church.

**Toleration** In the context of religion, the willingness of the state to grant the right to worship freely.

**Translation** In church terminology, the transfer of a bishop from one bishopric to another.

**Usurp** To take power to which one is not entitled.

**Vagrant** A wandering beggar.

**Veto** To forbid further action and/or to cancel what has previously been passed.

*Via media* Middle way between Catholicism and Protestantism.

**Visitations** Inspections of the churches and clergy in a diocese carried out by a bishop.

**Wars of the Roses** The struggle between the families of York and Lancaster for the kingship of England which culminated in the rule of the Tudors (1485).

**Welfare-state ideology** The belief that the state has a responsibility to look after those in need.

**'Whig' school of historical interpretation** A term used to criticise historians who allegedly distort their accounts of the past by imposing their liberal values on it. They are accused of implicitly judging historical figures on whether or not they contributed towards progress in the direction of liberal parliamentary democracy.

**Zealot** One whose commitment to a cause is extreme.

# Index